African American Women
and Social Action

Recent Titles in
Contributions in Women's Studies

Embracing Space: Spatial Metaphors in Feminist Discourse
Kerstin W. Shands

On Top of the World: Women's Political Leadership in Scandinavia and Beyond
Bruce O. Solheim

Victorian London's Middle-Class Housewife: What She Did All Day
Yaffa Claire Draznin

Connecting Links: The British and American Woman Suffrage Movements, 1900–1914
Patricia Greenwood Harrison

Female Journeys: Autobiographical Expressions by French and Italian Women
Claire Marrone

Excluded from Suffrage History: Matilda Joslyn Gage, Nineteenth-Century American
Feminist
Leila R. Brammer

The Artist as Outsider in the Novels of Toni Morrison and Virginia Woolf
Lisa Williams

(Out)Classed Women: Contemporary Chicana Writers on Inequitable Gendered Power
Relations
Phillipa Kafka

"Saddling La Gringa": Gatekeeping in Literature by Contemporary Latina Writers
Phillipa Kafka

Representing the Marginal Woman in Nineteenth-Century Russian Literature: Personalism,
Feminism, and Polyphony
Svetlana Slavskaya Grenier

From the Field to the Legislature: A History of Women in the Virgin Islands
Eugenia O'Neal

Women and Domestic Experience in Victorian Political Fiction
Susan Johnston

African American Women and Social Action

The Clubwomen and
Volunteerism from Jim Crow
to the New Deal, 1896–1936

Floris Barnett Cash

Contributions in Women's Studies, Number 188

GREENWOOD PRESS
Westport, Connecticut • London

Library of Congress Cataloging-in-Publication Data

Cash, Floris Loretta Barnett.
    African American women and social action : the clubwomen and volunteerism from
Jim Crow to the New Deal, 1896–1936 / by Floris Barnett Cash.
        p.   cm.—(Contributions in women's studies, ISSN 0147–104X ; no. 188)
    Includes bibliographical references and index.
    ISBN 0–313–31563–9 (alk. paper)
    1. Afro-American women—Political activity—History—20th century.   2. Afro-American
women—Societies and clubs—History—20th century.   3. Afro-American women social
reformers—History—20th century.   4. Social action—United States—History—20th century.
5. Volunteerism—United States—History—20th century.   6. Afro-American women—
Social conditions—20th century.   7. Afro-Americans—Social conditions—20th
century.   8. United States—Social conditions—1865–1918.   9. United States—Social
conditions—1918–1932.   I. Title.   II. Series.
    E185.86.C33   2001
    361.7′6′08996073—dc21   00–061719

British Library Cataloguing in Publication Data is available.

Library of Congress Catalog Card Number: 00–061719
ISBN: 0–313–31563–9
ISSN: 0147–104X

First published in 2001

Greenwood Press, 88 Post Road West, Westport, CT 06881
An imprint of Greenwood Publishing Group, Inc.
www.greenwood.com

Printed in the United States of America

The paper used in this book complies with the
Permanent Paper Standard issued by the National
Information Standards Organization (Z39.48–1984).

10 9 8 7 6 5 4 3 2 1

Copyright Acknowledgments

The author and publisher gratefully acknowledge permission for use of the following material:

Excerpts from the George E. Haynes Papers, Box 4, "The Public Welfare League," Nashville, Tennessee, 11 February 1918. Courtesy of the Special Collections Librarian and the Fisk University Library Special Collections.

"Brief History of the Harriet Tubman Community Club, Inc. of Hempstead," one page unpublished typescript. Courtesy of Mrs. Fay C. Latimer.

Excerpts from a letter to Mrs. H.R. Halloway, Plainfield, New Jersey, from Mrs. Booker T. Washington, 6 December 1895, Margaret Washington Papers, Hollis B. Frissell Library, Tuskegee University, Tuskegee, Alabama.

Excerpts from the Stewart-Flippin Papers, Box 97-105, Folder 85, letter to Carlotta Stewart (Lai), Hawaii, from Verina Morton-Jones, Brooklyn, New York, 31 October 1926. Courtesy of the Moorland-Spingarn Research Center, Howard University, Washington, DC.

Contents

Photo essay follows Chapter 5.

Preface

The feminist principle the "personal is political," or relating political actions to economic and social conditions as well as to personal situations, is expanded in this book which compares and places issues within the context of social class, race and gender identity. For most African American women, including myself, the personal is intertwined with multiple factors related to race, gender, and class. The nature of black women's historical experiences demonstrates that the multifaceted texture of their lives is related to their identity.

This book explores the experiences of middle-class women who were at the top of the black intellectual, social, and economic hierarchy. In my community, cross-class relationships frequently occurred through church activities and family ties. These women were intricately involved in and tied to the larger African American community. Black women leaders, middle-class and working-class, who engaged in volunteer activities for the benefit of the community were held in high esteem.

My interest in African American women's history stems from both academic and personal motives. The voices of family and community mentors were compelling factors in my life. I grew up in an environment that placed the church and school as the centers of community life for African Americans. Schoolteachers and Sunday school teachers, often the same persons, were my role models. Service to the community was not only encouraged but expected. In addition to my immediate family, an extended family kin, Dr. Ida Mae Hiram, invited me to spend a couple of summers with her while her daughter attended college. She was the first black woman to practice dentistry in the town and the first in the state of Georgia.[1] At the age of nineteen, Ida Mae Johnson married Lace Hiram, a local dentist. The daughter of Lafayette Johnson, a widower, Ida did laundry work to help her family financially. Encouraged by her husband, she graduated from Knox Institute and Meharry Dental School. I was influenced not only by her presence, but by the educational surroundings, especially newspapers, magazines, and books, in her home. The family had acquired an extensive knowledge base.[2]

The women in my family worked mainly in domestic and service occupations, practical nursing and midwifery, and had developed an intricate network. Midwives and older women with some knowledge of folk medicine have an honored place in the African American experience. I had a special relationship with my grandmother, Daisy Stroud, who was a midwife for forty years. One of seventeen children, she was the mother of six children.[3] Sometimes I accompanied her as she walked to visit a patient, even during inclement weather. Some mothers inquired about birth control, especially those who were unable to pay for one child before expecting another. Role models and observers Bessie and Sadie Delany, who came from a middle-class black family of ten children in North Carolina, concluded, "Some women tried to prevent pregnancies but in those days there was really not anything that worked."[4]

The caring relationship between a midwife and her patients forged a community. Midwives who healed and helped women treated childbirth as part of a woman's life experience. Midwives like my grandmother stayed with the mother during delivery and reported the birth to the doctor afterward. When each of the novelist Alice Walker's sisters and brothers was born, her mother gave the midwife a payment of homegrown or homemade items, such as "a pig, a quilt, or a jar of canned fruits and vegetables."[5] Thus, these working-class women formed a community based on shared interests. A midwife, as a medical caregiver and confidant, provided a sense of community where black women could talk about subjects ranging from childbirth to gardening.

No one from my immediate family had ever attended college, but my teachers and family friends encouraged me to attend because they thought that I had the potential to succeed. They gave me books to read and classical records to listen to, as I prepared to major in music. My class was the first to graduate from the twelfth grade at the segregated Industrial High School. I used the back door of the public library to get the required books for summer reading before college because the books were not in the branch library. Although I worked after school and during the summers, I did not have enough money for college and knew nothing about how to get into one. However, I did get a tuition scholarship, and my mother worked at night and most days to pay for my college education. She also earned her high school equivalency diploma during the same time. My mentors at Spelman College included not only professors but a dormitory residence director (called a housemother), Mrs. Aline Howard. A former schoolteacher, she became a friend who helped me bridge the cultural gap between my home experience and college. My most enlightening educational and cultural experience came from the newly established exchange program that I was selected to participate in when Spelman sent students to colleges and universities in the North and Midwest.

Today, it seems unbelievable to most of my college students that community leaders during the early twentieth century would voluntarily bring their sisters into contact with community resources, especially in the cities. I contend that many of the social problems among contemporary African Americans are linked directly to a lack of close community mentors. As the black middle-class increased many persons who had struggled for a higher social status failed to provide the leadership, support system, and opportunity structure necessary to prepare youth for upward mobility. I anticipate new experiences, cooperative relationships, and social configurations in this new millennium.

Acknowledgments

I have incurred many debts while writing this book. Very special appreciation is extended to my family, my husband Ernest, daughter Floris Kathleen, and son, Eric. I would like to thank my extended family, whose roots stem from the Stroud, Barnett, and Owen kin groups. They provided information, sometimes living accommodations and transportation to the various archives, and even prayers. To my friends and colleagues, whose support, persistent encouragement, understanding, and constructive criticism enabled me to complete this project, I thank you.

Chapter 1

Introduction

> The first and real reason that our women began
> to use clubs as a means of improving their own
> condition and that of their race is that they are
> progressive.
>> Mary Church Terrell, "History," 34-8.

Writers have long recognized the large numbers of programs, philanthropies, professional organizations, and clubs that are concerned with social problems in American society. Until recently scholars have not seriously considered the significant role of women in benevolent work and humanitarian reform, with black women's roles coming even more recently under study than those of white women. African American women have a continuous record of self-help, institution building, and strong organizations. Anne Firor Scott suggests that black women participated more in organized activity than white women. The lives of black women, their organizations, and their social actions are now being reconstructed.[1] As Rosalyn Terborg-Penn asserts, we must take control of our own destiny. We need to tell our own story and write our own history.[2]

Recent sources are examining the dilemmas and aspirations of African American women. Reconstructing womanhood embodies a feminist perspective that emphasizes the articulation of gender, race, and class.[3] This book seeks to analyze issues and provide insights on the social action of the pioneer black clubwomen in African American communities from the Jim Crow era to the New Deal. It is a contribution to the theoretical and interpretative insights of black women's history. Although black women and their achievements have been largely invisible in historians' accounts of progressive reform, several recent books have addressed the issue of black women as social activists:

Evelyn Brooks Higginbotham, in *Righteous Discontent: The Women's Movement in the Black Baptist Church, 1880-1920 (1993),* analyzes the role of black women in making the church a powerful institution for social and political change. The focus of her study is the National Baptist Convention, the largest religious movement among African Americans. The women's movement, particularly under the leadership of Nannie Burroughs, was largely responsible for making the church accountable for self-help and social welfare services. Higginbotham argues that black women traditional uplift activities can be categorized as the politics of respectability.

Jacqueline Rouse's book, *Lugenia Burns Hope: A Black Southern Reformer* (1989), chronicles the life experiences of one black settlement worker in the South. Hope established the Neighborhood Union to aid the poor in an Atlanta community that bordered the college community of Morehouse, of which her husband was president, Spelman College, and Atlanta University. It was one of the earliest social service institutions in the South.

Cynthia Neverdon-Morton's *Afro-American Women of the South and the Advancement of the Race, 1895-1925* (1989) argues that black women founded and headed most of the social service agencies in the South and responded to the urgent needs of the race. Neverdon-Morton examines the activism of black women in the South who organized school settlements and social service programs near institutions of higher education in Alabama, Virginia, Georgia, Tennessee, and Maryland.

Glenda Gilmore, in *Gender and Jim Crow: Women and the Politics of White Supremacy in North Carolina, 1896-1920* (1996), examines the pivotal role of gender and race in North Carolina politics from the disfranchisement of black men by 1900 until women were granted suffrage in 1920. A generation of educated black women emerged in the 1890s to become diplomats to the white community after their husbands, brothers, and sons, were disfranchised. Gilmore notes their struggles and efforts to forge ties with white women.

In *Black Neighbors: Race and the Limits of Reform in the American Settlement House Movement, 1890-1945* (1993) Elisabeth Lasch-Quinn analyzed the settlement house movement and demonstrated the reluctance of the mainstream National Federation of Settlements to extend its programs to the black communities. African Americans developed their own alternatives to help black migrants. Lasch-Quinn redefined the traditional view of settlement work held by the NFS to encompass the programs and activities of African American women.

Stephanie Shaw examined the lives of women employed in the feminized professions of teaching, social work, nursing, and librarianship during the Jim Crow era. She reveals how their families, their values, and their exceptions were formed and how they contended with race and gender discrimination. In *What a Woman Ought to Be and to Do, Black Professional Women Workers During the Jim Crow Era* (1996), Stephanie Shaw shows us what made these women exceptional and leaders in their communities as they struggled against Jim Crow policies. She demonstrated that families, communities, and schools encouraged self-confidence and social responsibility in African American women.

In Deborah Gray White's *Too Heavy a Load, Black Women in Defense of Themselves, 1894-1994* (1999) explores the history of black women explaining, defining, and defending themselves. She looks at black feminists up to the 1990s. To tell her story of African American women in the twentieth century, White analyzes the ideological bases of several black women's organizations, namely, the National Association of Colored Women, the National Council of Negro Women, the Ladies Auxiliary of the Brotherhood of Sleeping Car Porters, the National Welfare Rights Organization, and the National Black Feminist Organization.

Building upon the themes expressed by each of these writers, this book explores the role of African American women in the settlement house movement. Concurrently, it links the social settlement movement with the rise of the National Association of Colored Women in 1896 and the subsequent black women's club network. Educated beyond their race and gender and with a sense of responsibility, many black women turned to volunteer work. From their positions of leadership, they created social service institutions in African American communities. This book, while examining black women's involvement on a regional and national level in the social settlement movement, provides a comparative framework for analyzing the impact of the organizations and programs that the clubwomen created mainly for the migrant black population. This book further documents the centrality of the progressive movement in many areas of reform in black communities, particularly reform in the cities.

Problems of poverty, illness, and family discord are not new developments in human history. African Americans were influenced by the ferment of cooperation in American society. They followed patterns that were similar to those that other Americans used in developing organizations and institutions for self-improvement and protest.

African American women have a long history of social action to provide the basic survival needs of African Americans. These efforts were most extensive in black communities during the era of Jim Crow segregation in the South and customary segregation in the North. By the late nineteenth century, the National Association of Colored Women was the foremost voluntary association seeking to ameliorate social problems in black communities.[4]

Progressivism arose as an effort to cope with problems created by the impact of industrialization, urbanization, and immigration.[5] Women's clubs, black and white, had considerable social, political, and economic, influence during the era. Club work influenced the direction of social welfare work during the Progressive era. The social reform of black women occurred during the height of the women's club movement from the 1890s to World War I, when black and white women made an enormous impact on American life. Women voiced concern publicly in rural and urban areas in both the North and South about education, child care, health care, and family.

Emphasizing women and community work is one way of presenting the history of black women. Borrowing from the self-help theories of both W.E.B.

Du Bois and Booker T. Washington, black clubwomen envisioned leadership as a response to crisis circumstances that would require pragmatic solutions. They understood the African American population and the local communities where they worked and lived. The inventiveness of the clubwomen, particularly in social service, education, and health care, contributed to community survival. Inventiveness also encompassed race and gender consciousness.

At the turn of the century, racial uplift as practiced by the conservative clubwomen included not only institution building and community service but encompassed a missionary attitude in dealing with the poor. Facing Jim Crow segregation, sexual assault, and other racial injustices in the South, African American clubwomen transformed uplift into what Evelyn Higginbotham denotes as the politics of respectability.[6] Although the women rejected the culture of the masses, they were ostracized and held in contempt by whites. The clubwomen looked to progress and respectability to bring the masses in step with the values and attitudes of the middle class. The reform of individual behavior became a goal as well as a strategy of reform. The politics of respectability was a means of expressing black women's identity, discontent, and agenda for social action.

Recent scholarship challenges the ideology of racial uplift as an effective means of advancing the race.[7] The idea of racial uplift that gradually emerged in the late nineteenth century was inherently exclusionary and may not have been an effective means of advancing the race. To counter racist stereotypes, African Americans embraced higher education, middle-class values, and patriarchal families. Clubwomen, who regarded themselves as the "better class," saw class differentiation as evidence of race progress. This ideology was reflected in the gendered struggles of the clubs in the black communities.

The occurrence of a movement of women's clubs aimed at social reform was linked to larger political, social, and economic changes in American society that transformed African American communities. Depressions between 1873 and 1893 led to a need for cooperation and greater relief in society. Historian Rayford Logan describes the period 1877-1901 as the "nadir" of race relations, African Americans were dependent upon self-help for improvement.[8] The application of Darwinian concepts to justify laissez-faire in the business world to American society ushered in racism and a belief that some races were inherently inferior to others. Social Darwinist theory became an important theme for the legal, scientific, and business communities, with one reinforcing the other.[9]

The Supreme Court constitutionalized the encroaching segregation in transportation, education, and public facilities by grounding its rationale on notions of racial inferiority informed by social Darwinism. The federal case *Plessy v. Ferguson* (1896) legalized statutory segregation and created the conditions for the spread of Jim Crow legislation in transportation, education, and public facilities, including hospitals and orphanages.[10] Jim Crow segregation, or the physical separation of persons for reasons of race, became an effective method for maintaining race and class inequities. Racial segregation in the social, political, and economic domain was the main component of a new racism.

The new racism was hardened by a hegemonic consciousness that proclaimed that African Americans deserved their lowly status because they were an inferior race. Americans from white politicians to world's fair organizers and black leaders were influenced by this social theory. Although the ideology emphasized the personal interests of individual struggle for existence, it upheld racial and cultural evolution. Lee Baker argues that the latter focus emphasizes a hierarchy of races from the inferior savage to the civilized citizen. It views the poor as biologically unfit to struggle for existence.[11] Black and white leaders believed that progress should come through natural evolution.

Social thought of the nineteenth century did not insist on equal treatment for all who needed assistance.[12] The black poor, like other impoverished groups, suffered from substandard housing, poor sanitation, tuberculosis, and other social ills. Of the many voices raised for reform and social justice, only a few were directed toward the African American community. As a result, there was a dire need for public relief for poor African Americans, who were excluded from it.

As racial conflicts and urban problems intensified in American society, church workers, settlement workers, and temperance workers became part of a larger movement called the Social Gospel, which worked for social justice. Many of the northern white Social Gospel prophets were officers and supporters of the American Missionary Association and carried social Christianity into the southern missions and schools.[13]

During difficult times and periods of severe oppression, black leaders advocated self-help and collective efforts. African Americans attempted to assimilate into American society but became alienated when faced with lynching, convict lease, peonage, race riots, and increasing segregation. Black women used their clubs, conventions, and newsletters to bring these issues before the public. Excluded from first-class facilities on trains, such as ladies cars and Pullman berths, black women protested against these issues affecting their legal status and violations of black rights. Women in Louisiana and Tennessee petitioned their state legislatures to repeal the Jim Crow car laws.[14] Clubwomen in New York assisted destitute African Americans from Oklahoma and Arkansas who were stranded in Jersey City, unable to obtain passage abroad a ship to Liberia. Ida B. Wells led a campaign against lynching and proposed migration as a form of self-help.[15]

OVERVIEW

African American clubwomen provided leadership during a time when voluntary action was most frequently the only solution for solving problems in African American communities. In 1895, when the first national meeting of black women was held in Boston, it seemed that a large network of middle-class black women activists had emerged overnight. Yet the formation of a National Association of Colored Women (NACW) in 1896 marked the culmination of three decades in which black women attempted to band together to achieve common objectives. During those thirty years, black women were active in numerous local, self-help organizations. The association provided the infrastructure for local clubs to organize for the social, economic, and political improvement of black communities. By the turn of the century, the association claimed a network of 15,000 women. In less than 20 years, the number of members rose to 100,000.

The clubwomen were motivated by role models from the past and served as mentors for others. They drew on the values and motivation of black activists Sojourner Truth, Harriet Tubman, Maria Stewart, and Frances E. W. Harper. Harriet Tubman, abolitionist and Civil War activist, encouraged the clubwomen to follow her example and establish homes for the aged. Antebellum social activists, such as Tubman, Harper, Charlotte Forten Grimke, Fanny Jackson Coppin, and Josephine St. Pierre Ruffin, immersed themselves in the continuing struggle for social uplift and political equality for African Americans by supporting suffrage and the actions of younger women, such as Mary Terrell, Margaret Washington, Victoria Earle Matthews, and Maritcha Lyons. Many of the women, like Matthews, were journalists. Maritcha Lyons was connected to the earlier generation through the anti-slavery activities of her parents.

When the first national conference of black women was held in 1896, the club women were mainly young women. Margaret Washington was thirty years old. Terrell, the first president of the NACW, was thirty-three. Victoria Matthews, cofounder of a women's network in New York City, was thirty-two. Antilynching crusader Ida B. Wells was thirty-three. Selena Butler and Addie Hunton were twenty-four and twenty-one years old, respectively.

Scholars such as Trudia Hamilton and Gerda Lerner have documented the presence of middle class women in black women's clubs.[16] W.E.B. Du Bois speculated that the black women's clubs connected and empowered women across class lines.[17] However, cross-class women's clubs were not the goal of black women. Black women's clubs were led by middle-class women at both the national and local levels. Only in areas where there were no college-educated black women would working-class women compose the rank and file of the club members. Mamie Garvin Fields, who organized the Modern Priscilla Women's Club in 1927 in Charleston, looked for energetic women who wanted to do more than meet and socialize. She noted that many people in the community were not invited to join individual club, regardless of their ability, education, or readiness to serve, they could be excluded.[18]

Increased educational opportunities and urbanization broadened the social class stratification among African Americans and influenced the direction of black women's club work. The experience of slavery and segregation led blacks to use criteria other than education, income, and occupation to determine social status, including skin color and even manners and morals. Leadership positions in black women's clubs were generally awarded to the most prominent members of the black community. Like African Americans in general, black women could be categorized into the upper-middle class, the new professional middle class, and the lower-middle class.[19] Women in the latter category, who were underemployed because of race or gender discrimination, worked as domestics and seamstresses or in other skilled or service occupations. Upper-middle class black women, such as Josephine Bruce, Nettie Langston Napier, Helen Appo Cook, Mary Church Terrell, Gertrude Bustill Mossell, Joan I. Howard, Josephine St. Pierre Ruffin, and Fannie Barrier Williams, came from families that had already achieved either intellectual or financial status or both. They were members of a small cultural elite that flourished from the post-Reconstruction period to about 1920.[20] Many African American families established within their children a sense of social responsibility. Historian Stephanie Shaw argues that the child-rearing strategies of black families transformed individualistic notions of self-help and the Protestant work ethic into an ethic of socially responsible individualism.[21]

Clubwomen in the middle range, who graduated from the newly founded black colleges which emphasized self-help, received recognition from their achieved social status. Northern church groups established institutions for African Americans in the South that not only provided training for black teachers but developed a black middle-class ingrained with notions of respectability. Women, such as Nannie Burroughs, Mary Bethune, Margaret Washington, and Janie Porter Barrett, reflected the missionary spirit and zeal rooted in black education. By 1900 several entrepreneurial black women emerged, including Maggie Walker, Madam C. J. Walker, and Annie N. Turnbo Malone, who built economic institutions to serve African American communities and sought to steer the NACW toward economic development.[22] Among the few business enterprises of the NACW was a building and loan association in Philadelphia.

Members of the middle class attempted to gain privileges that had been denied to them by whites claiming to be the moral leaders of the black poor. Yet middle-class blacks, who were ostracized by the white society and also removed from the black community, sometimes showed contempt for the lower classes. Cross-class prejudice and in-group distinctions among the club leaders were interwoven within their community efforts.

The nineteenth-century idealization of true womanhood or Republican motherhood was characterized by the separation of the home and the public interests of the economic and political world. Kathleen McCarthy argues that under the banner of religion, the ideology of motherhood, and the cult of domesticity, women broadened their domestic responsibilities beyond the home to help dependents and the dispossessed. Republican motherhood emphasized the domestic domain of education and nurture and recognized women as the carriers of virtue.[23] By the mid-nineteenth century, this cluster of ideas designated the values and code of behavior that was extensive among the "respectable" middle class.[24] Glenna Matthews asserts that the flowering of public womanhood was both grounded in and constrained by domesticity.[25] Black women have a different cultural history from white women. The experience of black women scarcely resembled the established norms, yet true womanhood remained the ideal toward which all women should aspire.

Karen Blair identified white clubwomen as domestic feminists who increased their autonomy without challenging the cult of domesticity.[26]   Black clubwomen believed that it was their duty to encourage their poor sisters to accept the values of Victorian middle-class morality. The leaders emphasized moral issues, temperance, good housekeeping, virtue, and submissiveness, at a time when other American women were breaking away from outdated Victorian standards. They encouraged the Victorian model of home, family, and womanhood. Club leaders who had achieved upward mobility and a high status attempted to impose their cultural standards on their less-privileged sisters. They did not seem to realize that those black women who were poverty-ridden, overworked, and illiterate could not meet the Victorian standards.

The black women's club network originated during the late Victorian period and shared some of its thinking regarding social class. The age was characterized by its emphasis on morality, respectability, and a guarded reticence toward all matters relating to sex. The latter concept worked well for middle-class women, but there a double standard for the rich and the poor. The social code stressed cleanliness and neatness. Notions about social class can be compared to the views of the new middle classes of the Victorian period in England who were trying to establish themselves and therefore stressed their respectability.[27]

The clubwomen attributed many problems in their communities to previous inequalities existing in black families since slavery and maintained thereafter by race discrimination. The concern is whether they perceived real problems within the family and sought to cope with them or whether they were overreacting to stereotypical images assigned to black women.   Clearly, there was a need to shift the image of the new century's black woman away from stereotypes before the women could begin their social reform. Black women had to confront the dominant domestic ideologies that excluded them from the definition of "woman." As public women, the clubwomen had to prove that black women were virtuous. The image of black women in the United States has been tainted by the "myth of promiscuous black women." The most common form of attack on the image of black women was to portray them as immoral.[28] The clubwomen believed that improving the circumstances of women would dispel the notion that all black women were immoral and subject to sexual transgression. They were more concerned with correcting negative images than in attacking the source of problems.

Settlement house superintendent Victoria Matthews insisted that morality was a question of environment rather than temperament or innate characteristics. She attempted to improve the very real social and economic circumstances in the lives of black working women. When Victoria Matthews and white reformer Frances Kellor discovered that employment agencies directed black female migrants from the South to saloons, gambling houses, and brothels, they might have gone on a zealous crusade to stamp out sin and vice. As super moralists, they could have demanded that the women exhibit proper behavior and be chaste. As feminists, however, they established travelers' aid societies and the National

League for the Protection of Colored Women. Black and white women believed that they had an obligation to society and to their migrating sisters to expose the problem and offer them an alternative. Their tactics more closely resembled those of conservative social reform and racial uplift.

Gender and race identity are interlocking entities. The clubwomen were conscious of the meaning of gender and race injustice.[29] The roots of black feminism extend back to the 1830s. Maria Stewart, as well as the clubwomen realized that the forces oppressing black women lay outside themselves. In *A Colored Woman in a White World*, Mary Terrell discussed the impact of racism and sexism on black women's lives. Terrell found that in every aspect of life, black women were handicapped by their gender as well as their race.[30] Club activists Mary Terrell, Frances Harper, Ida Wells, and Anna Cooper championed equality for women and justice for all African Americans. Feminism was part of the clubwomen's self-perspective, and consciousness of gender and race compelled their activism.[31]

The 1890s was a period of optimism and change that Frances Harper labeled "the woman's era." The clubwomen refused to occupy the special "place" reserved for black women in the conventional views of race progress. Many women no longer believed they should be subordinate or inferior to men. "In our day, the woman's sphere is just as large as she can make it and still be true to the finer qualities of her soul," proclaimed Harper.[32] Josephine Ruffin, editor of the *Woman's Era*, popularized the idea that a woman's place is where she is needed and where she fits in. Several black clubwomen believed that although men and women were different, they, nevertheless, were equal.

African American clubwomen attempted to restructure the ways that black women identified themselves. "No other group in America has had its identity socialized out of existence as have black women," says feminist scholar belle hooks.[33] Black women were recognized neither as a part of the larger group of women in American society nor as a separate and distinct group from black men. As "useful" women, black women were expected to work for the black community in its struggle against racial injustice. The clubwomen, as Deborah Gray White argues, believed that their efforts to improve black women simultaneously improved all African Americans.[34]

Club work afforded educated black women opportunities for leadership that were denied elsewhere in society. Black women were attending the newly founded colleges for African Americans in increasing numbers. Many clubwomen were teachers prior to marriage and later volunteered in social service and community activism. Married women, black and white, who lost their jobs were penalized for their status as well as their race and gender. Presumably, employment and wifehood didn't mix; employment and motherhood were a worse mix. Although married women were legally barred from teaching in the District of Columbia, Anna Cooper could teach because she was a widow. Former teachers Janie Barrett, Fannie Williams, Elizabeth Davis, and Ida Wells-Barnett became volunteer social workers. Verina Morton-Jones, a physician, spent most of her professional career as a social worker. Since educational standards were not yet fixed place, the first generation crossed occupational lines with ease.[35]

As the black middle class increased, black women began to enter professional and skilled occupations in larger numbers. Gender and race limitations restricted black women to service occupations as teachers, librarians, nurses, and social workers. John Rousmaniere contends that American female leaders, regardless of their backgrounds, followed gender-specific roles for women. They channeled their intellectual energies into perpetuating women's service roles in society. Verina Morton-Jones continued to do volunteer work long after the occupation of social work had become professionalized. Black women who engaged in settlement work were moved by social conscience, whereas social science influenced the actions of later social workers.[36]

COMMUNITY WORK

African Americans had to create their own social service institutions to improve the black communities. In the South, black women sponsored community development projects and social services that were often located near black educational institutions.[37] This book examines social settlement work as a primary vehicle for racial improvement in both the North and the South. It is important to view black settlement houses within the context of the settlement house movement. Thus, it is necessary to broaden the definition of a settlement house beyond that of the National Federation of Settlements to include institutions that functioned as settlements in black communities. Missions, which appeared a decade or so after the origin of the settlement house movement, provided the foundation for black settlement houses. Janie Porter Barrett's Locust Street Settlement, Hampton, Virginia, 1890; Victoria Matthews' White Rose Mission, New York, 1897; Margaret Washington's Elizabeth Russell Settlement, Tuskegee, Alabama, 1897; and Lugenia Hope's Neighborhood Union, Atlanta, 1908, fall within the range of social settlements. The women established and supported settlement houses in rural and urban America to ameliorate the social problems they perceived in their communities and environment.

Black and white reformers in the South explored biracial solutions aimed at racial reform. Most black settlements were not accepted by the National Federation of Settlements, despite the fact that black settlement work combined social service with health, recreation, and education activities at the community level. The National Federation of Settlements' exclusion of "mission settlements" eliminated many black social service agencies in the South, regardless of how efficient and complete their settlement programs were. White churchwomen pioneered in settlement work in the South. However, they established segregated houses that did not threaten Jim Crow.[38] Conversely, black clubwomen and white churchwomen found commonality in the close relationship between social work and race relations. Settlement houses and other institutions established for blacks meshed with the self-determination of African Americans to strengthen their own standards, and to create their own organizations. The biracial staff, governing board, and welfare league associated with the settlements set a precedent for the post-World War I ideal of interracial cooperation.[39] While white women were willing to work with black women in a movement of interracial cooperation, it is easy to discern that they did not consider them their equal.

Settlement house workers played a major role in the Progressive era reform of the early twentieth century. By World War I, white settlements in the North had become the primary institutions for developing a philosophy of social work and social service. As historian Allen Davis asserts, settlement workers fought for better housing, public health, kindergartens, and sympathetic treatment to juvenile delinquents, and led the progressive education movement.[40] The settlement house was a unique form of social service in the reform era. By 1910 there were more than 400 settlement houses in the United States. Mainstream settlement houses established a national organization, the National Federation of Settlements (NFS; later the National Federation of Settlements and Neighborhood Centers) in 1911. Among the founders of the NFS were Jane Addams, Robert Woods, Albert Kennedy, Graham Taylor, and Lillian Wald. Although black settlement work combined social service with health, recreation, and education activities, most were excluded by the NFS. Did the individual settlement workers, especially those who had worked on equal terms with African Americans in black organizations, share the racist views of the NFS?

Some scholars have compared the actions of black club women to attempts of settlement workers to assimilate the "new immigrants" from Europe. Jane Addams, founder of Hull House in 1889, infused the settlement house movement with cultural pluralism. Yet she may be considered more of an assimilationist than a pluralist because she believed that the future would reveal the commonality of all people. Mainstream, middle-class assimilationist views welcomed newcomers only if they repudiated their language and culture and adapted to Anglo-American culture. Addams believed that every ethnic group should be allowed to express its indigenous culture. Hull House cooperated with a group of professors at the University of Chicago in forming a new view of immigrants that evolved into the theory of cultural pluralism. The new concept of American nationalism and culture was coined in 1915.[41]

Did the cultural pluralism embraced by settlement workers and extended to immigrants apply to African Americans? Given this commitment to pluralism and social change, historian Elizabeth Lasch-Quinn argues that the settlement movement failed to redirect its efforts from white immigrants to African Americans who moved North during and after World War I. The Great Migration of African Americans to the North and Midwest presented problems in the urban areas. Hundreds of thousands of black people left the South because of racial discrimination, poverty, and sexual exploitation. Ignoring efforts to conduct settlement work among African Americans, the National Federation of

Settlements left it up to the local settlements to respond to the influx of black migrants. When faced with changing neighborhoods, most settlement houses chose either exclusion of blacks, segregated activities, removal to white enclaves, or closure and only rarely attempted to integrate.[42] Black settlement houses, the Young Women's Christian Association, the National Urban League, and other social service agencies provided the transitional assistance for African Americans.

The United States became a culturally pluralistic society mainly as a result of immigration, migration, and urbanization. Each group within a diverse society enriched mainstream American culture in its own way. Cultural pluralism implies the maintenance of many cultural systems within a common economic and political system.[43]

The primary goal of black women in organized clubs was full acceptance and acculturation into mainstream society. They accepted the American values of liberty, equality, and humanitarianism. The efforts of the black elite to gain equality in American society coincided with the emergence of the American doctrine that required minority ethnic groups to assimilate into the dominant group and repudiate their cultural heritage. The social actions of the clubwomen refutes assertions that the focus on homogeneity in American society motivated middle-class clubwomen to deny their racial identity. Believing that blacks had something to contribute to America's identity, black women struggled to preserve their history, institutions, and cultural heritage.

Race and cultural identity have played a continuous role in American society, yet they are not the same. Equating class and culture is a common flaw also. Race became a metonyn for culture and class.[44] During the late nineteenth and early twentieth centuries, academics studied and ranked the people of the world. The word race came to mean a biological community with shared characteristics. In "The Conservation of the Races" (1897) W.E.B. Du Bois clearly distinguished between the cultural aspects of race and the social relations of race.[45] The importance of race in studying intergroup relations lies in the social meaning of race.

Race is important in the study of the historical experiences of African American women. Race is significant, declares Cornel West, because the flaws in American society are rooted in historic inequalities and long-standing cultural stereotypes.[46] Evelyn Higginbotham posits theories that will allow us to simultaneously discuss race, class, and gender. She denotes race as a global sign, a "metalanguage" that gives meaning to diverse expressions that would otherwise fall outside the definition of race. The language of race serves as a double-discourse, voicing both liberation and oppression. The totalizing effect of race obscures class and gender relationships from our view.[47] This may well explain attempts to universalize women's culture and oppression.

OUTLINE OF CHAPTERS

The Introduction provides the ideological foundation undergirding the clubwomen's self-improvement and social service work. Chapter 1 examines the historical context of black women's social action in organizing women's benevolent and mutual-aid societies and the generational links between the antebellum self-help efforts and organized black women's clubs. Chapter 2 denotes the urgent social needs nationwide that shaped the clubwomen's impulse for organization. Chapter 3 examines the scope and diversity of the volunteer activities of the clubwomen. Black clubwomen provided alternative institutions and services not because of a desire for segregation, but because they were excluded from nearly all public facilities. The educated, professional black women engaged in unpaid social work in numerous towns and cities to meet the increasing needs of African American communities.

Chapters 4 and 5, a primary focus of the study, present a comparative analysis of black social settlements founded by clubwomen in the South, North, and Midwest. African American clubwomen in the South established settlements that provided social services for black communities and helped to bond the institutions to their neighbors. The schools became centers for community organizations, women's clubs, and outreach activities. In the North and Midwest, clubwomen established black settlement houses to provide for the increasing black urban population. This analysis shows that the vulnerability of African American women in the South and in the North motivated the middle class women to provide for their welfare by establishing social service institutions.

Chapter 6 explores the process by which the male-dominated National Urban League (NUL) assumed much of the community work previously done by women. The establishment of social services, settlement houses, travelers' aid service, child and family welfare services, job training and placement, and preventive health care services initiated the emergence of professional black social workers. The Atlanta University School of Social Work was a direct outgrowth of the activities of the women of the Neighborhood Union led by Lugenia Hope. The gender shift in settlement leadership coincided with the increased presence of blacks in social work. The NUL and the profession of social work used scientific research methodology.

The clubwomen produced various strategies for community building from the 1890s to the depression. Chapter 7 examines the role of the clubwomen from the new black woman to the depression and New Deal. The depression destroyed the hopes of the female talented tenth, and the black working-class as well. College-educated black women, the Female Talented Tenth, symbolized the means by which the African Americans would progress. As the New Deal assumed more responsibility for providing work and training, race women no longer attempted to create a community by relying on race unity alone to uplift African Americans. African Americans empowered the language of race with their meaning and constructed the terms "race man" and "race woman" to symbolize their approval of leaders in the black community. The clubwomen demanded that African Americans participate in government programs and join labor unions. They publicly voiced opinions that supported employment and social programs for the working class. The clubwomen used a new language, that cut across race, to talk about unemployment and social programs. Yet Social Security excluded agricultural workers, domestic workers, laundry workers, and other workers. At least 80 per cent of black women were not covered.

Some scholars view the New Deal as a "revolutionary response to a revolutionary situation" and praise the permanence of its programs. Others attack the New Deal for having failed to solve the fundamental problems of race and economics facing the nation.[48] Of major importance was the genuine interest of prominent New Dealers in the status of African Americans. Historians credit Franklin D. Roosevelt with a successful appeal to the black urban masses and note that by 1936 African Americans had broken their historic ties to the Republican Party. August Meier and Elliott Rudwick argue that the New Deal social welfare programs, that were administered in the North with less discrimination than in the South, helped accelerate black migration and increase the number of African American voters in the Democratic Party.[49]

The Epilogue articulates the clubwomen's desire to serve their race and community as a persistent force among women in the NACW. It reaffirms black women's networks and its emphasis on "associationism for the common good." Yet black clubwomen's social action was not enough since they failed to attack the root of social problems that contributed to injustice in American society.

The clubwomen tried to embrace their humanity which had been suppressed by the larger society by placing themselves at the top of a racial hierarchy based on white middle-class morality and respectability. They interpreted freedom as the right to participate fully in American culture. Thus, they embraced patriarchy, patriotism, and other standards of American society. African American clubwomen's focus on doing things for poor women rather than with them and voicing their concerns rather than allowing them to speak for themselves undermined their efforts of institutional and community improvement. It implied that they knew and sought a better way for others. Race progress was related to racial uplift and the assumed need to civilize the black population.

Simultaneously, to solve the race problem, African American women organized a national network to engage in diverse social action that included social work efforts, institution building, and professionalization. In state after state the first social services available in African American communities for children, orphans, the elderly, and delinquents were initiated through black clubwomen's voluntaristic efforts. Volunteerism is the essence of a democratic pluralistic society.[50] This book examines the black clubwomen's legacy of social service and demonstrates that the activism of the women's voluntary association contributed to shaping the foundation for future social reform.

Chapter 2

Black Women and Social Action: A Historical Perspective

Colored women have never been backward in promoting charities for
their own race and sex.

Frances E. W. Harper, in *When and Where
I Enter*, Paula Giddings, 73.

African American clubwomen were influenced by a long tradition of
organizational involvement, institution building, and the ideology of self-help and
racial solidarity that manifested themselves through abolitionism and protest. Self-
help organizations and protest for civil rights formed a solid base on which black
women's clubs were established. Black women's civic and social work in
organized clubs and leagues arose against a rich background of women's
involvement in community activities. Pre-Civil War mutual-aid societies and
post-Reconstruction societies and clubs formed a foundation on which black
clubwomen built a social service network.

The dearth of social service institutions and the frequent exclusion of
Africans from those that were in existence raised the consciousness of black women
to community needs and influenced their decision to establish their own institutions.
Operating outside the framework of the social service system of the dominant
society, blacks were compelled to create their own service institutions. The
legalization of segregation in the South and racial discrimination in the North led
black women to challenge injustice. In response, they established their own
schools, orphanages, homes for the aged, hospitals, settlement houses, and social
agencies. Numerous social services were established during the late nineteenth
century.[1]

While white women were involved with charity organizations, black women were founding their own voluntary associations. This chapter examines black women's efforts at self-improvement and self-help in benevolent and literary societies, social services, education, and health care. The creation of these societies indicates that in most states, African Americans were entitled to minimal social service assistance.

Charitable and philanthropic organizations existed among black women prior to the 1890s. Did these organizations provide a model of compassion in African American communities as well as a cultural tradition of helping those who could not help themselves? Lacking outside support, northern blacks depended on self-reliance to help the poor and needy. African Americans developed mutual-aid societies in many cities to keep their members out of the poorhouse and the pauper's grave. The earliest black women's organizations appeared in the churches in the eighteenth century. Free black women organized benevolent organizations for racial, cultural, and self-improvement. Black women played a critical role in developing charitable, educational, cultural, and economic institutions to improve the material conditions and raise the self-esteem of African Americans. The earliest literary societies were expressions of the impulses toward organizations and educational and moral improvement.[2] In Philadelphia, New York, and New England, African American women developed the earliest mutual-aid societies among the free black population providing food, clothing, shelter, and other necessities. By 1830 there were more than thirty female-launched mutual-aid societies. These women were part of an urban community that was striving for freedom, culture, and respectability.[3]

Intertwined with self-help was self-culture. Increasingly as a second generation matured, benevolent and mutual-aid work was only one aspect of black women's activities as the number of self-improvement organizations grew.[4] Free African Americans were strongly motivated to show that they could be acculturated into American society.[5] While the idea of feminine respectability was widespread in the North, black women were believed to be "sexually promiscuous" and thus stood outside the ideal. They had to prove themselves. By forming their own organizations, black women could challenge the slander publicly and perpetuate the traditions of autonomous black organizations.[6]

Black women, who were strongly motivated by duty and obligation to form gender-specific mutual-benefit societies, were also seeking opportunities to exert autonomous leadership. They were conforming to the traditional conventions that emphasized gender differences rather than similarities.[7] In Philadelphia, the leading city for mutual-aid societies, more than three-fifths of the members of the city's benevolent societies were women.[8] The Female Benevolent Society of St. Thomas Protestant Episcopal Church, a mutual-aid society with extensive welfare functions organized in Philadelphia in 1793, was the first self-help organization established by black women.[9] The Daughters of Africa, a mutual-aid society of nearly 200 women, was founded in Philadelphia in 1821 to provide for the sick, bury the dead, and provide other welfare activities. Black women organized the African Educational and Benevolent Society in Providence, Rhode Island, in 1828, and the following year, in New Haven, Connecticut, women organized a similar society. The African Female Benevolent Society in Newport, Rhode Island supported the city's schools for black children until the city established a public school.

Secret and benevolent societies required a strong and intelligent leadership. Their social services for the sick, indigent, orphans, widows, and children established a precedent for black women's clubs. They contributed to a developing sisterhood and to a consciousness of the social reforms that became the aims of black women's clubs. Many of the female groups distributing food to the needy in Philadelphia were Dorcas Societies. The Dorcas Missionary Society, the most widespread of the women's groups to offer aid and assistance to the poor, was founded in 1824 by Sarah Bass Allen, the first missionary in the African Methodist Episcopal Church. The society, which made clothes for the needy and cared for the sick, was named for the biblical Dorcas who dedicated her life to doing good deeds.[10] Women like Allen who organized benevolent societies adhered to the traditional domestic roles associated with family and charity.

Black women, restricted by race and gender, often struggled against the most discouraging and desperate circumstances to provide for their families. In 1828 black women in New York City organized the African Dorcas Association, with the object "to afford relief in clothing, hats, and shoes to such children as regularly attend the schools belonging to the Manumission Society."[11] The large number of students who were absent frequently from the African Free School due to lack of suitable clothing led to the organization of the association. Encouraged to organize by the Manumission Society, the Dorcas Association accepted the gender conventions and sought assistance from male counterparts.

Early black self-help activities stressed direct assistance to maintain the integrity of the family and to provide available financial assistance for emergencies. Whereas black men established beneficial societies for economic reasons, black women emphasized morality and ethical behavior. Concerned about their collective image, black women placed exacting requirements on membership in the societies.[12] The Abyssinian Benevolent Daughters of Esther Association, for instance, was founded in New York City on 19 April 1839 for moral and relief purposes. Black women chose gender-conscious names for their organizations and many from the Old Testament, such as Dorcas and Esther. The latter name portrayed an image of black women who were strong and courageous. Membership in the mutual-benefit society depended on good conduct and moral behavior, whereas a woman was denied membership if she was addicted to inebriety, had a plurality of living husbands, or was guilty of improper conduct. According to the Benevolent Daughters of Esther: "The benefits of this society shall be extended to any member who shall be taken sick, confined to her bed. She shall receive $2 per week for six weeks, if not confined, but prevented from her daily occupation, she will receive $1 per week provided her sickness did not result from immoral conduct. She shall be allowed $20 for funeral expenses."[13]

Black women established the earliest literary societies to perpetuate self-improvement. Some African American men praised the work of women's societies, but the restrictive attitudes of most men forced the women to organize their own groups. However, the enthusiasm with which these women sought to cultivate their minds did not necessarily imply a rejection of traditional gender roles. By improving their minds, they were becoming more, not less, womanly.[14] The Afric-American Female Intelligence Society was both a literary and a mutual-aid group. Its constitution stated that "women of color of the Commonwealth of Massachusetts associated for the diffusion of knowledge, the suppression of vice and immorality, and for cherishing such virtues as will render us happy and useful to society."[15] Established in Boston in 1832, the society sponsored lectures enabling it to become a moral force in the community and provided health insurance for its members.

Race consciousness precipitated gender consciousness among African American women. Maria Stewart developed a strong consciousness of the intersection of race and gender inequities. Boston's Afric-American Female Intelligence Society sponsored Maria W. Stewart's ascent to the public platform in support of antislavery activism and woman's rights. Stewart ignored notions of woman's place in the church and society and publicly addressed the mixed audience as well as other male and female groups. While Stewart spoke out on behalf of all blacks, much of her message was woman-centered. Black women were subject to a domestic double standard. They were admonished by church and society to consider home their proper sphere, to demonstrate subservience to men, all of which suggested a protected dependency. Most black women had to work to contribute to the upkeep of their home. Moreover Stewart realized that no matter how hard-working or virtuous black women were they were always considered to be subject to sexual compromise.[16] She opposed the idea that morality and worth were inherent to a particular race or class. She projected a religious and moral ethic that provided a context for black women's feminism for succeeding generations. Stewart encountered hostility and alienation not only because of her political views regarding slavery but because she addressed mixed audiences of men and women, which was not considered respectable behavior for women.[17] Although Stewart's racial improvement efforts were welcomed by the black men of Boston, they were less complimentary a year later when she publicly chastised them for not doing all they could for the race.[18] Silenced and ostracized in Boston, Stewart moved to New York and taught in Brooklyn's Williamsburg Colored School from 1833 to 1853, immediately preceding the educational and public work of Sarah S.T. Garnet.

Public actions such as charity work, and campaigning for temperance, education, and moral reform were closely tied to women domestic responsibilities. During the abolitionist era, Shirley Yee argues that black women filled the expectations of womanhood, worked for racial uplift, and walked the fine line of female respectability. Among affluent African American women in the abolitionist movement, such as Sarah Mapps Douglass, Susan Paul, Sarah Remond, Caroline Remond Putnam, the Forten sisters, Margaretta, Sarah F. Purvis, and Harriet F. Purvis, and their niece Charlotte Forten Grimke, the woman's role was traditional. Women from prosperous families met the expectations of middle class womanhood and could devote time to community work. The sexual ideology of antebellum free black society, as embodied in white ideals of true womanhood, made community activism a special duty of black women and the basis for their involvement in abolitionism.

Many women who joined the literary societies also participated in antislavery societies such as the Philadelphia Female Anti-slavery Society and Boston Female Antislavery Society. Susan Paul was the vice president of the second annual Antislavery Convention of American Women and active in local temperance group. An advocate of women's rights and abolitionism, Paul was the the daughter of Thomas Paul, pastor of the Joy Street Church. Like Sarah Mapps Douglass, Paul was a pioneer in education for African Americans.

Black women were assets to the antislavery cause in a variety of ways. The wife and sister of abolitionist Charles Lenox Remond, Sarah Parker Remond and Caroline Remond Putnam, were in abolitionist groups and also acted individually to protest against segregation and discrimination. Black women participated in the rescue of fugitive slaves and provided refuge within their homes for escaped slaves. This is true for women involved in the Underground Railroad, such as Lettia Still and Catherine Delany of Philadelphia, and Anna Murray Douglass, Henrietta G. Ray, and Mary Marshall Lyons of New York. Shirley Yee argues that whereas the notion of submission and passivity might define white womanhood, it was less meaningful for black women, especially for the majority who helped support their households financially or for those who were encouraged by the men of their race to participate in racial activities.

Limited social services provided for African Americans before emancipation were forerunners of institutions established in the late nineteenth century. Catherine (Katy) Ferguson, a former slave freed by New York state emancipation in 1827, began an integrated Sunday school in her home in New York City that set a precedent for future efforts in child welfare services.[19] She took in or placed in private homes forty-eight children, of whom twenty were white, from the streets of her poor neighborhood and almshouse. Katy Ferguson understood the advantages of the "placing out" system over institutional care.[20] Katy Ferguson's School for the Poor was the earliest Sunday school in New York. Although she could neither read nor write, Ferguson committed much of the Bible to memory to teach the Scriptures.

Quakers in New York City founded both the Colored Orphan Asylum and the Colored Mission after the Civil War. Established in 1838, the orphanage existed until it was destroyed by the Civil War riots in 1863. Following the war, the institution was replaced by the Riverdale Colored Orphan Asylum and Association for the Benefit of Colored Children.[21] The orphanage received support from the Empire State Federation of Women's Clubs.

The Civil War impoverished the South, and by accelerating the process of industrialization and encouraging urbanization and immigration, it transformed poverty from a local to a national problem.[22] Following the Civil War, the task for blacks and whites in the South was to build a free-labor society through schools, churches, and employment and to reunite their families. Historian

Marable Manning asserts that many African Americans viewed America's experiment in social democracy during Reconstruction as a harbinger of a better life in their times.[23] Congress established the Bureau of Refugees, Freedmen, and Abandoned Lands in 1865 to administer a program of temporary relief during the war and for a year thereafter, and it was extended for six years.[24] The Freedmen's Bureau was a federal welfare agency established to function as an employment agency and a settlement agency, lease abandoned properties to black cultivators, to function as an educational agency, encourage the founding of black schools, and function as a health agency, maintaining and establishing hospitals and employing doctors. Yet the job of restructuring the South may have been more successful if placed in the Freedmen's Aid Society, organized by the Methodist Episcopal Church after the Civil War or the National Freedmen's Relief Association.[25] After the bureau was abandoned in 1872, and the limited institutional support by the government ceased, social services were not provided for African Americans by the larger community. African Americans, especially black women, shouldered the burden of providing for themselves.

Concern with ending exclusion led African American women to initiate early attempts at social service by establishing orphanages, homes for the aged, nonprofit hospitals, and other medical care facilities. In both the North and South, there was an urgent need to establish institutions for children whose parents were dead, missing, or working long hours as domestics. The Howard Colored Orphanage Asylum began before the Civil War in Sarah A. Tillman's home on East 13th Street in lower Manhattan. With the assistance of General Oliver O. Howard, this service moved to Brooklyn and was incorporated in 1869. The Brooklyn Orphanage served as a child-care center and offered trade skills for older children under the motto "to give a child a chance." Initially located at Pacific and Ralph Avenues, the orphanage moved later to the heart of Weeksville.[26] A women's auxiliary, led by Florence Ray, Maritcha Lyons, and other community women, raised funds to support the orphanage. Ray, the daughter of abolitionist Charles Ray, was assisted by members of the Woman's Loyal Union and local churches.

After the Freedmen's Bureau and northern societies closed their facilities in the South, African Americans turned to their own resources. In the South, the Carrie Steele Logan Orphan Home was founded in Atlanta in 1888 as an orphan home and nursery school for indigent children. A domestic servant in the train depot, Logan had learned to read and write while enslaved. She began her work in a two-room house with five orphans. Earnings from her job enabled Logan to purchase property on Wheat Street, construct a three-story building, and supported the institution through fund-raising. The board of directors consisted of businessmen and ministers from the black community. Prominent whites endorsed the institution which aimed to keep black youth out of jail and make them industrious, substitute for a Christian home, and provide domestic and vocational training. The home provided training in morals and religion, education, domestic training, and citizenship.[27] Since a primary goal of the institution was behavior modification and character development, it was not unusual that it received strong interracial support. After Logan's death her husband continued the work that she had started. The home became a part of the Community Chest in 1924.

Although orphanages occasionally accepted youthful offenders, there were no reformatories for African Americans during the post-Reconstruction period. Institutions for delinquents became an immediate goal of the clubwomen. Diana Pace Watts offered social services to orphaned children at what became the Reed Home in Covington, Georgia. The children taken in by Watts lived on a farm during the summer and raised their food for the winter.[28]

In 1890 the Leonard Street Orphan Home was established in a Fort McPherson army barrack purchased from Spelman Seminary. The Atlanta institution provided for underprivileged girls ages six to sixteen. Miss M. L. Lawson was the director of the home until failing health forced her to relinquish it to Amy Chadwick, an Englishwoman from the Northfield Bible Training School in Massachusetts. Since it was located near Spelman Seminary, Chadwick arranged for the children to be educated at Spelman while they were cared for in the orphanage. The original orphan home was the site of the orphanage until 1926. The children attended Spelman's day school program until 1928.[29]

For some black women, involvement in charitable projects, a shelter for the homeless, and care for orphans and the poor was part of their leadership in evangelism and public preaching. Evangelist Amanda Berry Smith combined preaching and social reform. In 1899 she received national attention after establishing the Industrial Orphanage Home for Colored Children in a temperance community near Chicago. As the number of black migrants increased so did the need for orphanages and homes for the elderly. While clubwomen in Chicago took the lead in developing day-care for black children, Amanda Smith led the fight to obtain adequate facilities for homeless children in Harvey, Illinois asserts scholar Wanda Hendricks. Smith, like Anna Cooper and Mary Terrell, also played a role in the developing feminist consciousness among black women. Dissatisfaction with restrictions on her preaching in the African Methodist Episcopal Church led Smith to become a missionary evangelist. Preaching in England, India, and Liberia, she used the money from her years of evangelistic work in the United States and abroad and the sale of her autobiography, *Amanda Smith's Own Story*, to establish and finance her institution.[30] She invested her life's savings of $10,000 in the home and was left penniless. Restricted growth and an inefficient staff limited the home's success and led state inspectors to threaten to close the orphanage.[31] Supported by the club women and other philanthropic groups in Chicago, the orphanage institutionalized black clubwomen's work when it became a state institution in 1914. In 1920 the Northside Women's Club of the Illinois Federation raised funds to build a new institution for the Amanda Smith Industrial Orphanage Home.[32]

COMMUNITY HEALTH CARE SERVICES

African Americans were excluded from nearly all community-wide health and social services.[33] Black women provided health care institutions, including hospitals, sanitariums, dispensaries, tuberculosis camps, and other self-reliant medical assistance. Poor health care combined with unsanitary living conditions and poor diet produced high mortality rates among African Americans. Sylvania Francez Williams, founder of the Phillis Wheatley Women's Club and the Phillis Wheatley Orphan Home for Girls, led a fund-raising campaign for the erection of a sanitarium (hospital) in New Orleans and to organize a training class for nurses.   Chicago clubwoman Fannie Barrier Williams assisted in the fund-raising campaigns for a nurses' training program which Dr. Daniel Hale Williams established at Chicago's Provident Hospital in 1891. Operating with white and black directors, the black facility was the largest medical institution in the North. Dr. Williams established a school for nurses at Washington's Freedmen's Hospital. The black community was responsible for building facilities and training its own people.[34]   Caroline Still helped establish a dispensary in Philadelphia. Hallie Tanner Dillon established a Nurse Training Program at Tuskegee Institute.

Hampton Institute established a nursing program and graduated its first class in 1897. Mary Susan Bailey, a graduate in the class, was the first matron at the Brooklyn Home for Colored Aged and the first registered nurse in the black community. Bailey, president of the Missionary Society of the First Episcopal District of the African Methodist Episcopal Church, combined health care and social work.[35]

Black women entering the profession of medicine often found refuge from race and gender discrimination as resident physicians in black colleges. African American women were the first females of any race to practice medicine in four southern states.[36] Included were Hallie Tanner Dillon in Alabama, Verina Morton-Jones in Mississippi, Matilda Evans in South Carolina, and Sara Jones in Virginia.   Dillon and Jones graduated from the Women's Medical College of Philadelphia. Hallie Dillon-Johnson practiced at Tuskegee from 1891 to 1894. Sophia Jones was the resident physician at Spelman Seminary.   Morton-Jones became the physician at Rust College in Holly Springs, Mississippi.

Both Verina Morton-Jones and Susan McKinney-Steward combined medicine with a keen interest in social action and community improvement despite gender and race prejudice.   A graduate of the Medical College of New York in 1870, McKinney-Steward was a founder of the Brooklyn Woman's Homeopathic Hospital and Dispensary (Memorial Hospital for Women and Children) and the physician for the Brooklyn Home for the Colored Aged.[37]   Dr. McKinney-Steward was aware of the role of women in medicine. She was indebted to Dr. Clemence Lozier, New England School of Medicine for Women, a white woman who had pioneered in the admission of women to medical schools.   As both female and black, Susan Smith initially found it difficult to find steady work. As one patient stated, "That isn't a doctor, that's a lady; doctors are gentlemen."[38] She was active in the Brooklyn Literary Union, the Women's Mite Society of the African Methodist Episcopal Church, the Women's Christian Temperance Union, and the woman suffrage movement.   Marrying Rev. William McKinney in 1871, she was widowed two years later. After her second marriage to Chaplain Theophilus Steward, Susan Smith McKinney-Steward settled in Ohio at Wilberforce University as the college physician from 1897 to 1918.

Trends in health care and emphasis on preventive medicine during the Progressive era included the visiting nurse, whose services were used in homes, schools, and settlement houses. Emphasis on the poor and environmental factors led many nurses to community work. Black nurses were unable to secure employment in public institutions, except in black-run hospitals. However, tuberculosis and other infectious diseases in poverty-stricken urban black communities motivated blacks and concerned whites to seek alternative medical assistance. Settlement house founder Lillian Wald, head of New York City's Visiting Nurse Service, sent black nurses into black communities to assist with health problems. From this effort emerged the first black public health nurse, Jessie Sleet-Scales. A graduate of Provident Hospital in Chicago, she was appointed to the Tuberculosis Committee in New York City in 1900. Near the same time Elizabeth Tyler, a graduate of Freedmen's Hospital, was the resident nurse for the Stillman Settlement, a branch of the Henry Street Settlement House.[39]

EDUCATION SERVICE

African Americans regarded education as the best strategy for racial progress. Even in the North, there were few schools for African Americans. In the South laws prohibited slaves from receiving an education. Mary Peake, a former slave, operated a school illegally for black children at Hampton, Virginia, during the Civil War. Sponsored by the American Missionary Society, she volunteered to teach at the Hampton Rhodes contraband camp at Fortress Monroe. Children and adults from ten counties attended the school. Peake taught the rudiments of education, needlework, and dressmaking.[40] In 1862 Peake died from tuberculosis at the age of thirty-nine. Had she lived, perhaps she would have been useful to the American Missionary Society's work of establishing black schools following the war.

Frances E. W. Harper was the single most important black woman leader in both the abolitionist and feminist reform movements.[41] Relying on traditional tactics, Harper helped lay the foundation for public activists of the next generations. From 1865 to 1871 she traveled throughout the South raising money for schools and hospitals and giving special lectures "in cabins, churches, and schools" to freed women and men. Her postwar activism revolved around social uplift, temperance, and women's rights issues.[42]

Most women, white and black, drew on the reverence for domesticity that emerged from a foundation in evangelical Christianity.[43] Harper was influenced by the ideals of evangelical reform. In a speech in 1875, she called the work of social uplift among the emancipated blacks a "glorious opportunity" for the youth of the race. She hoped that social advantages would not divert black men and women from helping the weaker and less favored of the race. Harper reflected the optimism of the postemancipation reform culture, which regarded education as crucial to group advancement.[44] She was active in the temperance movement, serving as a lecturer and field-worker. From her work before and after emancipation, Frances Harper developed fundraising skills that she used in her women's club work.

Fanny Jackson Coppin, a graduate of Oberlin College in 1865, made the Institute for Colored Youth in Philadelphia a training ground for a core of women teachers who raised the level of black schools and whose training could match that of female graduates of white seminaries. Coppin, a former slave, headed the Institute's Female Department from 1869 for over three decades.[45] An earlier graduate of Oberlin, Mary Jane Patterson, worked under Coppin's supervision for seven years before becoming principal of the M Street Preparatory School in Washington, D.C., from 1871 to 1884. Sarah Mapps Douglass, a graduate of the Ladies' Institute of Pennsylvania Medical University in 1858, taught science subjects at the institute for over thirty years.

Blacks in the South provided for their own education through self-help and northern philanthropy. Support for black education derived from a combination of northern white philanthropic funds and religious organizations. The American Missionary Society (AMS) ignored the early focus on black self-help activities of direct assistance to maintain the integrity of the family and to provide financial assistance in emergencies. De-emphasizing elements that African Americans considered crucial to their survival, the AMS did not provide burial services, payment of debts, or protection from peonage. Instead, it focused on the development of Christian education in black communities and the development of schools where this education could thrive.[46]

The missionary ideals of their New England teachers were instilled into the African American women trained in the schools established by the Freedmen's Bureau, American Missionary Society, and philanthropic funds.[47] The religious motivation of the teachers meant that religion, morality, and temperance formed the basis of the curriculum. The missionary societies emphasized the importance of the home and home life. The cultural values of piety, self-control, temperance, and the work ethic were thought to be important for economic independence and citizenship. In order to compete in American society, African Americans needed schools and colleges to prepare a minority of male and female students for professional and leadership positions. Black educational institutions founded by northern religious associations established a socioethical mission that promulgated values, a spirit of social service, social conscience, personal responsibility, and a sense of racial justice.[48]

Black schools and colleges founded by New England missionaries and white philanthropics promoted the process of acculturation that began before the Civil War. African Americans were simultaneously enculturated and socialized into their own culture and mainstream culture.[49] The concept of culture applied to strategies that helped African Americans survive and advance over time.[50] Historian Lawrence Levine asserts that despite racial, social, and economic injustice, African Americans forged and nurtured a culture.[51] Culture includes not only music and art, but specific skills, institutions, work habits, saving propensities, attitudes toward education and entrepreneurship, and other requirements for survival. Cultural values distinguished many black families from white families. The clubwomen promoted themselves as the civilizing agents bringing culture to black communities.

African American women graduated from educational institutions established by northern missionaries, such as Fisk University (Tennessee), founded in 1866; Rust College (Mississippi), founded in 1866; Howard University (Washington, DC), founded in 1868; Atlanta University (Georgia), founded in 1869; Spelman Female Seminary (Georgia), founded in 1881. These and similar preparatory institutions became colleges as they matured and abolished their secondary curriculum. Spelman Seminary opened in 1881 as a Baptist missionary school for women under Sophia Packard and Harriet Giles, who traveled south under the auspices of the Woman's American Baptist Missionary Society. Spelman Seminary extended its liberal arts program and granted its first baccalaureate in 1901.[52] By 1902 its graduates, trained as teachers and missionaries, were becoming the leaders and teachers of the race.

Between 1880 and 1915 largely as a result of support from the American Missionary Association, George Peabody Fund, Baptist Home Missionary Society, Julius Rosenwald Fund, John F. Slater Fund, and other philanthropic funds, the number of schools for blacks quadrupled, and the number of institutions capable of offering college-level instruction tripled.[53] Schools receiving aid from the John F. Slater Fund were required to provide industrial training. It increased the number of black teachers to about 30,000 by 1900, and also heightened the demand of philanthropic funds for industrial education for the black population.[54]

The industrial education idea, developed at Hampton and replicated at Tuskegee Institute, sought to prepare African American youth for economic self-sufficiency, usefulness to the community, and upright living. Many scholars have regarded industrial education as a product of compromise. Historians were influenced by the leading interpretation of industrial education that it was an extension of white supremacy, that it was designed to exploit black labor, and that it was outmoded even as it was being implemented. They rejected other views on industrial education. The term "industrial" had a different meaning in the early twentieth century from its current meaning. Industrial education was a moral program intended to inculcate the virtue of industry. Elizabeth Jacoway asserts that the advocates of industrial education worked to accomplish moral regeneration and social control.[55] Some scholars argue that the migration from the South to the North rendered industrial education obsolete as a method of integrating blacks into a biracial corporate state.

Self-help grew into a series of popular beliefs embracing race pride, solidarity, and economic advancement themes that were espoused by African Americans such as Booker T. Washington and W.E.B. Du Bois. African Americans were concerned about the best way to improve the race. Black leaders offered advice on how to deal with oppression and racism in American society. The central theme in the competing ideologies of Washington and Du Bois was education. Booker T. Washington's doctrine of industrial education was the main component of his program of race progress. In essence he believed that once blacks had proven themselves, the constitutional rights that they sought would be granted. Washington worked closely with the Afro-American Council, Negro

Business League, and the Farmers' Conferences, all of which promoted self-help. Washington believed that economic strength led to political and social strength. He supported the principle that "there is no prejudice in the American dollar."

W.E.B. Du Bois disagreed with Washington's concentration on industrial training for blacks and his accommodating approach to the loss of civil rights. While Du Bois supported thrift, patience, and industrial training for the masses, he argued that without equal rights, blacks could make no progress. He contended that cultivated highly trained African Americans, a Talented Tenth would lead the race.[56] Higginbotham argues the women's club network was the catalyst for a generation of black women, the Female Talented Tenth, that emphasized the importance of higher education to race survival and empowerment.[57]

African American clubwomen viewed Reconstruction as an aberration and refused to accept its failure. Using segregation to fight segregation, they created strategies and institutions that enabled African Americans to survive despite poor housing and neighborhoods and lack of health, educational, and welfare services. Their work demonstrated the belief that leadership arises out of the conflicts and crises of life. Although the Female Talented Tenth represented a diversity of backgrounds and attitudes, the women shared a public voice in black communities and a driving ambition that enabled them to overcome the obstacles of poverty and slavery. Despite the fact that they were encumbered by their tenuous position in society, they were aware of racial injustice and did protest against it. The roots of these elite, educated black women allowed them to understand the language of their constituents and what others perceived to be their limitations.

In essence, African American women of the 1890s expanded the club idea beyond the religious or literary societies. They formed their own organizations to meet local needs. Moreover, cross-class clubs, such as the Daughters of Zion of Avery Chapel founded in Memphis, Tennessee in 1867, gradually gave way to clubs with middle class black women.[58] In 1895 Alice Wiley Seay became president of the Dorcas Home and Missionary Society, a mutual-aid group to aid needy people in home and foreign missions. The society donated food, clothing, and money to members of the Brooklyn community and sent clothing and hospital supplies to Africa. The society was founded in 1877 by Eleanor Walker Hill, a member of the Concord Baptist Church in Christ. Under Seay's leadership, the Dorcas Society not only expanded its charitable activities throughout the city but became an association of the Empire State Federation of Women's Clubs. Thereafter, it gained an increasing membership from the black elite.[59]

Women in the North and South were involved in social action. Maggie Lena Walker engaged in extensive social service work in Richmond, Virginia. She was the daughter of a former slave, Elizabeth Mitchell, who was unable to make a living for herself and her daughter except as a washerwoman. Maggie graduated from high school and became a teacher in one of the public high schools. She was invited to become the secretary of the Independent Order of St. Luke, a women's sickness and death mutual-benefit society. The society, which was immensely popular and included many poor women like her mother, was founded in 1867 by a former slave, Mary Prout. In 1900 Maggie Walker took over the sisterly order, which had fallen into hard times. Eventually, it expanded to 100,000 members in twenty-one states. Among Walker's enterprises was the *St. Luke Herald*, a newsletter that gave notices of meetings and teachings on health, thrift, morals and education.[60] The St. Luke members, who were mainly churchwomen, struggled for gender and race justice while simultaneously maintaining traditional family values.[61]

The idea of an urban mission for African Americans was not new. Although settlement houses have been identified as imports from England, Jane Adams and other contemporary observers believed that missions provided the example. Missions, as proto-settlement houses, became an important part of the African American urban experience.[62] The ease with which Janie Porter Barrett established the Locust Settlement and the Industrial Home for Girls, and sustained the latter through interracial cooperation may have been inspired by Mary Peake's experiment at Hampton. The Colored Mission was a precursor of the White Rose Home for Working Girls. It was founded in 1865 as the African Sabbath School Association and incorporated as the Colored Mission in 1871. Its object was the religious, moral, and social elevation of black people. An increase in the black migrant population between 1870 and 1890 prompted the Colored Mission to become a social service organization. It helped African Americans from the South in getting jobs, housing, and child care for working mothers. During the depression of 1893-94, the Colored Mission distributed coal and barrels of food to black families.[63] Its mission work included a Sunday school, lodging rooms for women, clubs for boys and girls, an employment agency, visiting nursing, and sewing and cooking classes. In 1900 over 2,000 women were placed in jobs, 9,000 women received over-night lodging, and over 2,000 home visits were made.

In Washington, DC, Helen A. Cook and other black women served as volunteer workers with Associated Charities in the 1890s. These women were interested in the Home for Friendless Girls, established by Caroline Dean Taylor in the 1880s.[64] Anna Julia Cooper, Mary Church Terrell, and others supported the Washington Colored Settlement.

Atlanta's First Congregational Church was founded in 1867 by the missionary administrators and faculty of Atlanta University and the Storrs School. By the 1890s women in five black Atlanta churches were already performing beneficial and benevolent work. Women of Atlanta's First Congregational Church influenced the upper-class congregation to become the first black institution to enter social service through the establishment of a home for working girls and mission work in Atlanta's poverty areas. This community work by black women laid the foundation for the settlement work and social action of Lugenia Hope and other Atlanta women.[65] The Gate City Kindergarten was funded by the Congregational Church under Rev. Henry Proctor, the first black minister of the church.

The wide range of services conducted during this period shows that black women as much as white women were interested in humanitarian endeavors. African American women found themselves at a crossroads during the latter quarter of the nineteenth century. Middle-class black women were attracted to social reform, but they were rejected by nearly every organization as an equal participant. By 1896 African American women formed the National Association of Colored Women, through which they conducted club work, temperance, suffrage, and other reform work. They were encumbered by many things, including limited funds, little or no experience outside of church activities, and the promotion of self-interests. African American women organized themselves into a women's network and broadened the kinds of activities and scope of their work. The ideology of black self-help linked the work of the nineteenth-century women with that of the clubwomen.

Chapter 3

African American Women Organize to Ameliorate Social Conditions

We, the women of the Women's Era Club send forth a call to our sisters
who are members of circles, club societies, and associations to meet us
in Boston, 29-31 July 1895.

> Josephine St. Pierre Ruffin, "A Call," 3.

The elevation of the race will come only, and will come surely, through
the elevation of its women.

> Crogman and Gibson (1929), 191.

Women's clubs best exemplify the late nineteenth century organizations among African American women aimed at self-help and race unity. Black women across the country organized local clubs and leagues to aid in the social, economic, and moral progress of African Americans. The 1890s began a period of increased black awareness. It was a time of accommodation, mingled with hopes for racial justice and equality within American society. Black women, frustrated with the inertia of African Americans and the indifference of the white American conscience, formed clubs to ameliorate social conditions. The clubwomen recognized that it was in their best interest to take the initiative in resolving problems through pragmatic and innovative solutions. Therefore, they organized institutions and activities for the social improvement of their working-class sisters. They pooled their resources of time, money, and educational advantages to help others. The clubwomen concentrated on elevating women and children because they were the most disadvantaged.[1] Progressive women were identified by their capacity to form self-help institutions, such as women's clubs, which were the best example of the capacity of African American women for elevation. For African Americans, the community could rise no higher than its womanhood. The progress of a race is measured by the status of its womanhood.[2]

The organization of black women into clubs, leagues, and associations ushered in a new movement. The anxiety of an emerging middle class of black women was a vital motivational force for organizing local clubs and self-help organizations.[3] Although black women had created clubs previously, these race women linked club organization and community building. African American clubwomen launched an intricate task of establishing a community within a community.   For the first generation of African American women raised in freedom, club organization was the first step of community-building.[4] The challenge of the overwhelming task that lay ahead caused the clubwomen to be apprehensive as they attempted to build a sense of community and collective solidarity. In a positive spirit, speaking at her inauguration, Mary Terrell claimed that the magnitude of the work, far from depressing them, inspired the clubwomen to greater goals.[5]

Profiles of more than fifty African American women, that I compiled show the similarity and the diversity of the clubwomen in terms of education, marital status, regions, and other data. These women believed that they had a compelling mandate to work for the race, and most had the education and resources to do it. Nearly all of the women were graduates of a normal school, college, or professional school. Victoria Earle Matthews was one of the few self-educated leaders. Some clubwomen trained as schoolteachers attended Oberlin College, which recognized very early the necessity of closing the gender and race gap in education.   The Oberlin graduates joined the numerous graduates from the emerging black colleges.

More than half of the clubwomen married men who were prominent in their own professions, therefore, they had the time and economic security to do philanthropic work. Several women married ministers; Josephine Ruffin and Mary Terrell married men who became municipal judges; Elizabeth Lindsay Davis and Verina Morton-Jones married physicians. Nettie Napier was the daughter of a Reconstruction congressman, John M. Langston, while Josephine Beall Bruce married Blanche K. Bruce, who served in the U.S. Senate from 1875 to 1881.[6] Other club leaders married men who worked in business, journalism, city and municipal occupations, real estate, and building construction. Mattie Ison Heard, principal of the Newtown elementary school in Athens, Georgia and president of the Georgia Federation of Colored Women's Club from 1905 to 1913, was the wife of the city's only blacksmith.[7]

Mary Terrell, Josephine Ruffin, Ida Wells Barnett, and Fannie Barrier Williams, whose husbands were judges and lawyers respectively,   apparently engaged in social activism without threatening their husband's self-esteem. Some of the men who felt secure enough in their own profession offered physical support to their wives.[8] Although marriage symbolized respectability, a few women either postponed matrimony or separated from their husbands. In 1930, at the age of sixty-three, Elizabeth Carter-Brooks married AME bishop William Sampson Brooks. Mary McLeod Bethune separated from her husband, Albertus Bethune, in 1907. Charlotte Hawkins Brown's marriage to Edward Brown ended in divorce in 1915. Marrying men of achievement was part of black women's desire to be "ladies." Yet, many black women doubted the ability of most black men to view their women in the proper perspective of womanhood and to protect their virtue. Some black women believed it was their "duty to the race" to allow a black man to to feel protective regardless of his ability to exhibit these characteristics.[9] Christine Smith, a future national association president, believed that for a woman to develop to her greatest capacity, she must be allowed complete freedom. Why should a man be allowed to delegate to himself the power and the right to dictate to a woman her responsibilities, where her development begins, and where it ends?[10]

DEVELOPMENT OF BLACK WOMEN'S CLUBS

Was the development of black women's clubs a linear outgrowth of the benevolent clubs that arose during the pre-Civil War and Reconstruction eras? I have tried to answer that question by looking at the clubwomen involved in club formation as well as the structure of the clubs, membership, and club activities. Women were active in club leadership in the North and South prior to the formation of the NACW.   Local clubs were already in existence prior to the organization of a national association for African American women. Throughout the country, local clubs, societies, and leagues laid the foundation for a national black women's club network.

Opportunities for leadership came from the post-Civil War female organizations that were organized for temperance work, religious concerns, and cultural and social work efforts.   Among the clubs that grew out of temperance activities were the Harper Women's Christian Temperance Union (WCTU) in St Louis, founded in October 1888; the Woman's Club of Jefferson City, Missouri, organized in 1890; and the Woman's Club of Atlanta, established in 1895. The latter was an extension of the West Atlanta WCTU, which was organized in March 1887 at the Friendship Baptist Church.   Ella Branner Howard was the first president of the Atlanta Woman's Club. A member of the Big Bethel AME Church, Howard for many years headed the Daughters of Bethel.[11] This group was both a community organization and a church society.   Active members included Obediah Brown Carter, the wife of Rev. Edward R. Carter, pastor of the Friendship Baptist Church, and Selena Sloan Butler, founder of the National Colored Parent-Teacher Association in 1926.

Among the religious societies, whose membership included Fanny Jackson Coppin and other activist women, were the Women Mite Missionary Society of the African Methodist Episcopal Church and the Willing Workers Circle of the King's Daughters, an   interdenominational and interracial church group. Membership in literary and cultural groups broadened the intellectual horizons of black women and motivated them to later establish reading rooms in their communities. These libraries were important sources for community education. In 1892 Mary Terrell was the first woman to become president of the Bethel Literary and Historical Society.[12]

Yet black men have not always been willing to accept black women as equals.   Upon founding the American Negro Academy in 1897,   Alexander Crummell, W. E. B. Du Bois, Fancis Grimke, and other black intellectuals decided that black women were not competent for such an intellectual atmosphere and limited membership to African American men.[13] After protest from black women, namely, Anna Cooper, Alexander Crummell invited Maritcha Lyons to address the Academy and, along with W.E.B. Du Bois, wrote vigorous defenses of the lives of black women.[14]

BLACK WOMEN CAN "MAKE THEIR LIVES SUBLIME"

Monroe Majors, the most prolific defender of the virtues and strengths of black women, proclaimed, "A race, no less than a nation, is prosperous in proportion to the intelligence of its women." Noticing that the work and influence of black women were not   recognized, he   edited   *Noted Negro Women*.[15] Majors believed   the discourse between black men and women to be of great concern. Whether the leading race women had outdistanced the prominent men of the race was an important question. Majors believed the criteria for black civilization were intelligence, purity, and high motives of its women. Like W. E. B. Du Bois and the clubwomen,   Majors believed the educated black woman would save the race. Duty to the race prompted him to write about black womanhood, hoping to inspire black women to make their lives significant.

The immediate stimulus for organizing black women's clubs, however, was political, a need to protest the increasing number of lynchings that were occurring throughout the country, especially in the South. When black male leaders seemed unable or unwilling to protect their women or their race by taking action against lynching and other racial oppression, a spirit of unity galvanized black women to action. African American women gathered in a mass meeting in New York City to support one of their own sisters, Ida B. Wells, who was being oppressed because of her crusade against lynching. The meeting was called by two Brooklyn women, Victoria Earle Matthews, a journalist at the New York *Age*, and Maritcha Remond Lyons, a grammar school principal. Exiled from her Memphis home, Wells accepted a job from T. Thomas Fortune at the New York *Age*.[16] Other women journalist attending the affair were Josephine Ruffin of Boston and Gertrude Mossell of Philadelphia. Among the influential New Yorkers present were educator Sarah Smith Tompkins Garnet and her sister, Susan Smith McKinney-Steward, a physician.

As Wells created interest in her antilynching crusade, black women carried out the club idea for women's progress. They created clubs in New York, Massachusetts, Rhode Island, Connecticut, Washington, DC, and Chicago. Matthews and Lyons established the Woman's Loyal Union of Manhattan and Brooklyn two months after the gathering for Ida B. Wells. Matthews, whom the women identified as "a credit to her gender and the Queen Bee of our town," commanded the respect of the elite black women. The club began with seventy members, including teachers, doctors, journalists, women in business, homemakers, and seamstresses. The latter group included Carrie Smiley Fortune, the wife of Timothy Thomas Fortune and an expert in dressmaking and passementerie.[18] Club membership increased to 150 women within two years.[19]

The membership of the Woman's Loyal Union and other social and political clubs in Brooklyn and Manhattan was composed of culturally elite African Americans of old New York family backgrounds or migrants from the South who were generally well educated. Women in the club, such as Dr.Susan Smith McKinney-Steward, were both intellectually and financially able to assist the organization in pursuing its goals. Black women in Brooklyn were already politicized prior to Wells' testimonial event. Susan McKinney-Steward was the daughter of Sylvanus and Annie Springstead Smith, who were among the first homeowners in the historic black community of Weeksville, Brooklyn. Susan's older sister Sarah Smith Tompkins Garnet, an educator since 1854, helped make teaching a profession for African Americans.[20] Her pupils included the most competent teachers and leaders in the city, namely, Maritcha Lyons, Florence and Henrietta Cordelia Ray, J. Imogene Howard, and Susan Elizabeth Frazier, who graduated from Hunter College in 1888.

Typical of the club leadership was Maritcha Remond Lyons, a suffragist and one of the most brilliant clubwomen. Born into an old, established northern family, her father owned a seaman clothier's in New York City. Following the New York City Draft riots, Albro Lyons moved his family to Providence, Rhode Island, where he established a catering and confectionery business. A race man, he was interested in all civic and political matters pertaining to blacks. Maritcha's mother, Mary, studied with a French hairdresser and followed that business prior to marriage. Mary Lyons won a lawsuit against the state of Rhode Island that allowed Maritcha to attend the public high school and become the first African American to graduate from Providence High School. Later, Lyon's family left Rhode Island and settled in Brooklyn, where many of the city's black elites lived. By the 1890s Maritcha Remond Lyons, named for Catherine Remond [Putnam] of the abolitionist family, was a principal of an elementary school, a member of local clubs, and a volunteer fund-raiser for the Howard Colored Orphanage.[21] Leadership skills and the ability to command the respect of many black schoolteachers made Lyons an invaluable coleader in planning the mass meeting of black women at New York City's Lyric Hall in 1892.

Josephine Ruffin believed that clubs would make women seriously consider their future goals and make girls not think that marriage was their only alternative. In 1893 Ruffin organized the Woman's Era Club, in association with her daughter, Florida Ruffin Ridley, and Maria L. Baldwin. The aim of the Boston club was the "union of forces for the good of the race above all else casting aside all thought of self in order to do practical work." The local club was founded to promote the interests of African American women, primarily. However, membership was open to all women regardless of race. Members of the Woman's Era Club anticipated working with women for the benefit of all humanity.

Lucy Stone Blackwell, Edna Dow Cheney, and other white women representing the New England Women's Club attended the first meeting and congratulated the women on their broad approach to racial inclusion. They favored the idea of a club initiated and led by black women, but not necessarily a "colored woman's club."[22] The Woman's Era Club adopted the motto "Help to Make the World Better," the last words of Lucy Stone, an abolitionist and feminist who died on 18 October 1893. Despite its openness to diversity, in reality the Woman's Era Club was a black women's club.[23] However, Ruffin's association with liberal white women allowed her to become an advocate for black women among upper-class white Bostonians.

Josephine St. Pierre Ruffin was involved in community and national reforms prior to emancipation. She was the sixth child of an interracial couple, John and Eliza St. Pierre. Her mother was born in England, and her father, a clothes dealer, was a native of Martinique. Ruffin worked with the U.S. Sanitary Commission, and the Moral Education Association and was a visitor for Associated Charities for eleven years.[24] After the death of her husband, Boston's first African American municipal judge, she increased her charitable work outside the black community. The Woman's Era Club expressed race consciousness by publicizing civil rights and anti-lynching issues in the *Woman's Era.*

Black women in Washington, DC, organized the Colored Woman's League of Washington in June 1892. The league aimed to educate and improve black women, to promote their interests, and to form classes for educational and industrial work. Its leadership included the most prestigious women in the District, namely, Helen Cook, Charlotte Forten Grimke, Anna Cooper, Mary Terrell, Josephine Bruce, and Mary Jane Patterson. The league emphasized education, improvement of black women, and the improvement of their interests.[25] They were already engaged in charitable work in Washington.[26] The Woman's league provided racial uplift for Washington's black women. Under the presidency of Helen Cook, who had been involved in charitable work for many years, the Washington League established programs for community improvement. The league worked cooperatively with Washington's black churches and benevolent societies.[27] Anna J. Cooper later helped organize the first Colored Social Settlement in Washington. Cooper, Terrell, and others were among the many volunteers and donors to the social service center.

Ida B. Wells sought to establish a viable reform network of women from Massachusetts to Washington. She inspired women in New Bedford, Massachusetts; Newport and Providence, Rhode Island; and New Haven, Connecticut, to organize clubs to address grievances in community affairs. In 1893 following her antilynching campaign in Britain, Wells organized a women's club in Chicago with over 300 members. The object of the club was "the elevation and protection of African American women." The club, with Wells as president, attracted women from church and secret societies, schoolteachers, homemakers, and young women from high schools. The name was changed later to the Ida B. Wells Women's Club.[28] A member of the first Board of Directors of the League of Cook County Women's Club, Wells' extensive club work and community service earned her the title "Mother of Clubs."   Chicago became a club center, with the Ida B. Wells Club and the Phillis Wheatley Club as its oldest groups.[29]

Much of what we know about Ida B. Wells comes not from her personal life but from her public activities. She seldom wrote about her painful past: the deaths of her brother Eddie of spinal meningitis, of her parents and brother Stanley in the yellow fever epidemic of 1878, and of her crippled sister Eugenia and the abrupt termination of her education at age sixteen.[30]   Her father had been a member of the Fraternal Order of Masons, an organization pledged to assist the families of its members. Scholar Paula Giddings asserts that Ida refused the guardianship of this male organization but accepted its assistance in finding a job as a teacher at the rural one-room school.[31] At the end of the term, Wells moved to Memphis to be near her father's sister. Having studied in the normal school department of Shaw University (renamed Rust College), she continued her education at Lemoyne Institute and Fisk University to become a schoolteacher.

Wells based her self-definition and self-actualization on the personal aspects of her life. She was in constant conflict with the conventional female roles, which restricted a woman's desire for work and achievement. In the refined black society of Memphis, she felt dissatisfied with her life and lonely.   Even her network of journalists and friends, who supported her racial views, expected her to accept the conventional female roles of refinement and respectability. Wells gained admittance to Memphis elite black middle class, which was based on complexion, education, and talent. Although she joined a lyceum and edited its literary journal, the *Evening Star*, as a politically committed young woman she despised the superficiality of the black bourgeoisie culture.[32] Neither her gender nor her race kept Ida B. Wells from writing strong editorials on racial issues.

Meanwhile, the organization of local clubs spread rapidly among black women as prominent community leaders established clubs across the country. Under Victoria Matthews' leadership, the Woman's Loyal Union organized branches in many black churches in Manhattan and Brooklyn. As its membership grew, the New York Woman's Loyal Union formed sister clubs in Charleston, Memphis, and Philadelphia.[33] In 1893 Josephine Silone Yates organized a branch of the Washington league, the Kansas City League, with a membership of 150 women. Born in Mattituck, Long Island, New York, Yates was a science teacher at Lincoln Institute in Kansas City until her marriage to a high school principal. Sylvania Francez Williams, a teacher in New Orleans, organized the Phillis Wheatley Club in October 1894. Elizabeth Piper Ensley, a native of Boston, organized the Woman's League of Denver in 1894. Women in New Bedford, Massachusetts, organized the Woman's Loyal Union in 1894. Margaret Washington organized a Woman's Club at Tuskegee in 1895.[34]

TOWARD A NATIONAL WOMEN'S NETWORK

Realizing that a national organization was necessary to accomplish their goals, black women issued several calls seeking stronger ties and solidarity. The Woman's League of Washington was especially committed to organizing black women nationally. In the preamble of its constitution, the Washington league "appealed to black women of the United States to co-operate in forming a national league."[35] The Woman's League organized a dozen or more clubs in the South and West. Although it was the first black women's club to openly express the idea of national unity and to mobilize large numbers of black women, the Washington Colored Woman's League never became national in scope.[36] The Washington clubwomen turned to local work with fervor after 1896.

There was no national organization of black women at the time. Hallie Quinn Brown was an early advocate of a strong national organization for black women. She may have been influenced by her work as a lecturer and member of the British Women's Christian Temperance Union (WCTU). In 1893 she protested when the Woman's Board of Lady Managers of the Chicago Columbian Exposition rejected black women who applied to be managers because its members were selected "by organizations and not by individuals." A teacher at Wilberforce College in Ohio and former dean of women at Allen University and Tuskegee, Brown drafted a letter to each of the Lady Managers requesting the appointment of a black woman.[37] She maintained that if the woman's department proposed to represent the industrial and educational progress of the wage-earning women, the exhibit would be incomplete without the inclusion of black women. Following her protest Brown addressed many groups, including the Washington women, whom she urged to move toward making the league a national organization. It is likely that Brown had close connections with some Washington women, such as Mary Terrell and Anna Julia Cooper.

In 1893 the Women's Congress of Representative Women relented and invited Fannie Williams, Frances Harper, Anna Cooper, Fanny Coppin, and Hallie Brown to address a special session of the Columbian Exposition on the intellectual progress of black women. The World's Fair was a national forum to allow black women to defend their moral integrity and redefine the criteria for true womanhood. The black feminists earned the respect of black and white women for insisting that as American women they were entitled to attend the congress.[38]

Fannie Barrier Williams was the only black woman appointed to the planning committee for the woman's building at the Chicago World's Fair. Williams, whose parents and grandparents were free blacks grew up in the village of Brockport, New York. Her father, Anthony J. Barrier, was active in the local Baptist church and a partner in a coal business. Her mother, Harriet A. Barrier, was born in Sherburne, New York. Although Williams grew up in a white community, she experienced little racial discrimination because of her family's social position. Anna Cooper and some other clubwomen believed that Williams' light complexion, and northern, genteel background influenced her selection by the board.[39]

To understand the urgent need for a national organization, one must be cognizant of the many factors that only black women faced. In her speech on the moral progress of black women, Fannie B. Williams asserted that black women in the South continued to need protection. They were victimized by an environment that they had inherited from slavery.[40] Williams declared that the spirit of organization would be advanced when all women are coworkers. Black women were accused of having low moral standards, a condition caused by the heritage of slavery and made worse by their residence in one-room cabins. As a result of the publicity that Williams received, a great demand for her appearance as a speaker arose. She toured the country, urging all women to organize to effect reforms in education, home life, religion, and employment.

Speaking on the moral progress of the race, Anna J. Cooper stated that the black woman's history is full of heroic struggles against overwhelming odds to protect herself, struggles that often ended in her death. Much of Cooper's speech contained feminist themes expressed earlier in her book, *A Voice from the South* (1892). Cooper advocated a universal women's cause: "We want to go to our homes from this Congress demanding an entrance not through a gateway for ourselves, our race, our sex, or sect, but a grand highway of humanity. The colored woman feels that woman's cause is one and universal."[41] Cooper was advocating an egalitarian and inclusive theory that demonstrates a public voice for all women and all oppressed persons.[42]

Black women called for an egalitarian and inclusive political theory. Frances Harper envisioned women as potentially capable of transforming society. She challenged the Women's Congress to see themselves on the threshold of a new era: "Today we stand on the threshold of woman's era and the woman's work is grandly constructive. It is the women of a country who help to mold its character, and to shape, if not determine its destiny."[43] Harper asserted that if all women interested in social reform united, their cause would be advanced. The women wished to align women's cause with human rights issues, religion, and racial issues for social justice. Thus, the congress identified black women as public intellectuals, bringing recognition to their accomplishments as community leaders and prompting the National Council of Women to invite the Washington league, which they assumed was a national network, to join their group.

The quiet dignity and presence of the women led by Josephine Ruffin showed who they were and who they were determined to become. Ruffin, who had been associated with Julia Ward Howe, Susan B. Anthony, and Elizabeth Cady Stanton, challenged all women to join the black women's club association: "We are not drawing the color line; we are women, American women, as intensely interested in all that pertains to us as much as all other American women. We are only coming to the front, willing to join others in the same work and cordially inviting and welcoming any others to join us."[44] Ruffin was proposing women's organizations that could deal with broad-based issues. Hazel Carby contends that a major issue for the women attending the conference was the issue of exclusivity. Many African American women had experienced exclusion from white women's organizations, and they did not intend to discriminate.[45]

The defamation of black women's character immediately precipitated the call for a national conference in 1895 and hastened the beginning of club organization. Ruffin refused to publish a letter sent to the *Woman's Era*, of which she was editor, by the secretary of the British Antilynching Committee of London,

Florence Balgarnie, that assaulted the moral character of black women. The letter was written by John W. Jacks, president of the Missouri Press Association and a newspaper editor in Montgomery City, Missouri, a farming town about sixty miles southwest of St. Louis. In this notorious attempt to defame Ida Wells, Jacks attacked black women's character by denouncing all black women as immoral, liars, and prostitutes.[46] Jacks attempted to assault the character of the northern and British women who either worked for antilynching reform or associated with persons who did. Ruffin sent a letter to black women's groups and issued a call for delegates to convene in Boston.

The first national conference of black women was shaped largely through the communication network associated with the *Woman's Era* journal. With Josephine Ruffin's work in public affairs and as editor of the journal, it was natural for her to assume the lead in calling the women to organize. The need for representation at the national level, as in planning for the exposition, was one impetus for black women from many clubs to come together. Another was the women's clubs that had sprung up all over the country; they were an inspiration and preparation for a larger union. Josephine Ruffin noted, "Five years ago we had no colored women's club outside of those formed for special work; today we are able to call representatives from more than twenty clubs."[47]

Issues related to black women's sexuality provided the essence of the conference. Black women spoke with a collective voice that represented years of oppression. Organized clubs and individuals issued strong letters of protest against the insult to black womanhood. Responses came from women's clubs, and church societies, the women of the Bethel Church in New York City, and the Cleave Circle of Kings' Daughters of the Antioch Baptist Church, challenging Jacks for misrepresenting the moral integrity of black women. The Jacks letter projected a stereotyped image of black women that had existed since slavery and was perpetuated by newspapers and periodicals during the 1880s and 1890s.[48] It was essential to attack the racist thinking regarding the virtue of black women. Considering the notion of black inferiority and black immorality, it was not unusual for black women to condemn issues surrounding black female sexuality. The most common attack on the image of black women portrayed them as immoral, depraved, and loose. Clubwomen, who aimed to be respectable, refined, and cultured, denounced the image of black women as "wholly devoid of morality." Black women would create self-valuations that challenged externally defined notions of black womanhood.[49] They created their own identity.

The clubwomen, the women of the 1890s, would shift the image of black women away from stereotypes based on plantation stereotypes, and racist pseudoscience and rooted in social Darwinism.[50] As Ruffin acknowledged, the question of sexuality affected the very core of black women's organizations as well as their relationship to other national women's groups. Prominent black club leaders believed that the myth of black female promiscuity would impede racial advancement and progress. They that felt an assault on the moral character of black women would be detrimental to their agenda of reform. The clubwomen refused to adopt the attitude of silence.[51]   They voiced their opinions publicly despite the danger involved, and they established self-help programs, institutions, and activities for the economic, educational, and moral progress of African American women and the race.

Josephine Ruffin called for the formation of a national union for black women to exonerate their moral integrity: "A new era is here and we propose to ·protect ourselves," the women proclaimed.   Addressing the convention delegates in Berkeley Hall, Ruffin stated that black women could not expect to have unjust charges against them removed until they disproved them with their own efforts. She explained, "With an army of organized women standing for purity and mental worth the charges could be openly denied before the entire nation. All would work to elevate and dignify Colored American womanhood."[52]   Ruffin contended that if whites were asked to characterize black women in America, a common answer would be, they are mostly ignorant and immoral; there are some exceptions, but they don't count. Ruffin sought full participation in American society.   She challenged all women in clubs and organizations to join in a women's movement. African American clubwomen, like other middle-class women in American society, were interested in all social issues.   She stated that "we are not alienating or withdrawing, we are only coming to the front, willing to join any others in the same work and cordially inviting and welcoming any others to join us."

The National Federation of Afro-American Women (NFAAW) emerged from the Boston meeting in 1895. The NFAAW unified about thirty-six black women's local clubs under the presidency of Margaret Washington.   Victoria Matthews, head of the New York delegation, made the conciliatory speeches that softened the factions and made Washington's election possible.   The most prominent women attending the conference were Helen Cook, an intelligent woman who was familiar with parliamentary procedure;   Victoria Matthews, a gifted, fiery speaker and writer; and Margaret Washington, who was pleasant, practical, and generous.   Matthews was selected to chair the Executive Board.[53]   Selecting Margaret Washington for president acknowledged the cooperation and respect that she commanded from black clubwomen throughout the country.[54]

Meeting the NFAAW, Margaret Washington called for "unity in diversity " to link all women in a common cause of social reform. She called upon all women of the United States to lend their influence, interest, and aid.   She sought the leadership of the black middle class, especially the wives of bishops and ministers and the professional women to help their needy sisters.[55] Insisting that the middle-class women help their less fortunate sisters, she hoped that the women's clubs would foster cooperation through a national sisterhood.

Washington believed that educated women would save the race. Thus, her arguments were in the mainstream of black thought.   She indicated that it was not enough for the clubwomen to raise their own status; race progress entailed improving that of others as well. The elevation of all African American women was necessary to elevate the race. "Work for the masses and you work for the race. Only then will there be fewer outcries at the immorality of the race and there will be fewer lynchings of black men and women."[56]

The NFAAW consolidated the energies of black women into one sisterhood to promote needed reforms. With the formation of the federation the first conference of black women unified the local clubs into an ongoing national association. The conference revealed what they believed to be the issues of the 1890s. Their concerns, as indicated in their speeches, centered on education, temperance, social purity, homemaking, industrial training, black history and literature, and social uplift.[57] Still, it seems that black club leaders placed greater emphasis on achieving respectability than on reform.

Black women were interested in preserving their history and in shaping black cultural institutions to improve their gender and their race. Victoria Matthews, speaking on the "Value of Race Literature" at the National Women's Congress, praised the contributions of black women to race literature and race building. Matthews urged the women to examine African history and transmit the knowledge to future generations and show that African Americans have lived by this nation's democratic principles, Christian idealism, and self-reliance, and have contributed to the nation's progress. Matthews believed that literature would be the outlet for the suppressed lives that black women were required to lead. She asked, "What part will women play in the Race Literature of the future?" Matthews not only answered her question but stated the purpose of the newly organized club women: "Within one small journal, *Woman's Era*, we have created a record of Race Literature gathered from all parts of the United States, carefully selected by the ablest intellects of educated colored women determined to do their part in the future of uplifting the race."[58] Matthews was a regional editor of the *Woman's Era*. She believed that through their writings, black women could not only uplift women but destroy negative stereotypes.

The Colored Women's Congress of the Cotton States Exposition in Atlanta offered another opportunity for black women to meet on a national scale. Rosetta Lawson and Josephine Bruce chaired the Ladies Auxiliary Planning Committee for the Congress. Women from twenty-five states and the District of Columbia attended the congress, including Fannie Barrier Williams, Margaret Washington, Sylvania Williams, Lucy Laney, Lucy Moten, and Victoria Matthews. All were public women of national repute in educational, literary, and organizational circles. Lucy Thurman, a clubwoman from Jackson, Michigan, was elected president of the Congress. Although the Women's conference passed resolutions condemning segregated public transportation and the convict lease system, the clubwomen endorsed temperance and demanded the closing of a bar in the Negro Building that sold liquor and other intoxicants they believed were an insult to black womanhood.[59]

Thurman's selection to head the Women's Congress followed her appointment as national superintendent of Women's Christian Temperance Union (WCTU) work for African Americans and a trip to London as a delegate to the World's Temperance Congress. Black and white women campaigned against intemperance and saloons, especially in the South. In addition, white women blamed liquor as an influence in lynching and racial violence.[60] The clubwomen believed that the work of the WCTU was necessary for the physical, mental, and spiritual uplift of all people.   Founded in 1874, the WCTU campaigned against liquor and the people who sold it.   In the 1880s, under the direction of a former schoolteacher, Frances Willard, the WCTU became a powerful and influential organization.   Willard realized the importance of using politics as a vehicle for social change. Within a short period of time, not only was the WCTU in every state, but it had a membership of more than 200,000 women. Among the diverse women whom it attracted was the lecturer Frances Harper.[61]   Harper was a field-worker in the temperance movement and superintendent of the Colored Branch of the Philadelphia and Pennsylvania State Chapter of the WCTU from 1875 to 1882.   She headed the northern U.S. WCTU activities from 1883 to 1892.[62] Black clubwomen were split on the matter of support for Willard and the WCTU. Black women in the South and Midwest supported the W.C.T.U. despite the encroaching Jim Crow policy within the organization. By the 1890s local black units were separated from state bodies and designated as WCTU No. 2 Unions.[63] Ida B. Wells opposed the fact that black women were excluded from southern WCTUs and segregated in northern branches. Although the clubwomen knew that Willard was a good friend of African Americans, Wells believed that Willard was conservative and afraid to speak out on racial issues.[64]

Black representation was a major concern for African Americans at both the Chicago Columbian Exposition and the Atlanta Cotton States and International Exposition. The controversy over race and culture, which began in 1893 and broadened in 1895, produced arguments pro and con among African American leadership.   Indeed, African Americans had grounds upon which to build a reasonable doubt.   In the late nineteenth century, magazines and popular culture were filled with images, narratives, and representations that affirmed ideas about the racial inferiority of people of color. The media and "experts" appropriated the early anthropological notions of race to support their propaganda. World's fairs, magazines, and museum exhibits provided a scientific justification for Jim Crow segregation and imperial domination and simultaneously validated anthropology as a discipline.[65]   While African Americans felt that an exhibition of their skills, culture, and talents would improve conditions for them, the exhibition officials influenced by social Darwinist thought focused on how to exhibit their work without disturbing the racial custom. Exhibition officials spent $10,000 to erect a special building to house the exhibits from black educational institutions and organizations.[66]

With their exhibitions excluded from the main exhibition and the women's building, the clubwomen were divided in their support of black representation at the Atlanta Exposition in 1895. Some clubs, like the Phillis Wheatley Club of New Orleans, sent exhibitions despite the segregation. Club president Alice Ruth Moore stated, "The only way to convince our white friends that we can do anything is to show them; if separate provisions were not made Negroes would not be represented."   Moore and others felt that the strong presence of female black leaders interacting at a women's conference was commendable. Josephine Ruffin responded, "We cannot endorse the movement; separate exhibitions cannot do justice to the Colored people." Ruffin, who was noticeably absent from the Women's Congress, defined herself as an American.[67]

Far from launching a movement toward racial improvement, the Cotton States International Exposition promoted an attitude that encouraged blacks to accommodate white supremacy. In the most publicized address of his career, Booker T. Washington denounced social equality and urged blacks to pursue ownership of land, and habits of thrift, patience, and perseverance, along with high morals and good manners in an effort to gain respect from whites. Lack of social equality did not disturb Washington since he supported social Darwinism and believed that progress would come through the natural law of evolution.[68] Despite Washington's vision of economic opportunity for African Americans, there were serious race riots in Atlanta in 1898 and in 1906. A quarter of a century would pass before the Committee on Interracial Cooperation (CIC) and the Women's Council of the CIC would attempt to bridge the gap between the races.[69]

The National Association of Colored Women evolved from a merger of the National Federation of Afro-American Women (NFAAW) and the Colored Woman's League of Washington. Among the clubwomen attending the conference in July 1896 were the future organizational leaders: Margaret Washington, Mary Terrell, Victoria Matthews, Elizabeth Carter, Lucy Thurman, Ida Wells-Barnett (since her marriage in 1895), Josephine Ruffin, Addie Hunton, Lucy Moten, Alice Ruth Moore, and Selena Butler. Realizing the absurdity of two national groups working for the same objectives, the organizations united during their conventions in Washington, D.C.[70] A commission of fourteen women, seven from each organization, met to arrange for consolidation. The chair of the NFAAW's Executive Board, Victoria Matthews, directed the merger.[71] Matthews' astuteness as a politician, suggestions in the general meetings, service on the committees, and resourcefulness were invaluable in the formation of a new women's organization that became the NACW. Matthews was responsible for the most progressive thinking that occurred during the convention in 1896. Already experienced in club organization, she was selected the national organizer for the association. The clubwomen chose their motto, "Lifting As They Climb" to reflect their united goals and systematic effort in pursuing the moral, educational, and economic progress of African Americans. Although the motto, stressing "uplift," implied a sense of social distance between the members and the masses of black people whom they wanted to help, it also meant that the futures of both groups were intertwined.

The selection of a name for the association led to a spirited debate. Individual and organizational self-identity was significant for all African Americans, and both the federation and the league wanted its name adopted. Most clubwomen identified themselves as "Colored," a term that they associated with gentility and respectability. Some clubwomen, such as Josephine Ruffin, may have preferred the term "colored" to identify with international "women of color." Accepting a dual identity of African heritage and birth in America, Matthews asserted that she was not a colored American but an Afro-American. Identifying with race nationalist ideology and the militant T. Thomas Fortune, Matthews preferred to retain the term Afro-American.[72] An editorial in the *Washington Bee* declared that the club women should have spent more time deciding how to uplift their less fortunate sisters and less time on choosing a name.[73] The majority of the black population preferred "colored" and soon added respectability to the term by insisting that it should be capitalized.

Who would be the first NACW president? The names of each member of the joint committee were proposed for the presidency. Eventually, Mary Church Terrell was elected to lead the National Association of Colored Women. In her inaugural address, Terrell expressed concern about the uncertainty of the future. She stated that clubwomen, having overcome as a race and a sex so many obstacles that seemed insurmountable in the past, would neither be discouraged nor frightened. Terrell also encouraged unity and collective work: "In myself I am nothing, but with the loyal support of conscientious, capable women, all things are possible to us."[74] Mary Terrell believed that social problems would be ameliorated with the advancement of women. Throughout her presidency, Terrell addressed racial problems through programs and efforts designed to elevate and improve the circumstances of black women.

"SAW WOOD AND LET THE WOODPILE TALK"

Between 1897 and 1901 Terrell presided over three conventions. She established an official news organ for the association and organized the biennial conventions in cities with large black populations. The *Woman's Era* was the journal of the Woman's Era Club from 1894-1895. It became the official journal of the National Federation of Afro-American Women in 1895 and the National Association of Colored Women in 1896. The name was changed to the *National Association Notes* in 1898. The *National Notes* were published by Margaret Washington for 25 years, thus, she held control of the paper. Based in Tuskegee the newsletter reflected the conservative tendency of the NACW and its members who were content to "saw wood" or de-emphasize political activities.[75] In 1910 a controversy concerning the editor of the *National Notes* arose at the NACW biennial convention. There had been complaints about the irregularity of the paper and the frequent omission of items sent to the editor. The executive committee proposed that the editorship become an elective position. Ida Wells led the discussion. The effort was defeated by Washington's supporters. While not a monolithic group, the leaders of the national association were race-conscious. Terrell, as association president, believed that the well educated should provide opportunities to develop the capabilities of the untalented.

While black clubwomen were groping toward a strong national organization for unity in action and deeds, they were also building a consensus of thought and approach. They discussed specific issues of importance to all African Americans, such as temperance, morality, higher education, social hygiene, and domestic life.[76] Regional preference influenced the direction of the clubs.

Southern women insisted on industrial training and practical homemaking. Women in the West and Midwest were influenced by the temperance movement. Northern black women, like their white sisters, sought recognition in the professions.[77]

Regardless of their differences and preferences, black clubwomen were motivated by tension and anxiety. Black clubwomen were drawn to reform, yet they, too, were oppressed by social injustice. The clubwomen were among the new emerging and expanding black middle class. White women reformers who were concerned about their own loss of status and power were, in turn, better able to understand the perspective of those who never had power to lose.[78] Most black women emerged from a background of poverty. Discrimination and segregation prevented the clubwomen from elevating themselves beyond a certain point, but by working together they could "uplift" others and, conversely, themselves. Black women did not organize women's clubs solely to compete with white women or because they were excluded from white women's clubs. Organization among black women owed its particular character not so much to the fact that they were excluded from white women's groups as to the totally dissimilar circumstances of their lives.[79]

Clubwoman Fannie Barrier Williams proclaimed that the development of black women's clubs was the product of the "organized anxiety" of women who were intelligent enough to recognize their own subcultural status in American society and strong enough to initiate the forces of reform for improvement.[80] Adhering to self-help and collective efforts, the clubwomen of the 1890s created autonomous institutions to solve the problems associated with inferior education, economic deprivation, poor health care, and other neglected areas. Fannie Barrier Williams placed black women at the center of the African American's philosophy of self-respect that was prevalent during the late nineteenth century and the first two decades of the twentieth century. Williams believed that the black woman's club represented a "new woman" with new powers of self-help.[81] For the new black women who emerged during the 1890s, the women's clubs served both a political and a social purpose.

Chapter 4

Clubwomen and Social Action:
Volunteerism for the Common Good

We, the Colored women of America, stand
before the country today a united sisterhood,
to promote the welfare of our race. As a unit
we shall bend our energies to accomplish the
ends for which we have banded together.
　　　　Mary Terrell, *Woman's Era*, (1896): 3.

In the development of women lie the best
interests of the race; education is essential
to the highest type of womanhood.
　　　　　Anna Jones, *Notes*, (1904).

The organization of black women into a national association of women's clubs was
a distinctively forward move, elevating their philanthropic activities into a
systematic movement of social service and reform. In her first speech before the
National Association of Colored Women, Mary Church Terrell challenged the club
founders to succeed as women: "Through our united sisterhood, we hope to run the
whole gamut of human progress and reform having overcome as a race and sex so
many obstacles that seemed impossible in the past," proclaimed Terrell, the first
president of the association.[1] The woman's club association originated for the
social improvement of women and of the race.

　　　　The creation of the NACW ushered in a new era. "Our Association is
composed of women because the work which we hope to accomplish can be done
better by mothers, wives, daughters, and sisters of the race."[2] Black women
combined the force of a national organization with traditional American
methods of social reform. In speeches, mass meetings, and writings, they

represented the voices of African American women. The new leadership of the association, unlike Frances Harper, Sojourner Truth, and Harriet Tubman, had a forum and base to disseminate their ideas nationwide. In 1896 the organization of a national association vitalized a network of women's clubs across the country, uniting local clubs into a social reform movement.

The organization of women's clubs was a exuberant activity in the public sphere aimed at the progress of all African Americans, while simultaneously improving the status of women. The club, as black women's social space, was a vehicle for their public roles. Marginalized from leadership positions in male organizations, and kept out of other organizations in American society, black women created their own social space, the women's club. The women's club was a social space where African American women could develop their own sense of worth independently of their race and gender.[3] Since the churches were overburdened, the philanthropic efforts of black women would advance the race.[4] The NACW was the most effectively organized group among black women in the struggle for reform and woman's rights during the early decades of the twentieth century.

The clubwomen believed that there was no inherent inferiority that education could not remove. By the early 1900s nearly 4,000 women had graduated from normal schools and universities. At least 100 were from Oberlin College, and nearly 500 had graduated from the black colleges. Many of these women became leaders in the intellectual and philanthropical movement aimed at the moral and social uplift of the race.[5]

Women's clubs offered a professional status for such black women as Josephine Ruffin, Mary Terrell, Fannie Barrier Williams, and others. In 1896 there were nearly 5,000 women in sixty-seven clubs; in 1904 there were 15,000 women. In 1914 the national association represented 50,000 members in twenty-eight federations and over 1,000 clubs.[6] Where did the impetus for this organizing effort originate? Did the general encouragement of voluntary efforts to solve social ills that prevailed in the Progressive era contribute to the spirit of organizing among black women? Successful efforts in one place immediately triggered a response in another to solve their problems through the creation of women's clubs.[7]

Race work or social work was the primary focus of black clubwomen. Much was done through the women's clubs by women who were educated and had some leisure time for community improvement. Black women who worked for the race, such as Mary Terrell and Mary Bethune, were known as "race women." St. Clair Drake asserts that a race woman championed the rights of African Americans, but her role as uplifter was accepted generally with less antagonism than that of the race man.[8] Women stand out as a group distinct from the men engaged in community work. The community generally concurred with, and deferred to, the women's expertise. The community bestowed recognition and respect upon the volunteers and treated them as if they were professional social workers.[9] Working with community concerns that were public issues became a full-time job for many clubwomen.

The NACW gave coherence and significance to the club work of African American women by encouraging its members to embark on a broad program of activities and to address broad social issues. The association was stronger than individual clubs financially and therefore, able to broaden the scope of club work. Most of the work of the Association occurred on the local level. The NACW constitution, adopted in 1897, provides a convenient framework for examining the activities of the local clubs: to promote the education of women, to improve homes and homelife, to promote the moral, social, economic, and religious welfare of women and children, to provide job opportunities, to promote civil rights, to promote interracial cooperation.[10]   Interspersed throughout the   NACW constitution were the tenets of Republican motherhood.

There was no real model for a national organization for black club women. The organization of the local clubs provided some ideas for national organization. The earliest requests for advice were directed to the Woman's Era Club in Boston, the Woman's Loyal Union in New York, the Woman's Colored League in Washington, DC, and the Kansas City League. Thus, experienced clubwomen, such as Josephine Ruffin, Victoria Matthews, Mary Terrell, Josephine Yates, and Margaret Washington, emerged as leaders of black women's clubs.

The clubwomen supported race work, settlement work, and moral uplift. Josephine Ruffin, president of the Woman's Era Club, believed that every club should establish its own goals and adapt itself to the needs of its members. The Woman's Era Club had 150 members who were divided into literature, civic, philanthropic, domestic science, and race work (social work) committees. The club also sponsored classes in literature, music, and art.[11]

Margaret Murray Washington of the Tuskegee Women's Club promulgated educational work as the primary objective of black women's clubs. She believed that educated women would provide the best leadership for race work. Schoolteachers should establish mothers' clubs since they were generally the most capable individuals in the communities. Washington's main concern was self-help. She was committed to the idea of preaching black people to a higher social level. She believed it was the duty of the clubwomen to promote self-advancement among poorer women. As role models the clubwomen provoked inspiration from the community women but concurrently, they insisted upon home improvement, better child-rearing, and social purity talks."[12]   In a letter to a white benefactor, Washington stated her goals, "We have organized with the hope of lifting the masses beneath us and thus lifting ourselves. Necessarily, our work will be slow but I do not expect to become discouraged."[13]

Victoria Earle Matthews, president of the Woman's Loyal Union, emphasized charity, social work, and industrial education as goals for women's clubs. She suggested that the clubwomen form study circles and engage in some kind of philanthropy, hold vocational classes in their homes, visit the poor and unfortunate in the slums and in charitable and reformatory institutions, and provide nurseries for working mothers.[14] The Woman's Loyal Union members proposed establishing a reading room with books by black authors and a settlement house.

The latter goal was influenced by Matthews' tour of the South in 1895. Sponsored by the Women' Congress and the National Federation of Afro-American Women, the venture spurred her sensitivity to issues related to black women's image and sexuality. Tall, slender, with straight brown hair and a light complexion, Matthews spent several months on a fact-finding trip, traveling throughout the Black Belt of the South, including its red-light districts. Elizabeth Lindsay Davis suggested that Matthews' light complexion afforded her some protection while traveling.[15] Victoria Matthews preceded Walter White of the NAACP whose fair complexion facilitated his investigations of lynching. Her investigations uncovered red-light districts and the exploitation of black women in New Orleans, Charleston, and other southern cities and motivated Matthews to establish a home to rescue black women.

Immediate needs within the black community dictated the kinds of programs and actions that black women's clubs would provide. The women organized educational, philanthropic, and social service projects. The clubs emphasized household economics, night classes, free day nurseries, and kindergartens. Penny savings banks promoted self-reliance.

The condescending attitudes of the clubwomen were reflected in the mothers' clubs, established especially in the South, and in the homes for "fallen" women in the North. Conducted by the club leaders, the mothers' clubs were repositories of information on child raising and homemaking. Mary Terrell anticipated that Mothers' clubs would improve the moral standards of the "less favored and more ignorant sisters" because she believed that the world would judge the womanhood of the race through the masses of women. "Colored women of education and culture know that they cannot escape altogether the consequences of the acts of their most depraved sisters."[16]

Believing that music should elevate the race rather than disgrace it, the clubwomen formed music and literary clubs to promote the study of classical music.[17] They supported such musical groups as the popular Fisk Jubilee Singers. For the developing black middle class, indigenous forms of black music, such as ragtime and blues, were just another aspect of the "Negro world" that they wished to be rid of. Most respectable women considered ragtime and jazz obscene because of their origin in brothels. Thus, the clubwomen did not support the music that developed from the cultural traditions in black communities.[18]

Discrimination and exclusion caused the black women's clubs to support utilitarian projects to aid the indigent, orphaned, and aged. Most of the black women's clubs provided clothing, food, fuel, and other necessities for orphans and the indigent. The Tuskegee Woman's Club and the Sojourner Truth Club of Montgomery, Alabama, established the first libraries in their respective communities. The Phillis Wheatley Club of New Orleans established a hospital because colored patients were not received in the charity ward of other hospitals.[19] The Atlanta Woman's Club was interested in homemaking, better sanitation, and social service.[20] The Woman's Progressive Club, organized by Elizabeth Carter in 1898, supported a Home for the Aged. Elizabeth Davis and the Phillis Wheatley

Club looked forward to the establishment of a "settlement house."[21] Educated black clubwomen led the kindergarten movement in local communities.[22] Between 1900 and 1915 the clubwomen bought land for children's playgrounds, equipped schools with swings and gymnasiums, placed drinking fountains in schools, and established domestic science departments.[23] Like white female reformers in the Progressive era, black clubwomen in Chicago, Atlanta, Denver, and Pittsburgh waged successful campaigns for probation officers. Ida Wells-Barnett was appointed probation officer for juveniles in Chicago in 1913, and Alice C. Cary received a similar appointment in Atlanta.[24] Cary, the wife of the African Methodist Episcopal minister Jefferson A. Cary, was the first woman principal (dean of women) of Atlanta's Morris Brown College.[25]

To unify the clubs in a particular state or region, club federations were established. The earliest regional associations were the Northeastern Federation, organized in 1896, and a Southern Federation of Women's Clubs organized by Margaret Washington in 1899. Located in Alabama, Georgia, Tennessee, and Mississippi, the Southern Federation covered a larger area than any other regional unit and represented the most densely populated and impoverished belt of the black population. The southern women focused almost exclusively on the home and moral uplift because the members considered this the foundation for improving their race.[26] At the 1902 convention, 266 southern clubwomen attended the regional meeting.[27]

The Northeastern Federation of Women's Clubs was active in suffrage, woman's rights, and civil rights. Many of its members were among the founders of the NAACP and the National Urban League.[28] The strongest clubs in the federation and those most committed to education and charitable work were the Harriet Tubman Club of Boston, the Woman's Loyal Union of New York City, the New Century Club of Providence, Rhode Island, the Woman's Loyal Union of New Bedford, Massachusetts, and the Dorcas Missionary Society of Brooklyn.

Of the humanitarian projects sponsored by the state and regional federations, the work for Harriet Tubman by the Empire State Federation of Women's Clubs was the most historical. Alice Seay organized the federation in 1908 at the White Rose Home. Tubman was destitute and a patient in the home that she had struggled to maintain for the elderly.[29] She settled in Auburn, New York on several acres of land that she received from her friend William Seward, secretary of state under Abraham Lincoln. Other abolitionist friends included the Lowell family in Boston whom she often visited. The Northeastern Federation provided her with a nurse and helped Tubman settle a dispute with the federal government over the pension that she expected from her Civil War service. Although the Thompson Memorial AM E Church assumed the mortgage and gave Tubman a small pension, the clubwomen provided additional aid for Tubman and supported the home until her death from pneumonia on 10 March 1913.[30] Two years later the clubwomen in the Empire State Federation of Women's Clubs erected a monument over Harriet Tubman's unmarked grave.[31]

One main concern of the state federations was the establishment of state training schools for delinquent girls. Women of the Southern Federation, Janie Porter Barrett of Virginia, Selena Sloan Butler of Georgia, Charlotte Hawkins Brown of North Carolina, and Cornelia Bowen of Alabama led the fund-raising campaigns to build juvenile institutions through their respective state federations. The clubwomen, in conjunction with State Federations of Women's Clubs, established reformatories for black girls in Alabama, Virginia, North Carolina, Mississippi, Georgia, Missouri, and Texas.[32]

The clubwomen frequently sought assistance from the state legislatures in obtaining funding for reform schools. A club leader introduced a petition to the state legislature and attempted to convinced it that the institution filled urgent social needs. When the Mississippi legislature approved a request from the state federation for a probation officer and a home for delinquent girls, but deferred payment because of lack of funds, the women began their own campaign. Janie Barrett, president of the Virginia state federation appealed to the legislature for an annual appropriation for maintenance of the Industrial Home School. Since the project was new and plans for management were unclear, the legislators granted $3000 or only half the amount requested.[33] After Barrett had a dispute with the legislature and all state funds came to an end, she had to rely on the clubwomen to maintain the institution.[34]

Across the country, clubwomen established libraries to preserve black history and culture. Very early they grasped the historical significance of maintaining the physical residences of outstanding African Americans for future generations. They were involved for decades in projects to preserve the memory of Harriet Tubman and Frederick Douglass. The Northeastern Federation sent donations to the destitute daughter of John Brown. The women established the Paul Laurence Dunbar Memorial Association to care for the poet's mother, Matilda Dunbar, and to perpetuate his library.[35] Mary McCoy, the wife of the inventor Elijah McCoy and a founder of the Michigan State Federation, prepared a list of twenty-five black women inventors.[36]

African American clubwomen combined their interest in domestic popular culture, such as quilts, with their intellectual pursuits. In acknowledging fine needlework, china painting, drawing, millinery, cooking, and an extraordinary Bible quilt on display at the Atlanta Exposition in 1895, the women showed an interest in their heritage and the transformation of African cultural traits.[37] The quilt was made by an elderly woman, Harriet Powers (1837-1911), a former slave, who could neither read nor write. Powers memorized stories from church sermons and the oral tradition and transferred these to her quilt.[38] She lived in Clark County, Georgia, within close proximity to local churches and lodges. Powers' second quilt, depicting scenes from the Scriptures and natural phenomena, was commissioned by the interracial female faculty at Atlanta University.[39] Powers' heritage manifested itself in her tendency to draw upon the African tradition of recording history through natural phenomenon.

The first real challenge for the association in terms of programs was the Frederick Douglass Home, Cedar Hill. Located in Anacostia, Douglass and his first wife, Anna Murray, purchased property in the village across the river from Washington, DC, on the Potomac River. After Douglass' death in 1895, his widow and second wife, Helen Pitts Douglass, a friend of Jane Addams, struggled to preserve his home as a memorial to his life. As early as 1914, the NACW resolved to cooperate with the Board of Trustees of the home by sending a donation of $50.00.[40] In 1916 the club women assumed responsibility for the home and its preservation and restoration, which symbolized the goals and ideals of the association. Mary Talbert, head of the Douglass Memorial Association of the NACW, organized the movement to redeem the Home. The mortgage was burned during the tenth biennial NACW Conference in 1918.[41] Contributing $500 to the NACW, Madam C. J. Walker helped burn the contract. Following the completion of the restoration in 1921, the NACW gained prestige and power, and the public dedication event raised the consciousness of African Americans to the presence of black organized women. The Association dedicated the Frederick Douglass Home to freedom and progress in August 1922.[42]

Madam C. J. Walker, a member of the NACW, was known for her generous philanthropy to organizations and institutions in the black community. Despite her contributions to the Frederick Douglass Preservation Fund, to homes for the aged in St. Louis and Indianapolis, to numerous orphanages, to Tuskegee Institute, and to the NAACP, Walker was not completely accepted by the black bourgeoisie society.[43] Many African Americans accused Walker of trying to remake black women in the image of white women. Born Sarah Breedlove, Walker was orphaned at the age of seven and worked during her early years as a washerwoman. Although she was uneducated, Walker created a system of hair care and scalp treatment that not only provided black women with a grooming method but took them out of the washtub by opening a vocation in beauty culture and sales.[44] She promoted economic self-help for black women.

The clubwomen organized their biennial conventions in cities with large black populations: Nashville in 1897, Chicago in 1899, Buffalo in 1901, St. Louis in 1904, Detroit in 1906, Brooklyn in 1908, Louisville in 1910, Hampton in 1912, Wilberforce in 1914, Baltimore in 1916, Denver in 1918, and Tuskegee in 1920. Lacking a large meeting space and barred from most city auditoriums and public facilities, the conventions were held at black churches. There was continuity of issues because of repeated abuses of African Americans, especially women. At the same time, speeches on conservative topics as "Modesty in Manners and Dress," "Temperance," "Child Rearing," "Purity and the Woman," "Morality," and the "Home" indicates the interest of these bourgeoisie women and what they considered to be pressing needs of their people.[45] They considered themselves to be the moral guardians of the black communities.

The large number of respectable black women attending the conferences, along with the overall diversity of the conferees, served to counteract the social Darwinistic notion of inferiority. Both black and white women believed that they would be able to cooperate in social reform without regard to the superficial division of race. Among the white women attending the convention were Ellen Henrotin, former president of the General Federation of Women's Clubs, Jane Addams of Hull House, and Mary McDowell of the Northwestern Settlement. Addams invited the officers of the NACW to lunch at Hull House, where they found a real sisterly spirit.[46] In 1918 possibilities developed for cross-cultural sisterhood with Jane Addams, Grace Abbott, Edith Abbott, Sophonisba Breckinridge, Crystal Eastman, and Anna Strunsky Walling as affiliate members of the NACW.[47]

Although there was the appearance of a monolithic body at the national conventions, in-group divisiveness frequently surfaced. Ida Wells developed problems with both Mary Terrell and Fannie B. Williams. Although they had already gained prominence, Wells surpassed the women with her antilynching campaign. Wells was politically oriented, whereas the clubwomen emphasized domestic issues. Marriage in 1895 to Ferdinand Barnett did not close the "respectability" gap between Wells and the elite women. In 1899 Mary Terrell was a strong candidate for reelection even though she had already served three years. Ida Wells blamed Terrell after she was excluded from the planning committee for the Chicago Biennial Convention. Terrell claimed that the Chicago women on the ad hoc program committee, chaired by Fannie B. Williams, objected to Wells' involvement. Wells stated that this was a "staggering blow" because she had started these women in club work and assisted them.[48] The incident occurred one year prior to the break between the Barnetts and Williams in 1900. The oversight of Ida Wells-Barnett by Fannie Williams may have been an early indication of the rift that would develop between the Barnetts and Williams over ideology and patronage.[49] Ferdinand Barnett and S. Laing Williams were law partners before Williams and his wife became strong advocates of Washington's philosophy. Neither Fannie nor her husband completely succumbed to the Washington ideology, and both later returned to their protest activities.[50] Fannie Williams and Wells-Barnett continued their mutual activities in club and volunteer work.

Booker T. Washington's political pull was significant for many of the clubwomen. Considering his views on self-help and his access to white philanthropy, it is not surprising that there was a link between the Washington faction and the clubwomen.[51] However, this connection did not mean that the clubwomen were controlled by Washington. Black women acted independently of his influence. It was his policy of avoiding political and social equality that Terrell, Wells, and Josephine Ruffin rebelled against. Ida Wells-Barnett criticized Washington or suggesting that African Americans should pursue industrial training rather than college and university training, as well as his insistence on economic advancement over political equality. Wells-Barnett fought Washington's increasing control over the Afro-American Council. Indeed, there was a measurable distance on the stance taken by the association under Terrell's presidency and the public position of Ida Wells-Barnett on similar social and political issues.[52] Wells-Barnett and Terrell experienced a personality conflict rather than ideological difference. Mary Terrell, the daughter of a wealthy

Memphis real estate broker and a graduate of Oberlin College, was never firmly attached to Washington. She and her husband protested against discrimination despite the fact that Washington was responsible for Terrell's appointment as a judge in Washington, D.C. By 1903 Mary Terrell's loyalty to Washington was strained, and he was exasperated by the inconsistency of her speeches.[53] Moreover, his stand on the Brownsville riot of 1906 brought their relationship to a breaking point. Terrell openly criticized Washington after that.

The real contenders for the presidency in 1899 were Mary Terrell and Josephine Ruffin. Terrell was reelected for a second two-year term. When Elizabeth Carter was defeated for recording secretary, she threatened to withdraw the Northeastern Federation of Colored Women's Clubs. Both Carter and Ruffin resented the fact that no candidate from their regional clubs was elected to the association.[54] The dispute over the election of NACW officers lingered and nearly split the association. Ruffin, believing that club work was too important to be weakened by trivialities or personalities, urged the women to settle their differences.[55] Yet, unlike the controversy between Booker T. Washington and W.E.B. Du Bois, which divided the black community, the clubwomen compromised their differences in order to execute their club agenda of social action. Moreover, the club leadership slipped from the Northeast to younger women in the South, such as Margaret Washington and Mary Terrell, where the African American population was larger and in greater need of assistance.[56]

Despite dissent and disagreement among the leaders regarding the association presidency, the editorship of the *National Association Notes*, and other petty envies and jealousies, the conventions of the National Association were spectacular occasions during which respectable black women voiced their opinions and demands to the American public. The host community was usually overwhelmed by the numbers and diversity of black women.[57] The NACW's biennial conventions epitomized the politics of respectability. Not only were they a means of creating public awareness of black female leaders, but they provided an audience for conservative protest.

COLOR AND IDENTITY

Conscious of the stigma of color, some elite clubwomen attempted to deemphasize color distinctions, while others promoted color as if it were another quality to strive for. African Americans constructed a class hierarchy based on color as much as income. Divisiveness in the black community based on skin color began during slavery and became further entrenched in the decades following freedom.[58] Nannie Burroughs believed that it was preposterous for African Americans to set up color standards among themselves. Are fair-skinned Negroes better morally than black Negroes? She challenged blacks to think of character rather than color as the determining issue. She admonished black women to stop bleaching their skin and straightening their hair to alter their natural appearance.[59] In 1906 a dispute involving color prejudice erupted around the association. After serving two terms, Josephine Silone Yates could not be reelected. The women felt that Josephine Bruce, a presidential nominee with a very fair complexion, could not adequately represent the race.[60]   A younger generation composed of African Americans from humble backgrounds demanded a black club leader. Although Lucy Thurman was elected, this controversy might have influenced the election of darker, capable women, such as Elizabeth Carter (1908) and Mary Bethune (1924). Moreover, several of the most prominent clubwomen, such as Mary McLeod Bethune and Nannie Helen Burroughs, had climbed upward from from poverty and slavery and could be critical of some of their status-conscious sisters on class identifiers such as color.

"YOU'RE MY COLOR BUT NOT MY KIND"

African American club leaders insisted upon respectable behavior, which they perceived as essential to self-help and dignity.   The clubwomen objected to being forced into association with a certain kind of black person whose behavior was offensive to them.   Margaret Washington, advocating a dual class system on Jim Crow transportation, was attempting not to deny her racial ties and heritage, but to disassociate herself from those persons who she believed were beneath her. She would compromise the segregated railroad system as long as the interests of the middle class were protected.[61]   Were the goals of the elite club leaders aimed toward "uplifting" black women or protecting their own self-interests? Women such as Washington could be submissive to the system because they perceived the politics of respectability to be a viable weapon to change American race relations.

CROSS-CULTURAL GENDERING

The nineteenth century, an increasing number of organizations were run by women who were unpaid for their efforts. Women's clubs were the most active of those organizations. Black and white women were active in numerous women's clubs in both rural and urban communities. Women's clubs were established for cultural activities as well as for philanthropy and community service.   The membership of both the General Federation of Women's Clubs (GFWC), organized in 1890, and the National Association of Colored Women (NACW), formed six years later, consisted of middle-class, educated women who valued the Protestant work ethic, education, and material progress. Women from both groups believed in the importance of the home and the woman's moral influence in it. Moreover, the welfare records of the black and white clubwomen indicate class prejudice. Paula Giddings claims that both groups believed in the superiority of middle-class values and way of life.[62]

African American clubwomen were domestic feminists committed to Republican motherhood and the idea that women should improve the morality of the home and family life. Yet, black women had been slaves and were not able to socialize into the behavior of leisure class white women. They reshaped their language, actions, and practices in concurrence with the historical and cultural expressions of true motherhood and womanhood. Black women exulted their own version of domesticity, as they reiterated the primacy of motherhood and home life.[63] Mary Terrell asserted that it was only through the home that a people can become really good and truly great.[64] Most black women faced problems in trying to coordinate work and family life. The material conditions of black women's lives differed and therefore their expressions of true womanhood were not monolithic.[65] The clubwomen left their homes and enlarged their sphere in public life. Sharon Harley asserts that black women from upper middle-class families that would not suffer economically from having to choose between work and marriage confronted tension between the ideals for black women.[66] In her autobiography Terrell explained that she did not deliberately become a public lecturer. When she told her husband about the opportunity to bring a message to others, he stated that the lecture platform was the best vehicle for conducting the work that she wanted to do. "Some of my husband's friends warned him gravely against allowing his wife to wade too deeply into public affairs." They were not sure what evils Mary would encounter or under what circumstances, if any, she could maintain a home?[67] Terrell joined other women in transforming the women's arena from the world of domesticity into the world of politics.

In the North cooperation between black and white clubwomen began on the local level, with a few women joining sister clubs. Attempts to integrate the clubwomen at the national level began prior to 1893. When the Women's Club of Chicago refused Fannie B. Williams' application for membership, it ignited a bitter controversy. Williams had settled in Chicago and joined white women in reform work on a "common basis of fellowship and helpfulness." Ellen Henrotin and Celia Woolley presented Williams' name after she participated in the 1893 Columbian Exposition. The entire membership of over 200 women was shaken over the application of a black woman. Fourteen months later, Williams, an activist in civic and women's affairs, received membership in the Chicago Woman's Club.[68] The incident increased Williams' popularity among black women, who invited her to speak in Boston and other places.

Black women's struggle for recognition of their alternative form of womanhood was long and bitter. In 1900 another incident occurred at the Milwaukee convention of the General Federation of Women Clubs. Josephine Ruffin was a delegate of the Woman's Era Club, the Massachusetts Federation of Women's Clubs, and the New England Press Association. Denied entrance as a delegate from a black women's club, Ruffin would not enter the convention representing either of the predominantly white organizations.[69] Josephine Ruffin was outspoken and aggressive in her demand for social equality. She sought equality of opportunity based on individual worth as her goal. To most of the GFWC women, Ruffin did not understand her "position" in life.

A decision on the Ruffin incident was postponed for two years while Massachusetts and other states worked for a positive resolution of the issues. A compromise on the admission policy of the GFWC was passed in 1902. Basically, the compromise allowed clubs with black women to become members of the GFWC if they were eligible for membership in their state or regional federation, and where these organizations did not exist, eligibility would be determined by a majority vote of the GFWC clubs.

While fear of an influx of black women may have prompted the GFWC's decision to exclude black women, Mary Terrell attempted to lay to rest all fears regarding an inundation of black members in white women's clubs. She felt that only in places where the black population was small would they "seek the inspiration that might come from working with white women's women's clubs."[70] It would take at least two decades before the GFWC changed its policy of exclusion. Meanwhile, African American women set their own guidelines around their needs and the welfare of those of their respective communities.

The association became affiliated with the National Council of Women (NCW) of the United States in 1900 to strengthen "the bond of union between white and colored women of the country." The National Council of Women was the first white organization to open its membership to black women. Founded in 1888, the NCW was an organization of women's voluntary organizations interested in the social, educational, and political rights of women. The NCW was unusual in inviting all races and religious groups to join from its inception. Among its members were the National WCTU, National American Women Suffrage Association, National Women's Relief Society, National Christian League for the Promotion of Social Purity, and National Council of Jewish Women.[71] Terrell felt that it was important to become associated with an organization interested in women's problems and desirous of sharing the responsibilities in improving the role of women. The club leaders believed that they were American women and that the council existed to promote the welfare of all women. They assumed that black women would benefit from a closer relationship with organizations in the council.[72]

The philanthropic interests of black clubwomen led them into the major campaigns and movements in American society. During World War I, the increasing numbers of white women engaged in work, business, and industry convinced legislators that women were responsible in the public arena. A Woman's Committee of the Council of National Defense was established to coordinate the war activities of American women. It gathered information and attempted to place women in suitable employment. It encouraged all women to conserve food and fuel, plant victory gardens, sell Liberty Bonds, and become involved in the economy. The club leaders endorsed the Red Cross, Liberty Loans, the YWCA, Negro War Circle, and food conservation.

Interracial cooperation emerged during the war as black clubwomen interacted with the Women's Council of National Defense. Alice Dunbar-Nelson, an active clubwoman, educator, poet, and social worker, was appointed a field secretary in the Woman's Committee of the Council of National Defense. She took a leave from her job as head of the English Department at Howard High School in Wilmington, Delaware "to do war work."[73] The widow of Paul Laurence Dunbar married Robert Nelson, a newspaper editor, in 1916 and together they published the Wilmington *Advocate*. A national field agent, Alice Dunbar-Nelson traveled across the country, encouraging black women in the North and South to join the war campaign. She established a local chapter of the Circle for Negro War Relief. With members of the State Federation of Colored Women, she founded the Delaware Industrial School for Colored Girls where she taught after losing her job in the public schools.[74] She was the executive secretary of the American Interracial Peace Committee.

The increased participation of American men in the war after 1917 led the Red Cross and the YWCA to provide social services for troops in Europe and at home. Helen Curtis, a fashionable seamstress, was the first black woman to sail to Europe under the auspices of the YWCA. She returned to canteen service at Camp Upton, New York. Addie Hunton and Katheryn Johnson spent fourteen months organizing cultural, athletic, and religious activities for 2,000 black soldiers abroad. Black women's wartime philanthropic efforts included extensive fund-raising campaigns, especially the Liberty Loan drives. In the third drive, black women raised $5 million.[75]

Although African Americans had been involved with the American Red Cross relief efforts since before the Civil War, their services were mainly segregated and limited to black Americans. Susie King Taylor served as a nurse with Clara Barton during the Civil War. During World War I, many African American women were attracted to the activities of the American Red Cross. In many northern cities, black women merged with whites in the Red Cross units. In the South and in some Northern areas they formed separate auxiliaries to the local branches. Laura Williamson-Rollicks organized the Negro Women's Volunteer Service in New York City as a branch of the American Red Cross and operated a canteen for black soldiers.[76] Mary Waring directed the Red Cross Auxiliary work in Chicago. A practicing physician and former teacher at Wendell Phillips High School, Waring chaired the association's Department of Health and Hygiene.[77] At the 1918 NACW convention, Waring requested signatures to a petition for the more than 250 trained black Red Cross nurses who were available for overseas duty.[78] Despite promises, they never served their country abroad.

The War activities demonstrated the depth of patriotism that Afrrican Americans and black women felt for their country, despite discrimination and injustice. Maria C. Lawton, president of the Empire State Federation, appealed to club members to support the war activities. In a request to the women, Lawton called their attention to the need for warm clothing for men in the New York Fifteenth Regiment. "Everywhere, even on the streetcars, subways, railways, trains, women are knitting for their soldier boys. We are no less patriotic.[79]

World War I opened jobs for women in industry and government. As the men enlisted, white women stepped into government and skilled positions or went into unskilled wartime industries. Some black women held industrial jobs; others were employed as clerks, stenographers, and bookkeepers. The employment agency at the Colored Women's Branch of the YWCA in Harlem placed women as nurses, stenographers, factory workers, seamstresses, pressers, and milliners. The Manhattan Trade School placed black women as dressmakers and as operators of power machines in factories.[80] The Women's Trade Union League (WTUL), as well as the NACW, called for equal treatment of black women in the labor force. The American Federation of Labor (AFL) appointed a black social worker to direct its office for women.

Elizabeth Ross Haynes worked with the Department of Labor on the problems of women in the labor force. Before the war, most black women were in domestic service.[81]   Most black women and white working-class women found themselves in marginal positions. Many black women hired in industry were forced back into domestic work following the war.

The work of the NACW during World War I demonstrated the strength of the black women's clubs, but it showed also the limitations of cooperation between black and white women. Motivated by the democratic vision raised by the War, black and white women felt compelled to try harder to bridge racial boundaries.   Glenda Gilmore declares that the response of white women to the wartime emergency gave them confidence in their managerial abilities and made them question the male model of race relations.[82]

Following World War I, blacks and whites perceived that an improvement in race relations in the South would result only from interracial cooperation. Women, however, were not readily accepted into the Commission of Interracial Cooperation (CIC). Lilly Hardy Hammond, the first director of the Methodist Women's Bureau of Social Service, asserted, "The large movement toward racial adjustment of the last two or three years was initiated and is led by men. The Inter-Racial Committees, which have been formed in every Southern state and which are bringing the best men of both races into communication and cooperation, have no women."[83]   Initially, the CIC hoped to avoid fostering social equality through mixed-race and gender-cooperative relationships.   Hammond, whose husband became president of Paine Institute in Augusta, Georgia, outlined a program in her 1914 book, In Black and White, for ameliorating the conditions of blacks in the South. Her ideas were adopted for much of the work that was done in the twenties by the Commission on Interracial Cooperation.[84]

The interracial movement was built on the foundation laid by Southern Methodist women. Historian Anne Firor Scott has ascertained the importance of interracial work by white churchwomen. She emphasizes the significance of white churchwomen as agents of social change.   The leading female advocate of interracial cooperation, the Southern Methodist Home Mission Society, had been involved in the black community since the 1890s. Beginning in 1898 under the presidency of Belle Bennett, the Home Mission Society drew from both the Evangelical spirit and the social gospel to expand women's role in the church and in the social order. Inevitably, as their responsibilities expanded, the Home Mission Society confronted the race issue. Bennett urged the churchwomen "to redefine our relations to our colored sisters who live among us."[85]   Methodist women pioneered in settlement house work in the South and by 1920 had founded 25 facilities, including Bethlehem houses for African Americans in Augusta, Georgia (1912) and in Nashville, Tennessee (1913).

Gender gives women commonality, but race throws up barriers. The gap in race relations was closed partially by religion. By April 1920 several Methodist women felt that it was time to go beyond missionary work and establish their own separate Interracial Committee for Women. The proposal to create the Women's Committee came from Sarah Haskins, the former superintendent of Nashville Bethlehem Settlement House. At a meeting of the Women's Missionary Council, the group resolved to create "a commission of race relations which shall study the needs of women and children, and the methods of cooperation by which better relations may be brought about."[86]

Black clubwomen did more than any other African Americans to improve race relations through their speeches and lectures to interracial gatherings. The clubwomen Lugenia Hope, Margaret Washington, and Lucy Laney hoped to utilize the wartime contacts between white and black women to create a women's organization to improve race relations. In July 1920, when the NACW held its national convention at Tuskegee Institute, two Methodist women, Sara Estelle Haskins and Carrie Parks Johnson, who had chaired the Woman's Missionary Council on Race Relationships, attended the NACW's biennial meeting. Johnson addressed the gathering of 600 women on the theme of interracial cooperation.[87] The white women had experienced contact with blacks in church and community organizations, but never in a setting of mutual equality. They were impressed by the intelligence and seriousness of middle-class black women. An informal meeting followed at the residence of Margaret Washington attended by the club leaders who hoped to convince the white women of the need to find a place for interracial women's work through the Commission of Interracial Cooperation.[88]

Respectability mediated interracial relations between black and white women. The 1920 conference on race relations commanded the presence of four public black women, Mrs. Booker T. Washington, Mrs. George Haynes, Mrs. Robert R. Moton, and Mrs. Charlotte Hawkins Brown. The meeting of the women's conference in Memphis was sponsored by the Commission on Interracial Cooperation (CIC), Protestant churchwomen, the YWCA, and the General Federation of Women's Clubs. Apparently, race relations had improved enough to allow white women to invite black women whom they considered respectable and conservative to a conference to develop an agenda on interracial cooperation. Jennie Booth Moton, a former teacher at the Whittier Training School in Hampton, was suddenly elevated to leadership when her husband succeeded Booker T. Washington as head of Tuskegee Institute. Haynes was formerly with the Women's Bureau of the Department of Labor.

Both black and white women acknowledged a need for stronger efforts to bridge the gap between the races. Margaret Murray Washington was an adamant believer in interracial cooperation. A member of the Southern Interracial Commission, she was appointed chair of the Colored Women's work for the Interracial Commission of Alabama. Like her husband, her advice on race relations was frequently sought. Although Margaret Washington adhered to much in her husband's ideology, she had an assertive personality and a keen intellect which she used to act independently. Conservative in her approach, Washington steered away from politics and emphasized the home and family. Reluctant to blame anyone, Washington assured the women present that the "system" of racial practices had destroyed the black home. She believed that white women could play a role in the development of the ideal home for African Americans, especially plantation women and their children.[89]

Charlotte Brown was skeptical of whether racial integration could ever be achieved. Therefore, she accepted segregation in order to help her people, who were mainly in the South; her philosophy was that "neither position nor place could segregate the mind or soul."[90] In an uncustomary outburst, Brown tried to make the audience feel the reality of racial segregation. In her Memphis speech, Brown delineated the everyday examples of disrespect which black women regularly endured: for example, while traveling to the Memphis meeting, she was taken from the Pullman berth and escorted to the Jim Crow section of the train. Brown also spoke out against mob violence and urged the white women to join the campaign against lynching.[91] Secretary of the National Association of Colored Women from 1918 to 1922, Brown affirmed to North Carolina clubwomen that black women, having established their own society based on mainstream cultural values, were not seeking social intermingling but social justice.

Black and white women attending the Memphis meeting attempted to analyze social problems and present a program for social change. The groups worked together to issue a position paper to delineate interracial problems and to propose mutual action. The African American women were concerned about issues such as education, travel, child welfare, the treatment of blacks in the press, and suffrage. The Women's Committee of CIC discussed the issues proposed by the black women and added sanitation, housing, and justice in the courts but omitted suffrage. Brown and Hope demanded a version that protected African American voting rights and condemned lynching. NACW members blamed Washington and Jennie Moton for the diluted version of their statement that appeared in the final petition from the Women's Conference. After the proceedings the conference issued a statement pledging responsibility to work with black women "for a Christian settlement of the problems that overshadow the homes of both races."[92] Fear of social equality and strict adherence to Jim Crow clouded the agenda of the white women. The Southeastern Association of Colored Women's Clubs, founded by Mary Bethune in 1920, issued its own pamphlet and included the demand for the right to vote.

The Women's Council of the CIC, which emerged from the 1920 meeting, proposed better relationships between black and white women and a program of grassroots interracial work for community betterment. The Memphis Conference inspired blacks and whites to establish the Women's Council of the CIC. The Women's Council extended its organization to every county in the South where there was an extensive black population and anticipated peaceful race relations with cooperation on projects for mutual advancement. Carrie Parks Johnson, the first director of the Women's Council, helped organize interracial committees in every southern state. They worked cooperatively with black women on community improvement projects. The number of Methodist committees grew from 110 in 1922 to 606 by 1927.[93] While they did not challenge racial segregation, these developments were a new strategy in race relations in the Jim Crow South. By 1929 there were 805 interracial county committees in the South. Interracial cooperation on a local level, with increasing work by the state and national committees, continued to expand.[94]   The committees were primary factors in slowing the migration of African Americans from the South.

Interracial cooperation made its greatest inroads among African Americans through the leadership of the Southeastern Federation of Colored Women's Clubs, which was founded by Mary McLeod Bethune in 1920.   Judia Jackson Harris organized a grassroots campaign in the Georgia southern interracial movement.   President of the Athens Interracial Committee and vice president of the Georgia State Interracial Committee,   Harris published a booklet, *Race Relations*, emphasizing her own racial creed to promote better race relations.   She believed that ultimately right and justice would triumph.   She believed: "No country could achieve its goals with part of its citizens economically and industrially free and the other part deprived of the right and opportunity to obtain the same freedom;   there should not be a double standard of service to humanity; " the bigness and breadth of human character consisted of ministering to and elevating human life regardless of race and color."[95]

Judia Jackson Harris was an advocate for African Americans in her city and state.   Among her numerous interracial contacts were Will Alexander, head of the CIC, M. Ashby Jones, President of the Atlanta Interracial Commission, Morton Hodgson, chairman of the Interracial Committee in Athens, and other state and local politicians, businessmen, and educators.   Alexander asserted that blacks were not only speaking for themselves, but they had found new voices to speak for them, such as the clubwomen.   The clubwomen's activism in the local committees of the CIC helped reduce, but did not completely deter, lynching and other repressive measures in black communities. Between 1889 and 1918 Georgia led the South and the nation with 386 lynchings.[96]

Black and white women, while not equal participants,   deepened their ties to statewide and national voluntary organizations, building networks that institutionalized their dialogue.   Both the movement of interracial cooperation and the achievement of woman suffrage occurred in 1920.   Glenda Gilmore declares that white women's confusion over black woman suffrage underscores the limits of voluntary interracial work.   White women involved in interracial social service projects had allowed their racial practices to overshadow their racial ideologies of noblesse oblige.   Black women had to decide whether to register and risk endangering the interracial contacts that they had struggled for and to consider how their presence at the polls would affect black male voters.[97]

Passage of the Nineteenth Amendment was part of the Progressive agenda for social change and the culmination of a century-long crusade.   African American women had been involved in local and regional suffrage activities since the last decade of the nineteenth century and continued to the end of the suffrage struggle.   Black women viewed suffrage as a feminist issue and an instrument for achieving racial justice.   In 1896 the clubwomen organized a Suffrage Department within the NACW under the direction of Sarah Garnet as superintendent.   Equal Suffrage Clubs, like the Brooklyn Club, which Garnet founded, were soon found all over the country.   After Garnet's death in 1911, Verina Morton-Jones succeeded her as president of the Brooklyn Equal Suffrage Club. In 1912, with Adella Hunt Logan as director of the Suffrage Department, the NACW declared in favor of full woman suffrage.[98] Hunt, "lady principal" at Tuskegee, was the only woman in Alabama to become a member of the National Woman's Suffrage Association. It is interesting that the clubwomen recommended the formation of political clubs for black men to arouse their consciousness regarding their own welfare. Black clubwomen passed resolutions continuously supporting woman suffrage. Black suffragists and clubwomen insisted that the women who had struggled under race and gender injustice should be granted a political voice. Black women's clubs worked effectively at the local level in Chicago and New York; the women's participation made a difference.

Despite adversity, black women followed their own political agenda by organizing voter education groups in their own communities, running for public office, and fighting attempts to keep them from the polls.[99] Although they had some similar strategies, and there were coalitions between blacks and whites, the experiences of the two groups differed over time. Despite attempts in the South to nullify their votes, black women used the Suffrage Department of the NACW to make their vote count at the polls. Terrell, Addie Hunton, and Morton-Jones conducted voter education programs and documented discrimination throughout the South.[100] Historian Rosalyn Terborg-Penn asserts that black women's struggle for political equity since the ratification of the Nineteenth Amendment has been characterized by tension between their race and their gender.[101]

The Nineteenth Amendment gave women the right to vote, but it did not advocate gender equality for women. The most intense feminist group among white women in the 1920s was the National Woman's Party, founded by Alice Paul. Although black women sought the support of the Woman's Party, particularly for female voters in the South, they knew that Paul believed that discrimination at the polls was more a race issue than a gender issue.[102]

Ratification of the Nineteenth Amendment in 1920 increased black women's interest in the American political process. Mary Terrell's active involvement in the suffrage movement led to her appointment as the supervisor of the Eastern District among Colored Women. Terrell had helped organize the Women's Republican League in Washington, D.C. Long involved in the suffrage, in 1904 she had attended the International Woman Suffrage Alliance meeting and addressed the conference in German. The Southeastern Federation of Colored Women, headed by Mary Bethune, coordinated black women's efforts to register and vote. Mary Bethune concluded that black women had a heavier responsibility placed on them after enfranchisement. In 1920 she organized women's voter registration drives despite Klu Klux Klan terrorism. The presence of women at the polls, however, reduced the incidence of violence on election day, allowing black women and men to claim their voting rights.

In Nashville, Tennessee, black and white women became new elements in politics in 1920. Mattie E. Coleman, a physician and black state suffrage organizer, met with the white Davidson County Suffrage Committee in 1919 to organize efforts to register women to vote. Coleman encouraged the women in her community to register and support the white women's platform for more females on the city's commissions.   Club woman Nettie Langston Napier, who had organized women to work the Republican polls, helped to get black women involved in the voter registration drive.   Since they were exempt from the 1919-1920 poll tax, black and white women turned out in large numbers to vote, with more black women than white women or black men casting their ballots. Thus, the enfranchisement of black women did not cause friction between black male voters and black women in Nashville's Third Ward.[103]

The NACW was the leading organization for black women's political activities.   The association's Suffrage Department trained black women in the proper use of the ballot.[104] Women's clubs conducted meetings and classes to discuss national issues, candidates, and voting procedures.   As association president from 1920 to 1924, Hallie Quinn Brown mobilized large numbers of women at the community level.   Appointed director of the Colored Women's Republican National Committee, Brown circulated a newsletter to inform Republican women across the country.[105]   Brown utilized the organizational ability of clubwomen, such as Maria C. Lawton, who headed New York's Empire State Federation of Women's Clubs from 1916 to 1926.

Migration to the North increased the interest in voting, in spite of the small black population in that region. It was unnecessary for any party to recruit migrant constituency.   Black women composed a sizable portion of the migrants.[106] There were few black elected officials, even in the North, and no black person had sat in Congress since Reconstruction. It is unlikely that Oscar DePriest would have become the first black alderman in Chicago without the women voters. The entrance of women into the state electoral arena after 1920 opened new doors for black politicians.   In 1928 DePriest, a Republican, was elected to Congress with the help of Chicago women.[107]

A change occurred in the national association by 1926, following the death of well-known respectable leaders such as Margaret Washington and Mary Talbert. This left the club work to other women, including Mary Church Terrell and Mary McLeod Bethune.   Terrell used her speaking ability and written communication skills to promote reform and gender equality.   She created an exemplary record in human relations. Her contributions earned her a place beside prominent white women such as Jane Addams and Mary Richmond.[108] By the late 1920s, Mary McLeod Bethune was a dominant voice in the National Association of Colored Women. She believed that the clubwomen were at the forefront of social reform. With its headquarters located in Washington, the association became a visible force in the nation's capital. Bethune believed that race was no real barrier to advancement; it is merit that counts.[109]   Bethune's emergence as a young race leader during the depression and the New Deal is discussed in the final chapter. She developed an ideology and strategies that kept her in step with the changing times.

Chapter 5

Social Housekeeping in the South:
Social Settlements and School Settlements

> Look for the real heroines of the colored race in obscure
> places like Mt. Meigs in Alabama, the settlement in
> Georgia under the direction of Miss Judia Jackson, or
> the alleys in South Washington, where Mrs. Fernandis
> works, prays, and waits. Here you find women of
> real concentration and the true spirit of Jane Addams
> working with and for the unfortunate.
>   Fannie Barrier Williams, (1905), 401.

For Progressive reformers, black and white, the home and family life epitomized
middle-class morality and behavior. The cultivation of a Christian home, a major
tenet of the missionary schools, was regarded as a measure of race progress.
Reconstructing the home and family became the primary goal of southern
clubwomen such as Margaret Washington, Janie Porter Barrett, Cornelia Bowen,
Lugenia Hope, Sarah Fernandis, and Judia Harris. The strategy of social
housekeeping propelled these black female activists into the public arena.[1] Their
social settlements and schools provided mothers' meetings, night classes, home
libraries, home economics classes, and other activities for improvement.

Black clubwomen in urban and rural communities of the South, like their
counterparts in the North, were engaged in social service activities. African
Americans lived in rural communities throughout the South, while in the North
blacks were crowded into urban centers. Nevertheless, similar efforts in both
regions consisted of improving housing, sanitation and health conditions and
providing food, clothing, and shelter for the needy.[2]

During Reconstruction black women articulated a politics in which race, gender, and a history of enslavement were inseparable. Black women struggled to change negative images by emulating the mannerisms of white women. White society resisted as black women struggle to change the images of black female sexuality. Black women were ridiculed and victimized every where they went, on the streets, in shops, and in their work places. The women who suffered the most were those whose behavior resembled that of a "lady," particularly a black woman who was neat and clean in appearance and behaving in a respectable manner.[3] Women who acted in this manner were accused of "putting on the lady."

For the newly freed black men, more so than the women, liberation and American identity meant claiming the gender codes of American patriarchal society, including the acceptance of monogamous, male-dominated marriage as a symbol of civility.[4] In the post-Civil War period black women who decided to devote their time to their own households and children rather than engage in fieldwork outside the home were chastised by the farm owners.[5] Black women's rejection or withdrawal from fieldwork was seen by white plantation owners as the "evil of female loaferism."[6] Many freedmen agreed with the tendency of women to remain at home, but for different reasons. In their minds, a working woman undermined black manhood and the race. Eventually, a new labor system, family sharecropping, was imposed. Not only were black women forced to accept it for economic reasons, but they were tied to the sharecropping system through their husbands, who received the wages of the family unit. As families changed with the sharecropping system, nuclear, more male-dominated forms of family lifestyles emerged. Sharecropping households were organized patriarchally and, therefore, reflected the male-dominant gender focus of American society. Thus, assertive black manhood was expressed largely at the loss of equality for black women.[7] While conformity to American standards of behavior was regarded as important, there was a need to emphasize gender inequality within the context of racial injustice in the black experience.

The idea that men should play the dominant role in family life as providers and decision-makers on important issues permeated all social classes of African Americans during Reconstruction. The black press and leaders in the black community conferred to men the control on all issues other than those dealing with the household.[8] By the turn of the century educated black women were challenging the assertion that the ultimate authority on family matters should reside with men. While believing that women had a special role to play in maintaining the home, in raising the children, and in moral and social uplift of the race, middle class and upper class black women were convinced that women should have an equal voice in family matters.[9] It was left to black club leaders to redefine gender roles.

Although the club leaders offered advice through numerous articles and pamphlets concerning the family and children to poor women, it is doubtful whether the poverty stricken women read the materials or heeded the advice. Gertrude Bustill Mossell, a member of the middle-class black elite in Philadelphia, wrote *The Work of the Afro-American Woman* in 1892, which, from one aspect, resembled the advice manuals written by white women during the early nineteenth century.[10]   From another view the author gave a critical assessment of the sexist directives with which black women were bombarded.   For some years, every newspaper and magazine gave some teaching such as, "The wife must always meet her husband with a smile. She must throughout her married life do a host of things for his comfort and convenience." Men and women directed the moral advice toward women, rarely toward the men, and   women needed the teachings the least.[11] Mossell also provides a list of African American women in education, churches, missions, and social welfare. She directed the book to respectable black clubwomen who could serve as role models for their working-class sisters.[12] A race woman, Mossell promoted the cause of her sisters in a manner that would uplift the entire race.

While black clubwomen were conscious of race and gender domination, they were interested also in planting Victorian mores in the plantation women of Alabama, Georgia, and Mississippi. Margaret Washington, Janie Porter Barrett, Lugenia Hope, and others promoted social reform through the social settlements that they established in the South. Most of the community centers were extensions of colleges focusing on education and social services.[13] The southern and frequently rural location of these institutions should not obscure their settlement house functions. Jane Addams believed that certain characteristics were found in northern and southern settlements, namely, identification of the workers with local interests, permanency of the group of workers in residence, enthusiasm over the possibilities of one's neighborhood, and furnishing a stimulus in a community.[14]

Margaret James Murray Washington, the founder of the Elizabeth Russell Social Settlement, was a self-made woman who struggled valiantly to obtain an education and footing in life. In many respects, her life paralleled that of the women whom she helped during her lifetime. One of ten children, Maggie was born in Macon, Mississippi, at the end of the Civil War on 9 March 1865. Her mother contributed to the household with her earnings as a washerwoman. After her father died, Maggie was sent to live with a Quaker family of schoolteachers in the community. They had a tremendous impact on her life and at the age of fourteen she began teaching in a rural school. Maggie Murray entered Fisk University's preparatory class in 1881 as a part-time working student. She completed her studies after eight years, while working in faculty homes and teaching during the summers to pay college expenses.[15]

In 1889 Booker T. Washington, principal of Tuskegee Institute, delivered the commencement address at Fisk. While there he recruited one of their graduates, Margaret Murray. Although she was employed at Tuskegee Institute as a teacher of English literature, Margaret was soon promoted to "lady principal" (dean of women). By the time Margaret and Booker T. Washington were married in 1892, she was already committed to many doctrines of her husband's ideology.   A teacher, principal, director of industries for women, and the wife of the president, Margaret Murray Washington soon became a kind of "Mother confessor" to students and teachers at Tuskegee Institute.[16]   Margaret James Murray, Washington's third wife, outlived her husband by ten years.

The "uplift" program of the clubwomen emphasized moral and economic progress, middle-class virtues, and self-help. The idea of obtaining self-help and self-dependence reached a peak during the late nineteenth century in the writings of Booker T. Washington. While a student at Hampton Institute, Washington was encouraged to work hard and to develop habits of service, goodwill, and cooperation toward his white neighbors.[17] Hampton, which began in 1868 under the auspices of the American Missionary Association, was the first agricultural and industrial school for African Americans. Its founder, Samuel C. Armstrong, shared the traditional Yankee views of other missionary teachers. He assumed black people emerged from a culture which tolerated shiftlessness, extravagance, and immorality and to combat these tendencies, they must be taught to buy land, save money, create stable homes, and learn trades. Armstrong introduced a program of uplift which emphasized moral and economic progress, but ignored full citizenship rights.[18] Booker T. Washington's style was more secular than Armstrong's but his gospel of practical Christianity, a strong work ethnic, self-help, and education for service was for some individuals the best method of improving race relations.[19] These ideas, which contributed to Washington's immense popularity in the late nineteenth century, were not completely unlike those of the clubwomen.

Many institutions, black and white, emphasized household economics or practical housekeeping and homemaking for female students. At Tuskegee the female students majored in dressmaking, millinery, sewing, laundering, housekeeping, broom-making, nursing, cooking, tailoring, dairying, printing, or horticulture.[20] Margaret Washington, director of Girls' Industries, supervised the industrial training of over 400 women at Tuskegee. She placed each young woman in employment and supervised her work.[21] Along with her educational work, Margaret Washington placed primary emphasis on elevating the people of the community, which she accomplished with the assistance of the Tuskegee Woman's Club. The need for a Woman's Club originated with the exclusion of farm wives from the annual Tuskegee Negro Conference for the improvement of black farmers. During the session of 1892 Washington reserved a room in the center of town for mothers' meetings.[22]

Formally organized in 1895, the Tuskegee Woman's Club was composed of a small, educated membership of female faculty and faculty wives from Tuskegee Institute. The clubwomen's social work consisted of a Sunday school, jail work, temperance work, and social settlement work. They held mothers' meetings each Saturday afternoon in a large hall on Tuskegee's campus. The women provided religious services, fruit, and clothing for the prisoners at the local jail. Tuskegee women joined other clubwomen in the state in a campaign to build a reformatory for youth offenders. Washington and the faculty women loaned their books to the community women until arrangements were made for a free library in the town.

The club leaders used a modified "case method" to judge the effectiveness of their rural social work through home visits in the community. On one occasion, the "volunteer social workers" and educators visited over 100 homes in four weeks. The farm wives cleaned their yards, repaired their homes, and planted flowers in anticipation of the clubwomen's arrival.[23]

Margaret Washington envisioned the elevation of home and the black family as the solution to the race problem. In 1897 Margaret Washington began the Elizabeth Russell Social Settlement about eight miles from Tuskegee. Since most rural blacks were descendants of field hands, Washington believed that they would benefit from "missionary work." She believed that tenant farm wives lacked the fundamental knowledge of caring for their homes and families. The value and meaning of a stable marriage and closeknit family would come gradually to the "plantation women."[24] Members of the Tuskegee Women's club and other responsible community members provided leadership.

Assisted by the Tuskegee Woman's Club, Margaret Washington began to visit the Russell plantation. They converted an abandoned slave cabin donated by the plantation owner into a "settlement house." Margaret Washington organized mothers' meetings and instructed the women in home management and child care. She established a day and evening school for the parents and hired a Tuskegee graduate, Anna Rosetta Davis, as the teacher. The mothers were taught not only how to cook, wash, iron, and sew but how to live according to the values of the club leaders.[25]

The clubwomen attempted to persuade the farm wives to eliminate habits such as wrapping their hair, dipping snuff, smoking, and chewing tobacco, because it was harmful to their health and because it perpetuated the slave culture. In the Russell settlement, approximately thirty families lived in former slave quarters, consisting of one-room, windowless "huts." Because they had little money or no money, small children wore little clothing, women seemed to prefer bare feet to shoes, and they continued to wrap their hair. Wrapping involved dividing the hair into sections with string and twisting it. The strain straightened the hair somewhat, but Madam C. J. Walker discovered that it could damage the scalp. Conversely, wrapping hair, which was similar to today's hair-braiding techniques, such as cornrow hairstyles, connected the women to their African culture.

Middle-class black women incorporated social settlements into their program of "uplifting and improving" sharecropping families. The settlements were supported partially by donations from northern friends. To a great extent, this relationship with northern white philanthropy influenced Margaret Washington's efforts to change the behavior of the farm women to conform to the "middle-class ideal" of a wife and mother in American society.

The clubwomen disapproved of the living conditions and habits of tenant farm wives for health purposes as well as cultural reasons. Both Hampton and Tuskegee encouraged teachers to include the study and practice of hygiene in their curriculum. It was important for both blacks and whites in the rural areas, but especially for blacks, who had a higher death rate from disease and infant mortality. The high rate of tuberculosis among African Americans accounts partially for the concern for better housing.

The focus on social hygiene perpetuated stereotypes of the black family and the continued association of dirt and uncleanliness with disease. Stereotypes of blacks and black health were reinforced with the spread of syphilis in the African American population. Concern with venereal disease encouraged fears about class, race, ethnicity, and in particular, sexuality and the family.[26] Prior to the 1920s, teachers and clubwomen, when discussing family planning or family regulation, frequently combined the topic with issues related to personal hygiene rather than birth control.

The Tuskegee Woman's Club set examples for the farm women on the proper behavior in, and care of, public facilities. These lessons were aimed toward impressing whites in order to gain their respect. The Woman's Club reported that it furnished two waiting rooms, doing the same thing in both the black and white facilities. They hung curtains, scrubbed floors, washed windows, and put books and newspapers in the rooms. They placed pictures of eminent Americans on the walls. The clubwomen's willingness to accommodate segregation was a conservative approach to challenging racism.

The work of Margaret Washington, Cornelia Bowen, and other Tuskegee graduates brought recognition to Tuskegee Institute and Washington's ideology. During a series of meetings financed by the John F. Slater Fund, Booker T. and Margaret Washington spoke throughout Macon County, Alabama, and the South. Addressing black professional community leaders, they espoused themes related to health, education, and morality. Margaret Washington linked immorality to the inability to resist disease and crime. She stressed the importance of persuading poor women to practice good basic personal hygiene, to keep regular sleeping hours, and to provide nutritious meals for their families.[27] Washington reminded the middle-class women of their responsibility to the poor, but in asking the community leaders to stoop down and lift up others, she implied that the masses were beneath the clubwomen. No one referred to economics as the root of the poverty-stricken condition of blacks. Low salaries and employment in agricultural and domestic occupations primarily accounted for a large part of the problem. To some extent, the Washingtons were blaming the poor for their predicament instead of poverty.

LOCUST STREET SETTLEMENT AT HAMPTON, VIRGINIA

Janie Porter was born in Macon, Georgia. Her mother, a former slave, was a live-in servant in a white household.[28] Janie studied with the white children and absorbed the culture and refinement of the family. Despite "advice" from her employer that Janie should pass for white and attend a northern institution, her mother encouraged her daughter to attend a black industrial service-oriented college, Hampton Institute. While Janie was not prepared at first for the socialization process that motivated students to commit their lives to community service, the school's emphasis on duty to the race eventually raised her consciousness of social responsibility.[29]

Janie Porter Barrett transplanted Hampton's example in education and service to the black community. Teaching among sharecroppers in Dawson,

Georgia, and at Lucy Laney's Haines Institute in Augusta reinforced her vision of helping the poor and disadvantaged. She organized the Locust Street Social Settlement in 1890 and founded the Virginia Industrial School for Colored Girls in 1914. After her marriage to Harris Barrett, a business professor and bookkeeper at Hampton, she became involved in community service.[30] The settlement developed in 1890 from weekly meetings of neighborhood girls in the Barretts home. Lacking a clubhouse, Janie and Harris Barrett opened their own home as a model of housekeeping and homemaking. It became a "palace of delight" for the female youth of the community. Janie Porter Barrett aimed to help girls and women become good homemakers and to improve the social life of the community. "The Locust Settlement maintained a library, playground, instruction in cooking, sewing, quilt-making, embroidery, home-gardening, child care, and clubs for women and girls. [31]

Not until 1902 did Barrett obtain a settlement house. She sacrificed the money that she and her husband had saved for a bathroom to provide a clubhouse for the girls. Several girls' and women's clubs met there weekly, with nearly 150 members. Most of the youth clubs were conducted by Hampton students. The settlement conducted a Sunday School and afternoon services in the local churches. Female teachers from Hampton assisted Barrett, thus freeing her for fund-raising duties. Northern philanthropists, including Mrs. Collis P. Huntington of New York, donated funds for furnishings and maintenance.[32]

Education moved in new and important directions during the Progressive era. John Dewey, a leading progressive educator, perceived education as a means of reforming society. He disregarded knowledge acquired from memorization and learning by rote and insisted that children learn by playing together, making things, expressing themselves, and participating in group activities. In attempting to make the training of young girls relevant to their experiences, Barrett might have been influenced by John Dewey. The idea of working with one's hands was also part of Booker T. Washington's approach to education. Dewey's work ran parallel to that of Jane Addams, also a pioneer of progressive education. While teaching at the University of Chicago, Dewey was a member of the first Board of Trustees at Hull House. After moving to New York, he was involved with the Henry Street Settlement and Greenwich House.[33]

The Locust Street Settlement revolved around the activities of the Women's club. The clubwomen conducted social casework in individual homes in the local Hampton community. The child welfare department of the Homemakers' Club was one of its most important units. Other departments consisted of home gardening, poultry, flowers, quilting, and plain sewing.[34] The Women's Club sponsored an annual Flower Show and Community Fair, which was attended by local blacks and whites and helped to publicize the settlement. Barrett's work received national recognition in 1910, when she presented a lecture on her settlement work at an afternoon tea at Hull House sponsored by Jane Addams.[35]

Janie Porter Barrett organized the Virginia State Federation of Colored Women's Clubs during the Hampton Conference in 1908. The federation adopted two primary projects, the Locust Street Settlement and the Virginia Industrial Home School for Girls after Barrett became its president in 1913. The Virginia clubwomen began a fund-raising campaign to purchase land for a rehabilitation center for delinquent girls. Incorporated in 1914 and opened with two girls in 1915, it was the first home in the South for delinquent black girls. The Industrial Home for Girls was located near Richmond in Hanover County, Virginia. Practicing personal social work, Barrett viewed the Industrial Home as a "moral hospital" where each girl was carefully observed and given individual treatment. She emphasized individual responsibility over punishment.[36]   Barrett remained superintendent of the home until 1940.

Like Margaret Washington, Janie Porter Barrett emphasized interracial co-operation as a means of solving racial problems, especially through social service. The Industrial Home for Girls spurred co-operation between black women and influential white women in Virginia. The Board of Trustees, chaired by the white matron Mrs. Henry Schmeltz, worked with the Virginia Federation of Colored Women to further interracial cooperation.[37]   However, there is no indication that the interracial work solved any race problems.

COLORED SOCIAL SETTLEMENT IN WASHINGTON, DC

Not all blacks remained on the farms, despite Booker T. Washington's insistence on agriculture and rural land-ownership. Some migrated to southern cities prior to and during World War I, crowding into black communities and drawing on the meager resources. The majority of the African American population in southern cities lived in the alleys behind the white residential areas. The alleys, generally unpaved and muddy, were centers of disease, social unrest, and poverty. Thus, they often received national attention and were selected for self-help programs.[38]

The efforts of black clubwomen to improve housing and family conditions in Washington, DC, were linked to widespread gendered work in the cities during the Progressive era. The housing problem in Washington, DC, attracted the attention of members of Congress, eventually. Concerned whites had long sought assistance for the citizens of the District, whose alleys and slums were a national disgrace in terms of health, morals, and crime.[39] Charles F. Weller believed the alleys and shacks of Washington suggested the slave quarters of the Old south, where blacks lived near the master's residence but were separated and distinct.[40]

The Colored Social Settlement was established in Washington, DC in 1903 by black volunteer social workers. It was the first social service agency in the District of Columbia.[41] The settlement was the outgrowth of a Colored Conference Class, directed by Weller, the executive officer of the Associated Charities of the District of Columbia, which began in 1901. The object of the class was the enlistment and training of black friendly visitors, club and class conductors, and volunteers in personal service to neglected neighborhoods and needy black families. Black middle-class women in Washington did their best social welfare work in settlements. Anna J. Cooper and other club women contributed money and effort to support the settlement work. The settlement house was established to accommodate the black population that crowded into an area of Southwest Washington.[42] Much of the work focused on an area that bordered the city's open sewer line and was near alleys with deplorable housing conditions.   Volunteers came from women's clubs, church groups, and youth groups. Anna J. Cooper, the supervisor of the settlement, and Mary Church Terrell were trustees of the settlement. The object of the settlement was to help lower-class blacks attain higher standards and ultimately better citizenship. The black volunteers, with assistance from white philanthropy, secured a home in Southwest Washington for the settlement activities. Women volunteers investigated industrial conditions and social problems and sought to improve neighborhood and municipal conditions.

Anna Julia Cooper, known mainly as a black intellectual, was a social activist as well. Her life from her birth in North Carolina in 1858 to her death in Washington, DC, in 1964 was deeply centered in the virtues of home, religion, and proper conduct.[43] Her teaching career began when she was eleven years old and continued until she was in her eighties. In 1901 she was appointed principal of the M Street High School, a position she held until 1906, when the board refused to reappoint her. While some persons probably opposed Cooper because she was female, most likely she lost her job because she refused to use an inferior curriculum and textbooks.[44]   Although Cooper was committed to industrial education, she was a target of the Tuskegee machine mainly because she was well educated and a role model for her students. Cooper acquired social mobility and middle-class status through education. Her personal struggle accounts for her identification with oppressed black women. Likewise, it justifies her sensible reflections on the nature and necessity of work among the urban and rural poor.[45]

As a community leader, Cooper stood for education and service. She was a member of the Phillis Wheatley Branch of the YWCA, chaired the Alley Sanitation Committee of the Colored Women's League, and was a supervisor of the Colored Social Settlement in southwest Washington.   Cooper and other women volunteering at the settlement designed programs to help ease the transition of the migrants from a rural to an urban environment. Like other settlement workers, they attributed poverty to moral causes. Thus, they attempted to stimulate ambition, instill moral standards, strengthen character, and develop the incentive for self-help.[46]

The Colored Settlement hired Sarah Collins Fernandis as its head resident. Like Janie Porter Barrett, Stephanie Shaw notes, Fernandis moved easily from teaching to social work. Born in Baltimore and a graduate of Hampton Institute in 1882, Fernandis brought the pedagogical influence of that institution toward social service to settlement work. She worked under the Woman's Home Missionary Society in Boston and taught in the public schools in Baltimore. After marriage, she moved to Washington, DC where she attended conferences conducted by Charles Weller.[47]   Sarah Fernandis conducted the day-to-day activities of the settlement with the help of twenty-five volunteers.   After her arrival, the social settlement and social center conducted girls' and boys' clubs, vocational classes, a kindergarten, a day nursery, and a milk station to provide clean and safe milk. A doctor and nurse visited the settlement regularly. There were a branch of the public library, public baths, and a stamp-saving system for food, clothing, and fuel, which inculcated thrift and economy in the mothers and youth.[48]

A laborer with only twenty-five cents came to Fernandis and made his first deposit on a savings' account book. The stamp-savings was the best self-help activity offered by the settlement. According to the Associated Charities, the stamp program helped decrease the number of persons applying for charity. Sarah Fernandis brought the entire neighborhood into cooperation with the settlement.[49] The purpose of her "uplift" work was to change the standards of the homes through the children, and thereby improve the neighborhood.[50] The activities of Fernandis, Cooper, and other black women were not isolated experiences. They designed their grassroots public efforts to the needs of the African American community.

NEIGHBORHOOD UNION IN ATLANTA, GEORGIA

Lugenia Burns Hope was imbued with an independent spirit of social service when she went to Atlanta as the wife of John Hope, the first black president of Morehouse College and of Atlanta University. Anyone coming into Atlanta concerned about social service work among African Americans, was directed to Mrs. Lugenia Hope.[51] She became involved in northern humanitarian efforts before she ventured south. Born in St. Louis and raised in Chicago, Lugenia Burns developed altruism and an optimistic faith early in life despite struggle and personal sacrifice. Concern for improving the condition of working girls motivated her to join the previously all-white Kings' Daughters of Cook County, Illinois. She donated her services as adviser and friend to hundreds of working girls who came to the Kings' Daughters headquarters. Participation in the development of an apprentice school program, staffed by instructors from the University of Chicago, provided a foundation in community work for Burns.[52] According to historian Jacqueline Rouse, Lugenia attended high school between 1890 and 1893 and continuing education classes at the Chicago School of Design, the Chicago Business College, and the Chicago Art Institute.[53] She worked as a dressmaker and bookkeeper and in other employment in order to support herself and her widowed mother. Lugenia was the first black secretary for the King's Daughters, a charity organization that worked with the sick and needy, helped to bury the poor, and provided services to teenage working girls.

In 1897 Lugenia married John Hope, a young college professor. Two years later, they moved to Atlanta when her husband accepted a teaching position at Atlanta Baptist College. Within a few years, Hope became president of the institution (Morehouse College after 1913). As the wife of the president, Lugenia played a major role in the development of the college, particularly its social and cultural aspects. Moreover, she initiated efforts toward improving social conditions in Atlanta.[54]

Lugenia Hope's interest in social welfare issues preceded her move to Atlanta. In 1904 W.E.B. Du Bois invited Hope to the Atlanta University's Conference on the Welfare of the Negro Child. Du Bois sent invitations also to Victoria Matthews, settlement house superintendent in New York, and Jane Addams, settlement house director in Chicago, neither of whom could attend. The president of Atlanta University, Horace Bumstead, had asked Du Bois to direct the annual conference on urban Negro problems that the institution organized.[55] This conference was planned by Gertrude Ware, the first supervisor of kindergarten work in the Oglethorpe Practice School and the daughter of the first president of Atlanta University. Ware encouraged child care for working mothers.[56]

At the conference, a Board of Directors consisting of several mothers, Adrienne Herndon, and Lugenia Hope, was formed to establish the Gate City Free Kindergarten Association. Adrienne was the first black female teacher at Atlanta University. Her husband, Alonzo F. Herndon, founder of the Atlanta Life Insurance Company, contributed generously to the association's cause. Ella B. Howard, president of the Atlanta Woman's Club and wife of Atlanta's prominent mortician David T. Howard, was the first president of the Kindergarten Association. Lugenia Hope chaired the fund-raising campaign.

Hope's civic consciousness was heightened not only by the social condition of African Americans in the city but by the Atlanta riot in 1906. Two years later, Lugenia Burns Hope and a core group of women involved in community service established the Neighborhood Union Settlement in Atlanta, the first social welfare agency for blacks in Atlanta.[57] Hope remained its president for twenty-five years. The Neighborhood Union was an urban organization that closely resembled the university settlements in northern cities. Led by Hope, the union was the result of an organized effort of black women to improve the moral, social, and economic conditions of the city, especially Atlanta's West side. No other organization in the city was concerned with the welfare of blacks at the time. The union aimed to develop a spirit of cooperation and group consciousness among the people and to cooperate with the Associated Charities, the Juvenile Court, and other social service agencies.

As the wife of the president of Morehouse College, Lugenia Hope felt accountable to the college and to the community. Like other social workers, she investigated the problems of the community residents in order to assess their needs. The first meeting was composed mainly of faculty members and wives from Morehouse and Spelman Colleges. Hope attempted to impart to both the women and the students her vision of the needs of the community and the necessity of alleviating them. The colleges bordered on a slum of poor housing and unpaved alleys and streets. Aided by the students of the colleges, the members conducted house-to-house surveys to introduce the organization to the community. These visits allowed them to identify destitute families, provide assistance and casework services, and identify community leaders. As a result of the home visits, plans were developed to aid working mothers and their children. Relief was needed for the poor, sick, and destitute.[58]

The members of the Neighborhood Union secured a settlement house on Fair Street that was open to the community day and night. Individual members initially assumed the monthly rental fee of $130. Membership was open to any citizen who paid the $2.00 membership fee. The dues funded the organization and increased community participation. A charter covering several community services was obtained. The organizational plan was developed with its program agenda in mind: the city was divided into zones; each zone was supervised by a chairman, each zone was divided into districts, and each district had a presiding officer and a group of workers from the immediate neighborhood. The Neighborhood Union was governed through its Board of Managers, consisting of zone chairman, department heads, and presidents of the neighborhoods. By the time the leaders incorporated the Neighborhood Union in 1911, it had developed a very complex structure and accomplished many of its goals.[59]

The Neighborhood Union was a self-help settlement aimed at providing a spirit of cooperation among the neighbors and providing social services to the black community. The settlement promoted health and recreation and combated crime and juvenile delinquency. Its activities included lecture, playgrounds, and better sanitation of homes and the streets, abolishing houses of prostitution, and investigating dance halls, poolrooms, and vaudeville shows. By 1914 branches of the Neighborhood Union were established in other parts of the city.[60]

Lugenia Hope's position at the college as the wife of a powerful male leader and her influence in the black community provided access to the white community and membership in national and international efforts. She gained a larger audience and an interracial environment in which to conduct her social reform work. Jacqueline Rouse asserts that the new rights, privileges, and responsibilities that she gained as the wife of an emerging race leader and leading educator also stifled her independence.[61] Perhaps it motivated the fervor that Lugenia Hope put into her social service work.

Interracial cooperation in Atlanta increased in the campaign for better health and sanitary conditions. Members held lectures in public schools and churches to promote better health care practices. Annual clean-up campaigns, which were linked to environmental and health conditions, encouraged people to care for their yards and plant gardens. Lugenia Hope organized the Colored Department of the interracial Anti-Tuberculosis Association, through which all of the health work of the city for blacks was channeled, and formed its own health center to treat tuberculosis and other diseases.[62] Thus, the Neighborhood Union sought interracial cooperation on charitable and other causes rather than duplication of services for blacks and whites.

Lugenia Hope headed the NACW Department of Neighborhood Welfare by 1920. She was a pioneer social worker and a skilled community organizer. She convened the first social service institute for black people in Atlanta as a means of educating African Americans on health and social issues.[63] Although she directed a group of educated, middle-class African American women centered in the college community, large numbers of community leaders and volunteer campaign captains representing grassroots organizations and tactics joined the campaigns. Lugenia Hope raised the social consciousness of African Americans in Atlanta, and because of her efforts the Atlanta University School of Social Service emerged.[64]

SOCIAL SETTLEMENT WORK IN THE SOUTH

Social settlement work demonstrated the pragmatic thinking of the women and called attention to the emphasis that they placed on practical, self-help projects and grassroots organizing. Social settlements in the South and in the North were among the various ways in which club leaders rendered service to black communities. Margaret Washington, Janie Barrett, Lugenia Hope, and Cornelia Bowen were involved in self-help community service efforts in the South. Their campaigns for decent housing and nutritious food had far-reaching consequences, since tuberculosis and diseases resulting from vitamin deficiency were prevalent among the poor population in the South. Many of the southern settlement founders supported Washington's ideology but were not dominated by it. The clubwomen, like other black leaders in the South, used interracial cooperation as one means of obtaining desired goals.

Clubwomen Lugenia Hope, Janie Barrett, and Margaret Washington, who received inspiration from the club movement and personal achievements, used their skills to enhance their club efforts. Club leaders recognized a link between strong families and less poverty. The family is the largest social institution developed by African Americans. It was organized around labor, religion, and social associations before the independent black home was developed. Consequently, the establishment of strong homes among blacks in the South, the clubwomen believed, was an indication of progress since emancipation.

Conversely, the club leaders cast themselves as symbols of moral salvation. They considered it their mission to urge black women to strive for good morals and good homes. The clubwomen, therefore, dismissed the potential of working-class women, particularly tenant farm wives, to identify and pursue their own values and concerns.

SOCIAL SETTLEMENTS AND SCHOOLS

Black club women and community women established remarkable institutions, namely, training schools and industrial schools in the South. African Americans perceived education as a means to escape poverty, enhance employment opportunities, and redress social inequities and injustices. Cornelia Bowen, Judia Jackson Harris, and other clubwomen founded social settlements that became centers of education and community social service.

Many clubwomen who were committed to racial progress through education were influenced by their family backgrounds and a strong adherence to the Protestant ethic. Cornelia Bowen founded the Mt. Meigs Social Settlement and School. Born in 1858 in Tuskegee, Cornelia Bowen structured her life from values received in Sunday school, the Colored School at Zion Hill, and the Normal School after it was founded by Booker T. Washington. Graduating from Tuskegee in 1885, Bowen was dedicated to self-help, self-improvement, and industrial and agricultural training. Cornelia Bowen had grown up in the shadow of Tuskegee. She wrote, "My mother lived the greater part of her life as the slave of Colonel William Bowen, who owned the plot of ground upon which Tuskegee now stands. A seamstress and former house slave, she was never allowed to mingle with plantation slaves."[65] In addition to exposure to the Protestant ethic at Tuskegee, Bowen recalled that her early education came from a McGuffey Reader which was presented to her by a white woman from the town of Tuskegee. In 1888 a new plantation owner contacted Washington, seeking to employ a schoolteacher at Mt. Meigs and Bowen, whom he recommended, had been employed as the principal of the Children's House, the institute's training school.[66]

Cornelia Bowen went to Mt. Meigs to establish a social settlement for the impoverished black tenants on the plantation. She found the people burdened with mild peonage, debts, and low morals. Bowen called the peasant women together and taught them cooking, sewing, housekeeping, and child care. She instructed them in acquiring finer manners and improving relationships with their neighbors and between husbands and wives. She attempted to teach the women to eliminate habits that were unfeminine and unhealthful, such as dipping snuff and chewing and smoking tobacco. Grounded in middle-class values, Cornelia Bowen attempted to uplift the peasant women by organizing the Anti-wrapping Society.[67] As president of the Mt. Meigs Women's Club, Bowen made the following report in 1904: "We have committees appointed to attend to social work, namely, caring for the sick, organizing other clubs in different localities. The homes are neat and clean, pictures on the walls, flowers growing in the yards, and strings are no longer wrapped around the hair."[68] Serving in multiple roles, she became the school teacher, Sunday school teacher, substitute minister, and family counselor. Bowen taught bible classes in a church to mothers and fathers who attended with their children to learn to read or write.

Bowen, Washington, and other public women acted as advocates for the African American community. Cornelia Bowen established the Mt. Meigs Institute in a small rural farming district between Tuskegee and Montgomery with support from the black rural district, black churches, and white philanthropy. The Mt. Meigs community was one of a number of black settlements within a fifty-mile radius of Tuskegee Institute. Purchasing over forty acres of land, Bowen built a school and a model community. Tuskegee faculty members supervised her students in constructing a school building (with boarding facilities), a vocational education building, a girls' dormitory, and a home for teachers. Bowen held mothers' meetings regularly, and in a few years there were visible improvement in moral standards, and in the condition of homes and decreased illiteracy.[69] Some of the graduates of Bowen's school attended Tuskegee. A few became teachers; others took trades. Several became successful farmers. Cornelia Bowen, well known in her community and state, was principal at Mt. Meigs until 1922.

THE CALHOUN COLORED SCHOOL AND SOCIAL SETTLEMENT

Like Cornelia Bowen, Charlotte R. Thorn and Mable W. Dillingham brought the social settlement idea to a cotton plantation in Alabama. They established a southern mission that was "a community center, a farm, a home, a school, and a church."[70] Although Thorn and Dillingham were neither black nor clubwomen, the Calhoun Settlement best exemplified interracial cooperation in the rural South. Contemporaries and observers believed that Calhoun stood for friendly interracial contact. The settlement followed the model of education established by Hampton and Tuskegee Institutes. It was committed to the idea of furthering the work of the colleges by establishing a small efficient center in the county to benefit its residents. The purpose of the settlement was to help teachers and preachers identify with the community, encourage its residents to buy land and build homes, and to build pride and a sense of responsibility.

Lowndes, one of the poorest counties in the South, had a majority black population of approximately 28,000 peasants. Blacks in the county, located approximately twenty miles south of Montgomery, owned no land and had no training or educational facilities and, thus, no opportunity for improving their living conditions. This meant an enlarged environment of ignorance and poverty. In 1892 Booker T. Washington visited a rural district where he found forty or fifty tenant farm families praying for a school. The appearance of Mable Dillingham seemed to answer their prayers.[71] The farmers were barely existing in the crop lien system. Following Washington's speech at Hampton addressing the need for educational missionary work in the Black Belt, two young women from New England, Charlotte Thorn and Mable Dillingham, volunteered to go to the plantation to help people help themselves. The white faculty members, Thorn and Dillingham, were influenced by Armstrong's ideas.

Calhoun, under the direction of the principals, Thorn and the Reverend Pitt Dillingham, Mable's father, established a land company and purchased several plantations in the area. The details of the land buying scheme were worked out by John W. Lemon, a Hampton graduate and the farm manager of the Calhoun School for a decade. His presence and influence helped bring the community closer to the school. By 1904 the land company owned 4,000 acres of former plantation land. Of the eighty-eight families who settled on the land, sixty-six held the deeds for their farms.[72] The earliest homes were purchased through the thrift and economy of the mothers. Ideal standards of morality were not only expected, but demanded from the families.[73] A Farmers' Conference held annually for the blacks promulgated the economic gospel " Raise your own food and buy your land." By 1910 most of the families were property owners.

It was important also for the students to have the opportunity to purchase land. Industrial education was not enough. To keep the graduates from migrating to the city, mine, lumber mill, or the railroad, they needed their own land. It would make farm life attractive and anchor them to the soil.[74] Although this might not have been the purpose of the land scheme, the results reinforced Washington's idea of "casting down your bucket where you are."

Calhoun Settlement School, an industrial and agricultural school of about 300 students, established an academic department with classes from kindergarten to the secondary level.   The graded school became a social center for the community.   Later, a new school was constructed, and the interracial faculty expanded.[75] Vocational classes were required for all students, including practical courses in cooking, ironing, washing, and dressmaking for the girls. Calhoun sponsored an annual Teachers' Institute and the first summer Normal School for black public school teachers of Lowndes County.   A school nurse provided professional service in the school and helped reduce health problems throughout the community.[76]   Calhoun seeks not jealous or narrow competition of neighborhoods, but along with the union of farms, homes, churches, and schools of the community, the equally real union of communities for the common good of the country."[77]

The home-purchasing scheme, the health services, the farmers' conferences, and the interracial faculty bridged the boundaries of race and class at the Calhoun Settlement Colored School. As the center of activities, the Settlement School served as a base to develop the surrounding community. The multipurpose community center attracted the adults and children. Thus, the social milieu of the Calhoun settlement came from its Farmers' Conferences, thrift society, fathers' and mothers' meetings, community night school, celebration of national and Christian holidays, community activities, traveling libraries, and teachers' institutes. Numerous black and white leaders visited the interracial experiment, such as Mary White Ovington and Butler Wilson of the NAACP.[78] The school was maintained by donations and a small endowment fund. Booker Washington and William Jay Schieffelin of New York were members of its Board of Trustees. Although Mable Dillingham died in 1894, Thorn served as the dominant administrator for several decades until 1932.

The Calhoun School received outside funding from several sources from its inception: the Rockefeller Foundation, the Slater Foundation, and the General Education Board, along with churches, women's clubs, civic groups, and individuals.   Charlotte Thorn traveled easily within the philanthropic circles of northern philanthropists. Yet, there was never a feeling of stability.

The Great Depression publicized the poverty of areas like Lowndes County and increased the need for the federal government to participate in the relief. Will Alexander, director of the Commission on Interracial Cooperation and assistant administrator of the US Settlement Association, traveled to the South to learn how Calhoun helped farmers become landowners. Jessie Thomas, Southern Field Secretary of the National Urban League, believed that the key to Calhoun's success was its responsiveness to local conditions and culture. Calhoun was the center for relief efforts during the depression. With the growth of the state education system and the growing federal assumption of responsibility for extension and vocational work, the depression brought an end to a way of life that was outmoded in American culture.[79] The school became the property of the state of Alabama in 1943 and was supervised by the Lowndes County Board of Education.

JUDIA JACKSON HARRIS, "I'LL FIND A WAY OR MAKE ONE"

In a farming community near Athens, Georgia, Judia Jackson Harris carried concepts of self-help mingled with pedagogical doctrines that reflected missionary zeal. Education lagged behind in rural Clark County, which offered a three-month term for students who could attend school. Harris, a graduate of Atlanta University and advocate of self-help and economic independence, followed the school's motto, "I'll find a way or make one."[80] She was influenced by Hampton's emphasis on service after spending a summer at the institution.

In 1903 Harris established the Model and Training School (later the Teacher Training and Industrial Institute) on four acres of her own land in Clark County, about five miles northeast of the city of Athens. With a majority black population, there were 9,378 blacks and 8,230 whites in Clark County in 1900. Within a decade the population had increased to 11,767 blacks and 11,562 whites in the county.[81] To encourage property ownership among the sharecroppers, Jackson Harris organized Land Clubs (called Corn Clubs) beginning in 1901 to give them an economic foundation. She aimed to improve the homes of blacks and build a school that would be the center of community activities. Using the School as a base, Harris aided blacks in purchasing more than 2,000 acres of land.

The first Club contained ten members. They paid $100 in cash and obtained bond for title to a tract of forty acres (later increased to fifty-five acres) the purchase price being $350 for forty acres. During the next seven years, four other Land Clubs were organized, and by 1915, the organizations had acquired a total of 440 acres valued at more than $3000.[82]

Under Harris' direction, the clubs expanded their cooperative investments and purchased a community sawmill, a cotton gin, and a threshing machine. Eventually families, namely, the Neal, Young, Farmer and others, were among the largest property owners and independent black farmers in the area.[83]

Previously a principal of an Athens public school, Harris gave up a stable position with an assured salary to work with residents of a neglected rural community whom she thought she could help. There was no school nearby, and there was no way to get to a school. Classes were held in churches and in lodge halls. Because she believed in self-sufficiency, Jackson Harris made agricultural education and home economics part of her curriculum which included grammar, mathematics, Latin, and black history. Domestic science classes, in a separate building, taught the girls all they needed to know after marriage about keeping house, sewing, cooking, and planting flowers. She persuaded the girls to act in a ladylike manner and encouraged the students to come to school in clean clothes and to comb their hair each day. Harris was concerned about people and treated them all equally. "She didn't look down on persons who were beneath her, socially and economically. Most people liked her, but there were some who believed it was none of her business how they dressed or what they did."[84]

Judia Jackson's school was unique among the educational facilities in the area since she hired only college-trained persons to teach. She built the first school with her own money, a three-room wooden structure with an adjoining two-room home economics building. In 1926 a fire of mysterious origin completely destroyed the main building, and classes were held in the home economics building and in her home also on the Danielsville Road while she conducted a fund-raising campaign to rebuild the school. She mobilized both black and white support, attracting funds from the community and from white philanthropies, namely, the General Education Board, the Slater Fund, the Phelps-Stokes Fund, and the Julius Rosenwald Fund.[85] By 1929 a brick structure with a principal's office, library and auditorium had been constructed on the school campus. It was the largest school in Clarke County. As an observer from one philanthropic fund wrote: "The Training School is the only negro building in the county where the property is in good condition. The grounds are well kept and have flowers planted. The premises are kept clean of trash, and altogether presents a neat appearance."[86]

Judia Jackson Harris and her school encouraged interracial cooperation. She commanded the respect of whites and blacks in the area. The school auditorium, which held about 300 persons, was often filled with blacks and whites who attended plays, baccalaureate ceremonies, and musical performances. The school had an outstanding chorus. Harris wrote and produced four pageants, which had racial, historical, and religious themes.

Judia C. Jackson was born on 1 February 1873 in Athens, Georgia. She was the sixth child of Alfred Jackson, a day laborer, and his mulatto wife, Louise Terrell Jackson. Born Judy Jackson, she graduated from Atlanta University in 1894. By 1900 she was living with her married sister, Camilla, and her husband, Eugene Brydie, a barber. As in many black families, Judia had become a teacher, and her older sister was a laundress.[87] Judia was nearly forty years old when she married Samuel F. Harris, a widower and the principal of the first black public high school in Athens. The Harrises had no children, but he was the father of four children from a previous marriage. Samuel Harris died in 1934. Judia Jackson Harris was an activist throughout her life in club and interracial efforts. A founder and president of the Athens Women's Club, 1899-1900, she was a member of the Georgia Federation of Women's Clubs. Due to ill health, Harris retired from teaching in 1950. The school continued to operate until 1956, when the students and teachers were consolidated into the (black) county school system.

BETHLEHEM CENTER SETTLEMENT HOUSE, NASHVILLE

Most of the social settlements in the South were organized by African Americans, primarily black clubwomen. However, the Methodist Church established several settlements to serve African Americans. These settlements had interracial staffs with white supervisors. Historically, the settlements for blacks were known as Bethlehem Centers, and those for whites were Wesley Houses.[88]

Nashville's Bethlehem Center began when Sallie Sawyer envisioned a settlement house for African Americans in Nashville. Noting that the Methodist women had been assisting in the welfare of white women since the 1890s, she saw the need for a center in the black community. The women of the Methodist Episcopal Church established Wesley House in 1894, as the Door of Hope Mission, to provide a rescue shelter for girls and a free kindergarten. It was the first church-sponsored settlement in the South. In 1903, at the request of the Home Mission Board, the name was changed to Wesley House.[89] Sawyer, a member of the oldest African American congregation in Nashville, the Capers Chapel Christian Methodist Church (CME), sought the help of Estelle Haskins, the appointed and salaried representative of the Women's Missionary Council in the Methodist Training School. Haskins revealed: "It was nearly twelve years ago that she came to my office door in the Mission Training School to ask for help to do the things [for blacks] being done in the Wesley House in South Nashville for the whites. She wanted a sewing school in Capers Chapel for the children. And we responded gladly."[90]

In October 1913 Bethlehem Center Settlement House was cofounded by Sallie Hill Sawyer and Estelle Haskins as a well baby clinic, child care facility, and sewing circle in the basement of St. Andrews Colored Presbyterian Church. Haskins was the first head resident of Bethlehem House. Sallie Sawyer was the institution's first house mother. "To the whole community she was mother, comforter, and advisor."[91] Bethlehem House emerged partially as African Americans envisioned a settlement house for the black population in Nashville. Sawyer was partially motivated by personal reasons to establish a center since she opened her home from "sun-up to sun-down," to provide child care for black mothers who worked long hours as domestics. Sawyers received support from Mattie Coleman, one of Nashville's earliest black female physicians. Dr. Coleman was an activist for woman's rights within the Colored Methodist Episcopal Church (later the Christian Methodist Episcopal). She was active in the struggle of CME women to change the church's national program. Coleman was the founding president of its Woman's Missionary Council.[92]

The Methodist Training School cooperated with the Missionary Society of Capers Chapel Memorial Colored Methodist Church to establish a Bethlehem Settlement House in a black neighborhood. The house was located in the Fourth Ward, one of the most heavily populated African American communities in the city. In 1914 a building for the Bethlehem House was erected with $1,000 from the Tennessee Conference Missionary Society. The settlement conducted a Camp Fire Girls' group, kindergarten, Sewing School, Sunday Bible Story Hour, vacation Bible School, boys' and girls' clubs, and a Mothers' club. Through its many activities, the settlement touched every part of the city. The Bethlehem House became a meeting place for clubs, committees, and church societies. In 1915 the Women's Missionary Council of the Methodist Church began programming for the Bethlehem Center.

In 1920 an extensive study was conducted by Fisk University sociology students, the Methodist Episcopal Church South, and Bethlehem House, Nashville.

The purpose of the study was to discover the existing conditions in the Bethlehem Center community and to determine what the future programs should be.[93]   The report recommended that Bethlehem House cooperate with black churches in religious work, women's work, and children's activities. A playground and kindergarten would be the focus of the efforts.   In 1923 a permanent Bethlehem Center building was erected on Charlotte Avenue at Fifteenth Street. Programming included early training and housing on the second floor for college students involved in the program. Bethlehem Center constructed a gymnasium in 1930, which was funded by the Methodist Episcopal Church, South.

EDUCATIONAL INSTITUTION BUILDING

Despite the work of women institutional builders, the traditional work of institutional development has focused on men.[94]   The work of school founders such as Lucy Laney and Judia Jackson Harris in Georgia, Emma Wilson in South Carolina, Cornelia Bowen in Alabama, Charlotte Hawkins Brown in North Carolina, Nannie Burroughs in Washington, DC, and Mary Bethune in Florida has never been as widely known as the founding and building of Tuskegee Institute under Booker T. Washington. Although the women used programs and methods that were similar to Washington's and had vision, determination, and persuasive powers, it was more difficult for each woman to finance her institution. Women leaders led the protest against deplorable conditions in neglected schools for blacks, overcrowded classrooms, and an inferior instructional program, especially in rural communities. These teachers, who were also community leaders, became adept at raising funds to sustain poverty-stricken black institutions and thereby developed a skill that would be useful in their women's clubs.

Black schools in the South became community centers supporting many activities, including women's clubs and mothers' meetings.[95]   The schools established by Charlotte Hawkins Brown, Mary Bethune, and Nannie Burroughs were not social settlements. However, they offered social services for the immediate community.

Charlotte Hawkins Brown opened the Palmer Memorial Institute in Sedalia, North Carolina, in 1902. She established the school for approximately forty families in a rural community on fifteen acres of land given to her by the pastor of the dilapidated Bethany Congregational Church. Brown received a large donation from the Rosenwald Fund for her institution.

Requiring a rigorous academic schedule as well as service, Brown and her students participated in community action and efforts to improve the lives of the community residents.   Brown encouraged homeownership, better health care, improved farming methods, and political action. She insisted on proper behavior, and teaching respectability was part of the school's objective. Through her club work and academic work, Brown sought to impart Victorian sexual and social mores to black girls and women.[96]   Brown helped organize the North Carolina Federation of Women in 1909. She launched an interracial fund-raising campaign to establish an industrial home for delinquent black girls. She was president of the North Carolina Federation, the largest in the Association, from 1915 to 1936. During her presidency the Federation purchased 300 acres of farmland at Efland, North Carolina and built an Industrial Home for Wayward Girls.[97]   The Federation also established the Colored Orphanage at Oxford. Brown once declared that the industrial schools could do much to uplift the people and pave the way for interracial cooperation. By the 1940s Brown had changed Palmer Memorial Institute's emphasis from agricultural and industrial subjects to liberal arts. This modification contrasted with the vision of practical education for blacks held by most white philanthropists at the time.

In 1904 Mary McLeod Bethune established the Daytona Educational and Industrial Training School in Florida.   Mary was the seventeenth child born to former slave Samuel and Patsy McIntosh McLeod. She attended the Maysville Educational and Industrial School founded by Emma Wilson and the all-female Scotia Seminary (later Barber-Scotia College).   Mary Bethune established her school originally to benefit young girls, particularly the daughters of washerwomen and black workers building the Florida East Coast Railroad and other poor persons.[98]   Bethune aimed to help neglected girls by developing them into useful Christian womanhood.

Mary Bethune organized a Board of Trustees, which included black pastors from local churches, white philanthropists, and an advisory board of volunteers. She solicited the support of wealthy white women who spent their winters in Florida. Bethune's largest benefactor was James Gamble of the Proctor and Gamble Company of Ohio.

Some credit for Bethune's thriving institution must be given to Frances Reynolds Keyser, the former superintendent of the White Rose Home. Bethune met Keyser when she boarded at the home in 1912 and invited her to come to Florida. Keyser, who had worked previously at the Florida Agricultural and Mechanical College in Tallahassee, believed in the ideals that Bethune sought to instill in the girls who came to her institution. She assisted Bethune as director of the Academic Department, thereby allowing Bethune more time for a public role, especially in fund-raising.[99]   Keyser, who was older than Bethune and former head of the Empire State Federation of Women's Clubs, introduced Bethune to other clubwomen in the National Association.

African American women, such as Cornelia Bowen, Judia Jackson Harris, and Mary Bethune established schools that functioned as social welfare agencies providing services for black communities. Bethune's school, which became a college, provided academic, civic, racial, and interracial activities. A farm and livestock department provided demonstrations for the community. There were conferences on health, thrift, homeownership, gardening, property improvement, and other concerns. In 1911   the McLeod Hospital was founded as part of the extension work of the school.   The institution cooperated with the Associated Charities and the clubs of the National Association of Colored Women. The campus YWCA visited and assisted needy families. The College conducted home aid and child welfare work in rural communities. The college library was the only public facility of its kind open to African Americans.[100]   The social work continued after the school merged, under the auspices of the Board of Education for Negroes of the Methodist Episcopal Church, with the all-male Cookman College to become Bethune-Cookman College in 1923.

Nannie Helen Burroughs' ideas about work, female respectability, and self-help culminated in 1909 in the founding and development of the National Training School for Women and Girls in the District of Columbia. Burroughs emphasized the Protestant value system and a strict moral code for race advancement.   Her goals were to train women for missionary work, to prepare Sunday school teachers, and to train women for domestic service.[101]   The female institution offered courses in domestic training, dressmaking, printing, and beauty culture. The school published a newspaper and operated a laundry. Students attended from the North and the South ranging in age from twelve to forty-four.

The migration of blacks within the southern region and northward made Washington an ideal place for a vocational training school. Moreover, the District provided ample opportunities for domestic work.   Burroughs succeeded in establishing a practical school because of her remarkable success as secretary of the Women's Convention of the Baptist Church and in fund-raising.   At the time, black educational institutions were generally founded and managed by blacks, but mainly supported by white benefactors. A firm believer in self-help, Burroughs accepted the primary responsibility for managing and funding her institution.

Becoming dissatisfied with conventional philanthropic and social reform efforts, in 1920 Burroughs established a labor organization for women, the National Association of Wage Earners.   As president of the National Training School and prominent in the church and women's club network, Sharon Harley argues that Burroughs challenged some of the clubwomen to work directly with poor, workingclass women.[102]   Like the Women's Trade Union League (WTUL), Burroughs emphasized the importance of cross-cultural class cooperation.[103]

In 1920 Burroughs sought to professionalize domestic service to help improve the socioeconomic condition of working-class black women by providing job training to make them employable as skilled workers rather than menials. Membership in the organization consisted of local, state, and district unions of wage earners.   Females under sixteen were not admitted to membership.[104] Burroughs established a strong Board of Directors with the support of Mary McLeod Bethune, Maggie Walker, Elizabeth Carter, and Mary Church Terrell. Evelyn Higginbotham suggests that the professionalization of domestic service was the embodiment of respectability.[105] To professionalize an activity that was already in the domestic sphere was a conservative means of racial improvement.

COMMUNITY WORK

African Americans have a long history of social action and self-help, community development, and relief efforts.   In the South, black women were concerned about family improvement and community development.   Black clubwomen in the North, such as Victoria Matthews, were concerned about creating homes and improving the environment for working women. African Americans developed their own social settlements in several communities of the South. In addition to these social service centers, they created homes for the elderly and orphans, juvenile reformatories, and day-care centers for working mothers. They campaigned for improved education and better health care for African Americans and, in turn, supported a National Negro Health Week.

Black and white workers in social settlements in the South and in the North were middle-class Americans who used their education and skills as a means of achieving social change. Black and white settlement workers promoted a scientific approach to social service. A primary focus of all the social settlements, North and South, was their emphasis on housekeeping and domestic science. Women attempted to transform the traditional domestic housekeeping responsibilities into civic housekeeping. Mrs. Booker T. Washington, in her presidential address at the biennial conference of the National Association of Colored Women in 1914, proposed that the future work of the National Association of Colored Women should concentrate on civic housekeeping, YWCA work, cleanup days, and industrial high schools. Washington, therefore, linked the local community work of the black clubwomen with that of women on a national scale.[106]

This chapter reminds us that institutions for African Americans have either been ignored or underfunded or both by mainstream society. Black philanthropy and charitable giving usually assumed the form of small-scale, personal assistance and involvement. In most cases the women knew the individuals, families, or groups whom they assisted. Black women had to struggle to create their institutions. They performed a nearly impossible feat of education pioneering and entrepreneurship. Black women's philanthropy attempted to help African Americans survive and change their circumstances.

Mary Church Terrell, First President, National Association of Colored Women (NACW), 1896–1901. Courtesy of Moorland-Spingarn Research Center, Howard University.

Verina Morton-Jones, Founder, Lincoln Settlement House, New York, 1908. Courtesy of Moorland-Spingarn Research Center, Howard University.

Victoria Earle Matthews, founder, White Rose Home and Industrial Association for Working Girls, NYC, 1897. SC-CN-85-0262. Courtesy of Photographs and Prints Division, Schomburg Center for Research in Black Culture, The New York Public Library, Astor, Lenox and Tilden Foundations.

Janie Porter Barrett, Founder, Locust Street Settlement, Hampton, Virginia, 1890 and the Virginia Industrial Home for Girls (1908) near Richmond in Hanover County, Virginia. Courtesy of Hampton University Archives.

School Founder Judia Jackson Harris, and teachers Eli Jackson and Dora Sapp. Courtesy of Mrs. Helen Neal Joseph.

Lincoln Settlement House, Branch of Henry Street Settlement, founded 1906, New York City. Courtesy of Lillian Wald Papers, Rare Book and Manuscript Library, Columbia University.

Mary McLeod Bethune, Founder, National Council of Negro Women (1935); President, National Association of Colored Women (NACW), 1924–1928. Courtesy of Moorland-Spingarn Research Center, Howard University.

Maritcha Remond Lyons, Principal, P.S. 67, New York City, ca. 1910. Courtesy of Harry A. Williamson Papers, Photographs and Prints Division, Schomburg Center for Research in Black Culture, The New York Public Library, Astor, Lenox and Tilden Foundations.

The National Federation

......OF......

Afro-American Women.

Mrs. B. T. Washington, Pres.　　Mrs. U. A. Ridley, Sec.
　　Tuskegee, Ala.　　　　　　131 Kent Street,
　　　　　　　　　　　　　　　Brookline, Mass.

Mrs. Libbie C. Anthony, Treas.
　　　　Jefferson City, Mo.

Membership Application Form.

The *W. L. U.* of *New York City,*

No. of members *55,* Object *Vigilance in securing justice for all,*

Hereby make application to enter The National Federation of Afro-American Women.

Mrs. Victoria Matthews, President.

Miss W. Cordelia Ray, Secretary.

No. *311 East 62nd St,* (Address.)
N. Y. City.

DATE. *June 6 1896,*

* *Woman's Loyal Union*

The National Federation of Afro-American Women Membership Application Form, ca. 1895. Boston Public Library/Rare Books Department. Courtesy of The Trustees.

The National Association of Colored Women's Organization Meeting in Washington, 1896, National Association of Colored Women, Inc., 1896–1952. Courtesy of Sophia Smith Collection, Smith College.

Sewing Class, The National Training School for Girls, Washington, D.C. Courtesy of The Library of Congress.

Nannie Helen Burroughs, Founder, The National Training School for Girls, 1909, Washington, D.C. Courtesy of The Library of Congress.

White Rose Industrial Association Working Girls Home. Courtesy of Mrs. Mattie K. Daniels, former superintendent of the White Rose Home.

Northeastern Federation of Women's Clubs of the National Association of Colored Women, Inc., New York. Photograph by Austin Hansen. Courtesy of Photographs and Prints Division, Schomburg Center for Research in Black Culture, The New York Public Library, Astor, Lenox and Tilden Foundations.

The Children Wrapping a Maypole. Courtesy of Bethlehem Center of Nashville.

Phyllis Wheatley Home Association Officers. Courtesy of Chicago Historical Society.

Director, Forrester B. Washington, The Atlanta University School of Social Work. Courtesy of Robert W. Woodruff Library, Atlanta University Center.

The Calhoun School, Graduating Class of 1915. Courtesy of State of Alabama, Department of Archives and History.

Pupils and teacher from the second and third grades in front of a log cabin school built by students from the Calhoun School carpentry classes, 1916–1917. Courtesy of State of Alabama, Department of Archives and History.

Neighborhood Union, Atlanta, Georgia, Founded by Lugenia Burns Hope, 1908. Courtesy of Neighborhood Union Collection, Archives and Special Collections, Atlanta University Center, Robert W. Woodruff Library.

Irene McCoy Gaines. Courtesy of Chicago Historical Society.

Leonard Street Orphanage, Atlanta, Georgia. Courtesy of Robert W. Woodruff Library, Atlanta University Center.

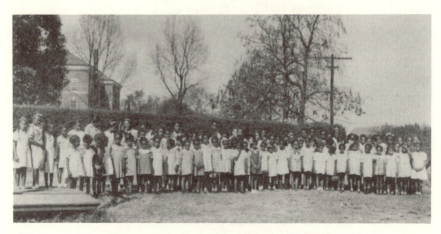

Chadwick School, Atlanta, ca. 1933. Courtesy of Robert W. Woodruff Library, Atlanta University Center.

Judia Jackson Harris School, Founded in 1903, Clark County, Georgia. Courtesy of Mrs. Helen Neal Joseph.

Chapter 6

Black Bourgeoisie in the Slums or Helping Women: Paradigms of Black Settlement Houses in the North and Midwest ·

> We are appealing to people who are contributing to educational and philanthropic institutions. Our work aims to help the "strange girl" who comes into the city, to provide a home for her, a job for her, and keep her away from the snares and pitfalls of life. Our work is not only helpful to her, but an asset to the city.
>
> White Rose Industrial Association, *Appeal*, 1920.

Middle-class black women made the settlement house a catalyst for community development and social change.[1] They were conscious of the leadership role that the institutions could play in African American communities. Although black women volunteers were generally not settlement house residents, the institutions constituted a woman's space where a women's culture did develop. Settlement houses served a dual purpose as both lodging facilities for black women and community centers. Settlement houses were unique institutions established by black women to facilitate their participation in public affairs. Race progress among black women turned occasionally to the state for support to represent the interests of their race and gender.[2] Black clubwomen used the settlement houses for political and cultural affairs. African American women have historically used community institutions as places to develop an alternative black women's culture.[3]

Black clubwomen's most successful and effective philanthropic activities were conducted in settlement work. Poverty and poor conditions impelled black women to establish and promoted social settlements in the North and in the South in the 1890s. Coincidentally, Victoria Matthews began her settlement work in the North the same year that Margaret Washington began working among tenant farm wives in the South. Programs in the North, like those in the South, were designed to serve the poor and modify unfavorable social behavior. The social service and self-help programs established by black women in the North were modified to meet the conditions of the urban environment. Both rural and urban social service programs emphasized vocational education. Southern clubwomen networked with educational institutions in their outreach efforts to poor rural families.[4] In the early years, social settlements in both the North and the South received donations from white philanthropy. In the South some of the institutions received local funds and became members of the Community Chest. Northern clubwomen relied on a network of women's clubs and urban institutions such as the YWCA, churches, and the National Urban League. Although the work was similar, the efforts of the women's clubs in the North helped to modify regional and cultural differences between the clubwomen and the women whom they helped.

Nathan Glazer and Daniel P. Moynihan contended that the black middle class contributed very little in terms of money, organization, or involvement to the solution of social problems in black communities.[5] They did not emphasize the historical contributions of African Americans to the tradition of self-help and institution building. The work of black clubwomen disproved the assertion that African Americans lacked the community self-help agencies that fostered stability among other racial and ethnic groups. The clubwomen's work, especially with social settlements, indicated that black women were autonomous, active people.

Of the various settlement houses in New York City catering to African Americans around the turn of the century, the White Rose Mission was unique because it was the earliest black settlement house in New York City. Self-help and institution building were not new measures among African Americans, but the image of black women engaged in organized action to meet group needs was new. Victoria Earle Matthews established the White Rose Mission in New York City in 1897 as a shelter for young black women and a settlement house. It was incorporated in 1898, with a biracial Board of Directors, as the White Rose Home and Industrial Association for Working Girls. Northern settlement houses emerged for community improvement and became centers for women migrating from the South. They provided lodging, night classes, and job placement. Northern settlement houses for blacks developed activities that closely resembled those for European immigrants.

Settlement workers were at the forefront of the social welfare sector of the Progressive movement. Jane Addams' Hull House in Chicago and University Settlement in New York became "spearheads of reform" in the Progressive era. Settlement workers were young, educated, middle-class persons who lived in slum neighborhoods in efforts to restore communication between those who were college-educated and working and the working class and to help improve conditions in the cities. They hoped to improve the lives of the working class by helping them obtain an education, an appreciation of the arts, better jobs, and better housing.[6]

Like the black clubwomen, settlement workers also attempted to remake the working class in their own middle-class image. Jane Addams looked at social problems as a middle-class woman visitor and she perceived that only women could see the true vision of a democratic society.[7] In nearly every settlement in the United States was a shifting ethnic population. This complicated the settlement ideal of creating a neighborhood spirit in a crowded section of a large industrial city. Historian Rivka Shpak Lissak asserts that Jane Addams believed that American society failed to adapt its institutions to the economic and social changes created by urbanization, industrialization, and immigration. These changes included the emergence of a large, underprivileged working class suffering from lack of equal opportunities and social disorganization in the slums. Class conflict, social antagonisms, and a disintegration of morals and social norms were the result. Addams proposed extending democracy beyond its political expression to a universal moral code to produce democracy. The better element in society, the educated, middle class who possessed merit and virtue should have the major role in curing the ills of American democracy.[8] Addams believed that the immigrants were entitled to preserve their cultural identity, their language, customs, and tradition.

This chapter is mainly concerned with black settlement houses and black settlement workers, most of whom were clubwomen. There was an intensification of social reform within black communities between 1890 and 1910.[9] By the late nineteenth and early twentieth centuries, African American women increasingly joined the movement of social reform. They developed their own organizations and institutions for improving the lives and status of African Americans. Urban reformers were interested in improving housing, employment, child care, recreational facilities, health, education, and sanitary conditions, particularly for migrants to the city. Many New York reformers attempted to uplift the masses by establishing settlement houses.

WHITE ROSE HOME FOR WORKING GIRLS

Black clubwomen displayed considerable interest in seeking to protect decent, lower-class girls and "rescue fallen women," a social service that had excluded black women. Matthews dedicated her life to race work after she lost her only child at an early age. She volunteered for club work, settlement work and social service activities with enthusiasm and devotion. Matthews founded the mission to establish and maintain a Christian nonsectarian Home for Colored Girls and Women and to train them in the principles of practical self-help and right living.[10] Social work was needed among women who arrived in urban areas seeking employment. The mission engaged in a variety of settlement activities, including travelers' aid service in New York and Norfolk, Virginia.

Victoria was influenced by her mother's self-determination and perseverance. Born in Fort Valley, Georgia, 27 May 1861, Victoria was the youngest of nine children born to Caroline Smith. A former slave, Caroline attempted to escape several times before finally succeeding during the Civil War. She left her children in the care of an old nurse, made her way to Virginia, and worked for eight years before saving enough money to return to Georgia to get her children. When Caroline arrived, she found only four of her children living. After a legal struggle, Caroline gained custody of her two fair-complexioned daughters, Anna and Victoria Smith, who were being raised in the home of her former master. Caroline, who was originally from Virginia, migrated with her daughters to New York in 1873.[11]

Victoria had no opportunity to attend school until she reached New York, and then she was about twelve years old. She attended Grammar School 48 in New York City until the illness of someone close to her, probably her mother, forced her to leave. Largely self-educated, she acquired knowledge from independent study, lectures, and contact with educated persons. Marriage at the age of eighteen enabled Victoria to escape her home life but it led to an unhappy and perhaps lonely domestic situation.[12] Victoria and her husband, William Matthews, a coach driver, moved to Brooklyn, which was the home of a small group of black elite men and women.

The constant motivating factor in Matthews' life was her writing. During the early years of her marriage, she wrote stories about her childhood that were published in weekly journals. In 1893, under the literary pseudonym Victoria Earle, she published a slim volume, *Aunt Lindy*. Matthews' popularity with the press stemmed from the fact that much of her early work was in dialect. She did freelance writing for black and white newspapers. Matthews' writing linked her to prominent women, black and white. Like Josephine Ruffin, she was invited to join the predominantly white Women's National Press Association.[13]

An activist and social reformer, Matthews helped organize the first woman's club in New York City. The Woman's Loyal Union became involved in protest and woman's issues, such as access to better jobs and fair wages. Matthews' social work in New York City allowed her to exchange ideas with white reformers and social workers and to raise her own consciousness regarding moral reform and the condition of African American women.

In 1897, the same year that she founded the White Rose Mission, Matthews spoke before the mostly white Society of Christian Endeavor meeting expressing indignation over the attacks on black females as immoral women. Fannie Barrier Williams had written that the black woman was the only woman for whom virtue was not an ornament but a necessity.[14] Nearly every black female leader, including Mathews and Williams, defended black women from charges by a patriarchy that first enslaved black women and then criticized them for the effects of slavery, especially illegitimate births. They argued that black women, having been degraded by slavery, could not exhibit the same qualities of virtuousness that was expected of white women.[15] At a time when the popular literature of the day attempted to create for white women an image of "true womanhood," chaste and loving, at the center of marriage, home, and family, black women were exploited as sexually promiscuous   and disinclined toward the virtues of true womanhood.   Matthews' lecture, "The Awakening of the Afro-American Woman," affirmed that the African American woman was just awakening to her rights and responsibilities. She believed that both black and white women should assume some responsibility for the less fortunate. She admonished both groups to join in elevating African American women.[16]

Matthews and other black women skillfully navigated the hurdles of race and gender. Like Cooper, Harper, and Wells, she realized that despite the need for a black women's organization, alliances with white women would be necessary to change the political and social condition of black women. She stated that it was the responsibility of white Christian womanhood of the country to join black women in elevating the mind and the soul of Afro-American womanhood. Matthews believed that black women deserved the cooperation of all the female forces in the nation, in religion, in education, in temperance, in industry, and in combating (negative) public opinion and laws that degrade black womanhood.

Professional women, who were the club organizers and leaders, established social settlements as boarding facilities for working women and community centers for neighborhood women and children. Domestic service was the main occupation for black women in urban areas. In Chicago and other large cities, an army of day workers and live-in domestics worked as cooks, housekeepers, and laundresses.[17] Black women actually obtained more freedom and control over their lives through day work experiences.[18]

African Americans had been migrating to cities outside the South since the 1880s, and the movement gained momentum in the 1890s. Many of the migrants were women.[19] In New York City most blacks lived in distinct pockets in the present-day midtown area between Twentieth and Sixty-fourth Street.   The lower part of the area located between Twentieth and Fifty-third Streets, was called the Tenderloin, and the upper part from Sixtieth to Sixty-fourth between Tenth and Eleventh Avenues was known as San Juan Hill because of the racial tension that occurred with the influx of new arrivals. With jobs scarce and rent high, the migrants found relief in narrow, unsanitary tenements and the lodging system. Two out of five or 40 percent, of the working-class households in the Tenderloin and San Juan Hill areas took in lodgers, and in only a few cases were the lodgers and the host families related.[20]

Black and white women were influenced by the social purity movement, which began in New York City in the 1880s. Social purity alliances focused on a range of interests, including moral education, child-raising theories, organizations for the protection of women travelers, and the abolition of prostitution.[21] Black clubwomen addressed such issues as "Purity and the Negro" and "The Colored Race and Moral Reform." Mary Terrell spoke at the National Purity Congress in 1905. For poorer women purity often translated into coercion. Moral purity crusades reinforced a stereotyped sexual image of black women.   Redlight districts revealed loose moral restraints and urban decay. Those created between 1890 and 1918 limited vice to black neighborhoods while protecting others.[22]

Victoria Matthews anticipated transplanting the "Tuskegee system," with a few local additions, on 97th Street in New York City.[23] By the late 1890s many black families in New York City were crowded into older housing. In 1896, Matthews began her social work by visiting black families between 59th and 127th Streets from Park to First Avenues to improve their home conditions. Many of the 6,000 blacks crowded there had been driven from Bleecker Street. Matthews attempted to assist the mothers with meal preparation and household tasks and to give them economical and healthful alternatives.[24] Working-class black women in the North and in the South were encouraged to improve their living conditions. Regardless of her good intentions, Matthews displayed a condescending attitude toward the poor.

The social work exhausted Matthews, as she worked alone to complete the tasks. Therefore, she organized a women's network composed of ten women from various black churches and proposed a general program of operation for her mission. Holding mothers' meetings in their homes, the women formed committees to study the conditions of blacks in the city, to contact teachers, and to locate a place to house the organization. Impressed by the work of the tiny mission, Winthrop Phelps, a wealthy apartment owner on the Upper East Side, provided space rent-free for a community center.[25]

By 11 February 1897 Matthews' experiment in social service and reform became a reality. The following year, the nondenominational mission was incorporated under the laws of the state of New York. Organized under the "settlement plan," the White Rose Mission offered vocational courses in home economics to prepare black women for domestic work. Ruth Alice Moore, then a Brooklyn schoolteacher and boarding in Matthews' home, taught the kindergarten class. A native of New Orleans and graduate of Straight University (now Dillard University), Moore married Paul Laurence Dunbar in 1898. Both Dunbar and Booker T. Washington frequently participated in the settlement's lecture series. To further race consciousness, Matthews established a library of African American books and taught a class in black history.[26] Neighborhood children from other ethnic groups were welcomed to the mission. Children, from three to fifteen, were taught the American values of decency, order, and thrift.

Matthews' work with the White Rose Mission took her in two directions that had national implications, the settlement house movement and travelers' aid service. News spread about Matthews' work and her mission. In the spring of 1898 Matthews went to meet a young woman who was arriving from Florida by boat. Missing for three days, the woman was "lured" away by unethical employment agents. Matthews decided to do something to help other female travelers avoid similar circumstances.[27]

The White Rose Home operated with a Board of Directors and a regular membership. Several white women joined the White Rose Home Association board, including progressive reformers Mary Stone, Grace Hoadley Dodge, Frances Kellor, and Mary White Ovington. Stone was both vice president and later president of the White Rose Home Association. Other patrons and board members were Adam Clayton Powell Sr., pastor of the Abyssinian Baptist Church, Booker

Washington,   and Mrs. Collis Huntington, the wife of the New York philanthropist.[28] The White Rose Home Association was dependent on voluntary contributions for social services. The White Rose Home moved from its original location at E. 97th Street to E. 95th Street where it remained for seventeen years. In 1918 the association, joining churches and other   institutions, relocated to Harlem and purchased a brownstone at W. 136th Street.[29]

Seeking to protect black women, settlement houses like the White Rose Mission engaged in rigorous supervision. Matthews, the superintendent, enforced the rules of the home. Strict rules, curfew, and punctuality were methods used by middle-class women to integrate the underprivileged into the mainstream of American life. The White Rose Mission admitted all women seeking shelter, especially migrant women seeking employment who were without relatives or friends.[30]   Curfew was eleven o'clock each night, unless the superintendent received notice otherwise. The settlement provided lodging mainly to working women aged fifteen to forty-five. The peak months for lodging were June through December. Overcrowding during this period required limited stays for the women at the home and compelled many to board with families.

Working girls' homes, like the White Rose Home and Industrial Association, offered a collective living arrangement for the women boarders. It consisted of a shared kitchen, a laundry and sewing room, communal bedrooms, and bathroom. There were fourteen beds upstairs and a common reception room on the first floor. Although this sisterly arrangement was temporary, it enabled feminine institutions, such as the White Rose Home, to present an alternative to an environment that was unsafe and inhospitable for young black women.[31]

TRAVELERS' AID SERVICE

Matthews established the White Rose Travelers' Aid Society in 1905. The New York agent, Dorothy J. Boyd (later Brown), a Sunday school teacher at Mount Olivet Baptist Church, was placed at the Old Dominion pier in that city, and Hattie Proctor was placed at the same line in Norfolk, Virginia.[32]   Due to Matthews' organization skills, the travelers' aid service functioned like a "perfect chain of white roses." Thus, she coined her social service the White Rose Mission. The name symbolized the nineteenth-century Victorian emphasis on "purity, goodness, and virtue."[33]   It showed, also, that black clubwomen held these characteristics of respectability in high esteem. Matthews's older sister Anna Rich assisted her in providing travelers' aid service. Experienced in public service, Anna was the first black woman to manage the Brooklyn Home for Aged Colored. As dock agent at the Old Dominion line, Anna helped all women seeking assistance. Within approximately ten years, the society met 50,000 women. Of these, the White Rose Mission sheltered at least 5,000.[34] Grace Dodge was one of the strongest supporters of the travelers' aid work. Impressed with the White Rose Travelers' Aid Society, she stated, "If it's a good thing for colored girls, it is good for all girls." Dodge organized the New York Travelers' Aid Society, which she expanded into a national service.[35] For years Dodge had advocated associations as a form of self-protection among working women. Interested in preventive social work for preserving morality, she inspired collective moral action among working-class white women.

Women's club minutes and records of local churches and other institutions may provide an invaluable glimpse of the kinds of young black women who went to New York City during the Progressive era. Some educated women arrived at the White Rose Home, although most were illiterate and destitute. Upon arrival, the settlement house workers counseled the women and prepared them for employment in domestic service. To ensure domestic jobs, better wages, and better working conditions, the White Rose Home had its own job placement service.[36] Of the approximately 300 annual lodgers at the White Rose Home, before 1920, the majority, or 75 percent, previously worked in domestic service. Matthews was not unlike other black club women in supporting Victorian ideas regarding black women's sexuality. Concerned with improving moral behavior, she challenged her club sisters to keep the working girls who migrated to urban centers from going wrong. A member of the Standing Committee and a participant in Hampton's second Negro Conference on how to improve the conditions of blacks, Matthews presented a paper on the dangers faced by southern black women who migrated to northern cities. She aroused the consciousness of the conference attendees, who expressed concern by organizing volunteers at the Norfolk docks to counsel the black women.[37] Matthews believed that knowledge of working conditions, the work available, and the circumstances in the cities would deter many female migrants.

Upon arriving in the North, black women were employed predominantly as domestics. Most migrants experienced difficulty finding employment and housing. Some women were taken advantage of, lost their money, or were drawn into vice, crime, and even prostitution. Young women were often victimized by procurers disguised as legitimate labor agents. Black and white agents went into the rural districts to recruit women and pressure them to migrate to the North.

Responding to these problems, women's organizations in many urban areas set up special programs to protect newly arrived single and widowed women. Chief among these were settlement houses with boarding facilities, travelers' aid services, and the League for the Protection of Colored Women, whose primary functions were travelers' aid and job placement. Of the migrants to New York City, "nearly three in ten women aged fifteen or older were lodgers or lived alone." Large numbers of migrants were single women who were attracted to the potential job opportunities in domestic service.[38]

Matthews and other investigators found that employment agencies in New York, Chicago, and other cities received large fees to send black women seeking work as domestics to houses of ill repute. Pretty girls were always in demand, but not as domestic servants. The young female recruits lived in deplorable conditions. Most of the women were not placed until they had depleted their resources. If a woman who had been pressured into prostitution attempted to leave, she was threatened with a suit for breach of contract.

"The tenderloins must be purified." Matthews had two motives for her message, simply that the path taken by many young migrant women from the South was immoral, and she feared that no one would hire such women because of their tarnished reputation. Matthews used her skills as a newspaper reporter to help her gather evidence. Through personal investigations and contacts, she found similar conditions existing for black women in New York, Boston, San Francisco, Chicago, and other urban centers. She believed that persons in fraudulent employment agencies should be accountable for their acts.

Lack of economic opportunity in the South was a primary force motivating migration. Most migrants came from the rural South and from areas dominated by sharecropping and tenant farmers. Whether in the South or in the North, most black women were employed in domestic service. Single black women coming from the South were often accused of having poor moral character.[39] Although the migrants were poor, they were not necessarily immoral. Industrious, hardworking women left the South in large numbers.[40]

Historically, black women adhered to a cult of secrecy, a culture of dissemblance, in responding to assaults on black sexuality. This was one way to fight back and to deconstruct society's candid use of race.[41] The clubwomen were conscious of the historical abuse and exploitation of black women, but they seemed more concerned about introducing standards of Victorian moral conduct. Matthews believed that bringing young women from the South for immoral purposes affected the reputations of all black women seeking employment. She advised women without enough money to survive to remain in the South.

For the most part, on a national scale, the social service institutions established during the Progressive era served whites only. Settlement houses throughout the country primarily provided services for European immigrants. Nearly a decade after the White Rose Mission was established, at least ten social settlements that served black neighborhoods were organized jointly by white social workers and black community leaders. Progressive reformer Celia Parker Woolley established the Frederick Douglass Center in April 1904. Lillian Wald organized Stillman House, a branch of the Henry Street Settlement for blacks, in New York City in 1906. In Boston the South End House established the Robert Gould Shaw Settlement House in 1907. A few of the settlements did provide interracial services, such as the Wendell Phillips Settlement. Hull House residents staffed that settlement with black social workers.

Individual Progressive era settlement house workers rejected inequality in both the National Federation of Settlements (NFS) and American society. Progressive reformers Jane Addams, Frances Kellor, Mary White Ovington, Lillian Wald, Sophonisba Breckinridge, Florence Kelley, and Mary McDowell opposed racial discrimination. They were active in the NAACP, the National Urban League, and other civil rights organizations supporting racial liberalism. Sympathy and perception helped Lillian Wald bridge the racial gap. In May 1909 Wald held a reception for the founding conference of the NAACP at the Henry Street Settlement, one of the few places where an interracial group could meet. Even these liberals, however, did not advocate racial integration.[42] Jane Addams, conscious of her father's abolitionist background, opposed nearly every injustice to African Americans of which she was aware. She realized that blacks faced residential segregation and political and economic discrimination. Race oppression distinguished African Americans from other ethnic groups.[43]

Although Jane Addams worked on behalf of African Americans, she supported Jim Crow facilities in black districts. Most white settlement workers before World War I believed that segregated facilities for blacks would better serve their needs and interests. Settlement workers were exposed also to the scientific justification for Jim Crow that permeated American society. In his sociological study of blacks in Boston, John Daniels noted that whatever there was speculation that the Negro, armed with equal rights, would rise to the level of others in the wider community it was replaced with the notion that the Negro was from a lower gradation. While this opinion supported the attitude of the South, it was more than merely accepting sectional prejudice. Scholar Lee Baker contends that it represented an acceptance of the South's anthropological theory that blacks belonged to a dissimilar race, unequal in intelligence and responsibility, and therefore constituted a major problem.[44]

FREDERICK DOUGLASS CENTER

Celia Parker Woolley founded the Frederick Douglass Center on the fringes of Chicago's South Side to promote integration. Woolley was a minister in the Unitarian Fellowship. Her religious background probably influenced her thinking regarding interracial equality. Woolley, however, had little interest in the conditions of poor African Americans. She admonished American society for barring refined, middle class blacks from social and economic equality. She believed that blacks were "as wise and good as their white neighbors." To borrow from ideologue Frantz Fanon, she conceived the ideal black as a white person in black skin.[45] Woolley dimissed both the racial and cultural heritage of African Americans. Celia Woolley, who viewed her settlement as an experiment in interracial relations, held forums and interracial teas to promote her idealism.

A member of the Chicago Woman's Club and the Woman's City Club, Woolley's interest in the club associations of the NACW motivated her into affiliation with the Illinois State Federation of Colored Women's Clubs. Woolley's activities appealed mainly to middle-class black women. An interracial Woman's Club did most of the work for the Frederick Douglass Center. Ida Wells-Barnett, the club's vice president, led the fund raising efforts to purchase a building on Wabash Avenue. The center sponsored children's classes in domestic science, music, and political equality. It was associated with charity relief, legal counsel, child welfare, and playgrounds. The Frederick Douglass Center expanded its services after Fannie Barrier Williams became president of the Woman's Club, a position that Ida Wells-Barnett declined. During World War I, Elizabeth Davis directed the center's War Office. In 1918 the center opened a relief station during the influenza epidemic.[46]

WENDELL PHILLIPS SETTLEMENT

The Wendell Phillips Settlement was founded in 1907 by a group of twenty African Americans. It provided blacks with social services similar to those provided for the poor by settlements in other neighborhoods. Its interracial Board of Directors included Sophonisba Breckinridge, Grace Abbott, and Louise deKoven Bowen. It was supervised by black social work students, Sophia Boaz and Birdye Haynes, who lived at the settlement and did their fieldwork there. Both women received certificates from the University of Chicago in 1913 and remained at the center, Haynes as head resident and Boaz as her assistant. The center conducted a variety of classes and clubs for children and adults and provided a meeting place for the community. Haynes described it as a "center from which constructive social work could be done to improve conditions for the African Americans on the West Side (of Chicago)."[47] Its location adjacent to the Black Belt rather than in it, Anne Meis Knupfer asserts, reflects its emphasis on social class. Although Haynes was trained, her work was scrutinized by Abbott and Breckinridge and the Board refused to adequately finance her recommendations for social services.[48] Birdye H. Haynes left for New York and became the head worker at the Lincoln Settlement House in Manhattan.

STILLMAN SETTLEMENT HOUSE

In December 1906 a black nurse from the Henry Street Visiting Nurses staff, working in the San Juan Hill district, felt it was necessary to launch a larger welfare effort. The Stillman Settlement House was an extension of the nursing service that began in 1905. It was located in a multiracial neighborhood that included migrants from the South and from the West Indies and was known as New York's "Black Belt" prior to 1922. The first director, Ida Morgan, formerly at Haines Institute, supervised an integrated staff of paid and volunteer workers.[49] The Board of Directors, headed by Lillian Wald, included Eugene K. Jones, executive director of the National Urban League.

Stillman House, at 154 W. 62d Street, provided free health care for mothers and children. The center of activities was the Mothers' Club, made up of working-class women earning a living as laundresses and domestics. The settlement program offered vocational courses, a kindergarten, a playground, a Penny Provident Fund, and a summer camp outside the city. Renamed the Lincoln Settlement House in 1897, the Stillman Settlement House was an example of interracial cooperation. A fund-raising campaign for the Manhattan settlement advertised a rebellious neighborhood that had become a cooperative, influential center for black people.[50] Ironically, San Juan Hill was renamed Columbus Hill to indicate racial cooperation and advancement.

The Urban League, in cooperation with Lincoln House, Children's Aid Society, and other social service agencies, conducted cases in the Columbus Hill district related to domestic relations, legal matters, housing, and employment. Eugene K. Jones praised the Lincoln Settlement House as doing more for people in the community surrounding it than any other settlement in America.[51] Lincoln Settlement also cooperated with the Union Baptist Church and public schools. Yet the board experienced financial difficulties in maintaining the settlement. In 1919 the Union Baptist Church, from whom the Settlement leased its building, increased the rent.   Wald, who was head of the Board of Directors, found it difficult to find suitable rooms at a reasonable price. In March 1922 the Lincoln House Settlement changed its program, including   a reduction in space, retaining only the kindergarten room and a smaller office, and discontinuing the all black staff.[52] The Board of Directors assumed that Birdye Haynes, the supervisor of the settlement, would not be satisfied with the changes.   Birdye, who was respected by blacks and whites, was befriended by both Mary Ovington and Addie Hunton.[53] Matters deteriorated further when Haynes, resigned. Only the kindergarten, domestic service class, and the Mothers' Club remained.   By the end of March, the income for the settlement was cut in half. The Lincoln House Committee recommended that the neighborhood people become involved and assume more responsibility. The Lincoln Settlement House finally persuaded the Union Baptist Church to reduce its monthly rental fee to $75.00 for the kindergarten room.[54] The Directors of the Lincoln Settlement House continued to struggle with financial problems throughout the 1920s.

ROBERT GOULD SHAW HOUSE

Boston's first settlement house, Andover House, was launched in 1891 by Professor William Tucker of Andover Seminary. Three years later, it was renamed South End House.   The South End Settlement organized a branch for African Americans in the heart of the Roxbury district. The Robert Gould Shaw Settlement House was founded to do social work among African Americans. Recognizing the diversity of Boston's neighborhoods, the founders attempted to give African Americans the same privileges that were extended to other ethnic groups. Concerned mainly with the activities desired by the people, the settlement stood for justice and equal opportunity for all irrespective of race or color and aimed to promote amicable relations between white and black individuals.[55]

Between 1800 and 1900 most of Boston's African American residents lived in the West End, between Pinckney and Cambridge Streets and between Joy and Charles Streets centered on the north slope of Beacon Hill.   Around 1890 blacks began to leave Beacon Hill and move into the South End. Located in an area that was in constant change, Shaw House aimed to help African Americans obtain better educational and social opportunities. The settlement house provided home economics for girls and vocational courses for boys; clubs for mothers, girls and boys.   There were a day-care program, a kindergarten, a playground, an employment agency, and a library. Shaw house sponsored classes in drama, music, elocution, and folk dancing. While lecturers gave presentations on personal hygiene, child care, and similar topics, there is no evidence that the residents or clients welcomed their advice.[56]

Programs at the Shaw Settlement House emphasized self-development and race improvement. Black and white individuals did volunteer and paid work. Isabel Eaton, who succeeded her mother in leadership at the settlement, was appointed the first resident director in 1910. Not until 1933 was a full-time secretary (director) hired at Shaw House. Financial support for the Robert Gould Shaw House came from donations. Several elite black Bostonians were on the Board of Directors, including Maria Baldwin, Florida Ruffin Ridley, the daughter of Josephine Ruffin, and Olivia Ward Bush. All were members of the Woman's Era Club.[57] Bush, who trained as a nurse, was a resident worker and assistant dramatic director at the Robert Gould Shaw House. Maria Baldwin, a grammar school principal in Cambridge, died suddenly in 1921 while speaking in behalf of the settlement's appeal for funds.

Shaw House filled special needs in the black community and its place and purpose there steadily increased. Not all members of the community were satisfied. In 1909 Monroe Trotter accused the settlement house of perpetuating segregation. Theoretically, it was, but in practice it offered many social services that would not be available otherwise. In 1912 Booker T. Washington was a speaker at the institution, which was growing in prestige. Shaw House provided special social services during World War I. In 1928 it established interracial student forums. During the 1930s the Boston Tuberculosis Association assisted the settlement house in giving health talks to the Mothers' Clubs. By the 1960s the charitable corporation was a member of the National Federation of Settlements and Neighborhood Centers, the United Fund, and the United Community Services of Boston.[58] The Robert Gould Shaw House, Boston Urban League, and Harriet Tubman House had centralized their social services. From 1907 to the 1970s the Robert Gould Shaw House was a major social service agency for African Americans.

While the Robert Gould Shaw House was launched by the South End Settlement House, the Harriet Tubman House was established by a small group of black women. In 1904 using the self-help initiative of the abolitionist Harriet Tubman, the House was founded in Boston's South End by African American women. They donated their time, resources, and property to assist working girls from the South in charitable ways.[59] This small group of women attracted friends from the community and wider metropolitan area. In 1909, Mrs. Julia Henson gave her home at 25 Holyoke Street for permanent quarters. Boston's Harriet Tubman House offered friendship to girls coming to the city seeking work or to students seeking lodging, offering the protection they needed in the new environment. The Traveler's Aid Society referred many girls to the House and contributed to its residence program. The founders held teas, bazaars, suppers, and concerts to maintain the home. Like other settlements, their program included sewing classes, music, drama, art classes, clubs, and a choral group.

By World War I, assistance came from many sources, including the Women's Groups of the Charles Street Methodist Church and the Massachusetts Federation of Colored Women's Clubs. With growing demands for service, the Harriet Tubman House expanded to a second residence, added a playground, and nursery school for working mothers.   In 1950 it was included in the newly formed Federation of South End Settlements. A strong council readily contributed the special qualities of the House to the new configuration.   In 1960, USES (United South End Settlements) was formed and a single board created.[60]

Frequently, the settlement houses created for blacks by whites and those established and managed by black women had inter-racial boards with prominent blacks and whites. In all cases, a small group of middle-class blacks lived and worked within close proximity to the poorer population.   Black club women volunteered and took leadership roles in all of the settlement houses designed to meet the needs of black communities. The women used community resources and the women's network to finance and support their programs. As a result of middle-class and working-class black women living in close proximity, black women leaders united for racial and community improvement while maintaining social distance from their poorer neighbors.

THE LINCOLN SETTLEMENT HOUSE AND ASSOCIATION

In May 1908 Verina Morton-Jones, Mary White Ovington, a white social worker, and other black and white intellectuals formed an association that led to the organization of the Lincoln Settlement House . It was organized as a self-help measure among blacks in the Brooklyn borough of New York City in response to urban problems. The primary sponsor was Verina Morton-Jones, an established physician who made the down payment on the property for the institution. Twenty years later, she was a founder of a settlement house in Hempstead, New York.

Black physicians emerged during an era in which the black community was struggling for freedom and dignity.   Thus, black female doctors were motivated to serve their communities and the struggle social justice. Verina Morton-Jones' medical practice was intertwined with her social work to the black community. A clubwoman, Verina directed the NACW's Mothers' Club in Brooklyn. Often referred to as a "race woman," Dr. Morton-Jones was active in community service and efforts to advance the race. She was president of the Brooklyn Equal Suffrage League and a founder of the Brooklyn NAACP, the National Urban League, the Association for the Protection of Colored Women, and the biracial Cosmopolitan Society of America. Called the Cosmopolitan Club, it was organized to promote interracial understanding and to combat racial discrimination in public facilities in New York City.[61]

Who was Verina Morton-Jones and how did she acquire the strength and resilience that allowed her to help herself and others survive?   Born in Columbus, Ohio, in 1857, Verina Harris was the daughter of free blacks who had migrated to the North prior to the Civil War. Her father, Robert O. Harris, was a minister in the African Methodist Episcopal Church and her mother, Kitty, was the daughter of John C. Stanley, a wealthy mulatto barber and plantation owner in New Bern, North Carolina. When the war ended Verina's parents went to South Carolina to teach the freedmen. Because of her middle-class background, Verina was able to attend college and a prestigious medical school. She graduated from Benedict

College in South Carolina and taught school for two years before attending the Medical College of Pennsylvania. She practiced medicine at Rust College in Mississippi prior to marrying a Brooklyn physician, Walter A. Morton. Following the death of both an infant daughter and her husband in 1895, Dr. Morton and her son moved to Mississippi's Rust College where she had practiced prior to returning to New York. She later re-opened her Brooklyn office and married Emory Jones in 1901.[62]

The Lincoln Settlement was the first social service organization in Brooklyn to attempt to deal with the needs of the black working class. Initially, the black population consisted largely of middle-class African Americans who had moved there from Manhattan seeking better housing, less crowding, cleaner air, and open spaces. By 1890 African Americans in Brooklyn had settled in the Eleventh, Twentieth, and Seventh Wards. Many of the 65,000 black residents of Brooklyn were newcomers and in "dire need of social services and moral uplift." In the immediate vicinity were located "some of the worst slum dwellings where the bravest efforts at cleanliness meet with discouraging results."[63] The tenements and frame houses were breeding grounds for disease, crime, and vice. Problems associated with health, housing, employment, and child care were common. While these conditions were typical in other areas, there was no government response to these problems for at least thirty years.

The Lincoln Settlement House emerged from a consolidation of the Lincoln Kindergarten, which began as the Brooklyn Free Kindergarten Association in 1896 at the Siloam Presbyterian Church, the Colored Day Nursery, and the Visiting Nurses Services of the Brooklyn Bureau of Charities. The purpose of the Brooklyn settlement house was to aid its neighbors physically, morally, and intellectually. It did not expect to solve the race problem, but to alleviate conditions through interracial cooperation and bring respect for persons who work together for the common good.[64]

Dr. Morton-Jones was concerned about the welfare of southern female migrants to Brooklyn. Lincoln House offered vocational classes to provide the necessary skills for employment in domestic service or other unskilled jobs. Although the settlement work was principally aimed at the youth, the settlement offered a day nursery for working mothers, a kindergarten, and a visiting nurse's service. It sponsored debating and choral clubs and a woman's club. Courses were taught by Pratt Institute faculty and volunteers from Manhattan institutions.

The Lincoln Settlement began in Brooklyn at 129 Willoughby Street. After it was incorporated in 1914, it moved to a larger building at 105 Fleet Place with space for a playground. Its program of charitable services cooperated with the Brooklyn Urban League after it was founded in 1916. Through the Lincoln Settlement Association, the Urban League, and Big Sister Organization, black women conducted social work among blacks in Brooklyn.[65] Although the Lincoln Settlement House functioned as a community house, the White Rose Home provided boarding facilities. Both institutions received support from white and black donors. During World War I, the black settlement houses interacted in providing activities for black troops stationed on Long Island.[66]

Despite its successful comprehensive programs, the Lincoln Settlement was plagued by financial problems. Brooklyn's black population rose to 75,000 as the migration from the South increased due to the industrial opportunities. Long-standing charitable institutions and civic organizations, like the Lincoln Settlement, were flooded with applicants. Overburdened and with fewer resources, they refused to specialize.[67] Verina confided to her niece, Carlotta, "We finally failed to raise money for the settlement and had to turn it over to the Urban League."[68] Together, they formed the Brooklyn Urban League-Lincoln Settlement Association, Inc., a branch of the National Urban League. The league became the center for relief and social services for the Brooklyn borough.[69]

HARRIET TUBMAN COMMUNITY CENTER

The Harriet Tubman Community Center demonstrates the direction of black settlement houses after World War I. Verina Morton-Jones began a second career in 1927, when she established the Harriet Tubman Community Center in Hempstead, New York. She went to treat a patient, who was also her friend, and liked the quiet serenity of the suburbs. More importantly, she found a community that needed her professional services. At the age of seventy, Dr. Morton-Jones resumed her medical practice, which she had suspended as responsibilities associated with her settlement work in Brooklyn increased. At such an advanced age, it was unusual for a community to welcome any woman, black or white, into its inner circles, yet she was the first black woman physician in Hempstead, and her role as caregiver to African Americans was essential. Known for her practice in obstetrics and pediatrics, she delivered many babies in the local community.[70]

African American women frequently focused on club work and practical activities such as kindergartens, childcare centers, clinics, hospitals, and settlement activities.[71] Dr. Verina Morton-Jones' work in the National Association of Colored Women, the Empire State Federation, and the Northeastern Federation of Women's Clubs brought years of experience and community service to the Long Island community. She exerted leadership in a strong network of black women. Not only was Morton-Jones the catalyst for the establishment of the Harriet Tubman Community Club and the Harriet Tubman Community Center, she was the bonding thread of the club's fabric.[72]

Visionary community leaders led by Verina Morton-Jones crossed class boundaries in providing assistance and social services for working women and mothers. Thus, a small group of women organized the Harriet Tubman Community Club as a community social club on 26 April 1928 in the home of Maggie Broglin of Hempstead. Among the charter members of the community organization were Della Ballard, Cornelia Brewster, Annie Noble, Julia Pinckney, Annie Gaines, and Rose Harvey. The clubwomen ranged from housewives, beauticians, and seamstresses, to domestic servants. There were no black teachers in Hempstead until 1960. Thus, these women, considered middle-class in the black community, reflected the tendency of African Americans to use criteria other than income and education to determine social status. The community club, which met regularly for business meetings, held monthly literary programs and invited both black and white speakers to public meetings and forums.[73] It was incorporated in 1931 under the name Harriet Tubman to commemorate the freedom fighter on the Underground Railroad and Civil War veteran.[74]

Verina Morton-Jones became the resident director of the Tubman settlement house. In 1933, after the Harriet Tubman Community Club rented a two-story building at Mill Road and Grove Street for club and community activities and lodging for women, she moved to that facility. As its head supervisor, she took care of the center's business and directed its activities. The community center provided a homelike environment and wholesome recreational activities for working girls and those temporarily unemployed.

Dr. Morton-Jones had an outgoing, assertive personality. Her profession, her social position, and her community leadership enabled the settlement to attract people of diversified talents and backgrounds to the community house. Among the speakers were Congressman Oscar De Priest of Chicago; Jessie Fauset, a Harlem Renaissance writer and literary editor of the NAACP journal *The Crisis*; and Matthew Henson, the Harlem resident and Arctic explorer who, with Robert Perry, discovered the North Pole in 1909.[75]

The Harriet Tubman Community Center was a settlement house because its programs and services closely resembled those provided by settlements for European immigrants. Unlike Jane Addams' Hull House, however, the director, Dr. Morton-Jones, was the only resident at the Harriet Tubman House. The women's club provided the community of women that managed the settlement house. The Harriet Tubman House was modeled after the settlement houses established by black clubwomen such as the White Rose Home and the Lincoln Settlement House in New York City.

Black women migrated from the South for noneconomic reasons such as the desire for personal autonomy and to escape sexual abuse.[76] Harsh agricultural labor and fieldwork also contributed to the migration of black women from the South. Hattie Bell Johnson, a Hempstead resident left Batesburg, South Carolina in 1928 at the age of seventeen, and went to New York as a "sleep-in" domestic in East Williston, Long Island. Recommended by a friend, she migrated to the North to find a better life. Hattie was disappointed with the isolated suburban environment, but "at least she was not in the fields all day." She earned forty dollars a month, and was off every Thursday and every other Sunday. Hattie Johnson married Pope Williams the next year, joined the Union Baptist Church, and left her domestic position.[77] Not all migrants were so fortunate.

The black women who migrated to the North were mainly employed in domestic service work, the only employment open to them. Although the local clubwomen initially planned to provide child care and other social services to the community, they soon became interested in the plight of black women working in domestic service. Some were sleeping in damp basements; others had lost their positions and were in need of temporary housing. The Harriet Tubman Community House developed a dual purpose to provide settlement activities for the local community and to provide lodging for "girls in the (domestic) service" who migrated from the South to Long Island. The initial boarders were employed in domestic service in the surrounding affluent villages and towns.[78]

In 1935, the local club women acquired a building and expanded their social services. Like other clubwomen, members of the Harriet Tubman Club held dinners, rummage sales, card parties, teas and other fund-raisers to pay off the mortgage. Churches and civic groups contributed bed linens and other items to the center. Many programs were open to the public. An interracial advisory committee provided a sustaining fund for the club's welfare work.[79]

The Harriet Tubman Community Club, the backbone of the settlement house, was an important social service agency in the local community. Contributions from friends, fund-raising of the club members, and donations from the local churches sustained the institution. Members of the community club led the churches in fund-raising efforts. Churches indirectly associated with the settlement house were the Jackson Memorial AME Zion, St. John's Episcopal, Union Baptist Church, and the Antioch Baptist Church.[80]

Interracial cooperation linked the Harriet Tubman Center to other social service and educational organizations such as the American Red Cross and the Parent-Teacher Association (PTA). These organizations brought health care and vocational educational to the black community. The most valuable service of the settlement house was a Red Cross course in home nursing and care of the sick, provided by the Nassau County Chapter of the Red Cross.

Lobbying, petitions, voting, and personal contacts were used by settlement house workers and clubwomen to achieve community improvements. Their tactics for survival included political as well as social goals. The opening of the new Harriet Tubman Community Center in 1935 attracted the village officials, including the mayor of Hempstead who joined the residents of the community in a formal ceremony.[81] The trend of political activism escalated as the demands of African Americans increased, along with a growing black population. This trend influenced the politicians and caused them to see African Americans as a viable force with which to be reconciled.

The Harriet Tubman Community Center received support from the federal government during the Franklin D. Roosevelt administration. The social work and social services offered by the community center attracted the attention of the federal government, which placed a youth project in Nassau County. The National Youth Administration (NYA) program employed a social worker, established a day nursery, and incorporated a full schedule of activities. More than sixty children in the village of Hempstead were inoculated for diphtheria.[82] Clubs and classes were organized for the youth of the community.[83]

Scholars have pondered whether the urgency for social settlements declined in the 1920s. The Tubman Community Center shows that social service institutions served a purpose well beyond the 1920s. Verina Morton-Jones retired from public work in 1939 and returned to Brooklyn. The center became affiliated with the Community Chest, and the settlement house could guarantee a director's salary and employ a small staff. Unfortunately, it was too late for Verina Morton-Jones and other community activists who had volunteered their time and service.

PHILLIS WHEATLEY HOME FOR GIRLS AT CHICAGO

African American settlement houses provided not only shelter but protection for young women seeking domestic work and for boarding students. This service was needed for female students in Chicago, Boston, and other cities. In Chicago the students attended Crane College, Chicago Teachers' Normal College, and various business colleges. At least 1,286 girls stayed at the Phillis Wheatley Home for Girls in 1927.[84]

In Chicago, white settlement workers and black social reformers occasionally worked together, but most often the settlements and other social institutions were segregated. Between 1905 and 1918 poverty, segregation, and discrimination increased in the city's African American metropolis. In 1908, to alleviate the living and employment conditions for newly arrived black women, Elizabeth Lindsay Davis and the Chicago clubwomen organized the Phillis Wheatley Home for Girls. It was incorporated in 1915. Born in Peoria County, Illinois, in 1855 to Thomas and Sophia Lindsay, Elizabeth was a schoolteacher prior to marrying William H. Davis, a Chicago chiropodist.[85] Davis organized the Phillis Wheatley Club in 1896 and was its president for the next twenty-eight years. She was national organizer of the association and president of the Illinois State Federation from 1910 to 1912. Prior to the establishment of the settlement house, the clubwomen were concerned about the home environment of poor black women. Their awareness of the double burdens of race and gender led them to reach across, rather than down, to their less fortunate sisters.[86]

Like the White Rose Home, the Phillis Wheatley Home was established by Chicago clubwomen "to give shelter and protection to young Colored women who wandered into Chicago unacquainted with the snarls and pitfalls of a great city." For thirty girls, it provided living accommodations, social facilities, and an employment agency for single black women who were excluded from the YWCA because of their race. Some women were led into disreputable homes, entertainment, and employment because of a lack of protection that Elizabeth Davis believed was not the same for "strange girls" of other races; unfamiliar with the city.[87] The clubwomen purchased a home in a desirable neighborhood for self-supporting women and girls. The home, located in "a comfortable brick building, was furnished plainly, and offered a home for young women until they have secured employment." While the first matrons were volunteers, and, later, others like Florence Johnson were paid to assist and guide the girls.

The Phillis Wheatley Home Association was formed by women from various club federations of the NACW. Among the women in the Association were Irene McCoy Gaines, the treasurer, and Davis, chair of the Board of Directors, and Fannie B. Williams, corresponding secretary. In 1915, there were seventy women's clubs listed under the Chicago Federation.[88] The Phillis Wheatley Home attempted to promote, provide, and maintain a residence of culture for young women; to surround them with refined and uplifting influences; and to participate as an association in the welfare of the community. The residents of the home came through the Travelers' Aid Society, letters from friends or relatives, and information from the home.[89]   In conjunction with churches and other organizations, the Phillis Wheatley Home was supervised by black women and financed by African Americans. It offered a domestic science class and social-education meetings every fourth Sunday. A Public Welfare Committee handled the cases of women in financial need.[90]

Respectability was important to the Phillis Wheatley Home Association. Young women went to Chicago for advancement, often without friends, relatives, or money. The home provided a Christian influence for women of good character and helped them find employment. Since respectability entailed responsibility, the home committee provided an example for the young women by cleaning and furnishing the home and fund-raising. They investigated welfare cases, contributed to the home's upkeep, and solicited support from clubs and churches.

Discrimination based on a stereotypical image of black women prevailed in the North as in the South. The Phillis Wheatley Home and other working girls' homes, provided an alternate cultural space for black women who were excluded from mainstream institutions, including the YWCA. Ida B. Wells, the founder of the Negro Fellowship for young men, complained that the women's Model Lodging House offered accommodations "to all women who needed a place to sleep except drunkards, immoral women, and negro women."[91] Unlike immigrant women who could be denied services because of immorality, black women were excluded solely because of race. Thus, race, sexuality, and behavior were primary factors in denying respect to black women.

With the migration, a spatial pattern developed within Chicago's black community that was similar to that of New York and other cities. There were pockets or "zones" in the Black Belt based on socioeconomic status. From 1890 to 1915 the black Chicago population rose from 15,000 to more than 50,000. After 1915, when 65,000 migrants went to Chicago within five years, housing became critical.[92] The social conditions in poor black communities were deplorable. The residents had high rates of sickness and death and low socioeconomic status. Many discriminatory practices prevailed, especially in housing. The black community was impoverished, unsanitary, and crowded. High rental fees forced many African Americans to take in lodgers.

As the migration escalated social class separation increased, with poor blacks directed to districts with vice and redlight districts. Often found in these neighborhoods were African Americans who had the least political influence. Respectable society wanted to avoid any visible evidence of prostitution and vice. It was understood in police circles that if persons engaged in prostitution confined their business to certain areas, they would be immune to police harassment. In Chicago and New York nearly all of the domestics of brothels were black women. Ruth Rosen in *The Lost Sisterhood* (1982) implies that most reformers, black and white, complained about the effects of prostitution on the black community, but they did little to alter the environment of its residents.

Respectable institutions, such as the Phillis Wheatley Home, black churches, and black-staffed Provident Hospital existed beside night clubs and other illegitimate establishments. The work of the Phillis Wheatley Home increased as the southern migration continued. Young women were referred to the Home Association by the Travelers Aid Society. The Phillis Wheatley Home for Girls was the primary concern of the Phillis Wheatley Woman's Club of the NACW for thirty-seven years.[93]

BOURGEOISIE IN THE SLUMS, OR HELPFUL WOMEN

The mission of some settlement workers was to promote culture to less fortunate women by exemplifying its beneficial effects. They organized libraries, music programs, dancing, elocution, and special lectures. Some clubwomen used their work in voluntary associations as an opportunity to exert a sense of superiority over young women.[94] Fannie Barrier graduated from the college department of the State Normal School at Brockport, New York and taught for ten years in Washington, DC before marrying in 1887 and moving to Chicago. She and her husband organized the Prudence Crandall Club, a literary society that attracted socially prominent African Americans. Both Fannie and S. Laing Williams, a prominent lawyer, served on the board of the Frederick Douglass Center. Williams believed that the best whites and the best blacks were involved in the center, where she also organized women's clubs. She carefully distinguished between educated and successful African Americans and the impoverished masses. She demanded equal treatment for African Americans, especially for those who had achieved middle-class success. In 1906 Williams stated that her settlement work was not "organized to do slum work but to be a center of wholesome influence to the end that well-disposed white people may learn to know and respect the ever-increasing number of colored people who have earned the right to be believed and respected."[95] Williams' views emphasize her status as a bourgeoisie reformer who engaged in social uplift more for her own benefit than for the benefit of the working class.

African American women in the North and the South established settlement houses and drew on the talents of philanthropic and educated race leaders to provide vital services to needy people. In the North black settlement workers attempted to impart-middle-class values and modify the lifestyles of the migrants to urban centers. Although the social settlements showed the ability of middle-class women to provide for their own people by establishing reputable social service institutions, the elitist clubwomen used their organizations to promote middle-class concepts of morality, cleanliness, thrift, and respectability. Working-class women subscribed to the same values, but they were not always able to live up to the standards because of poverty.

Conversely, we cannot dismiss the humanity and significance of the migrants' consciousness of their own experience, kinship networks, cultural beliefs, and attitudes.[96] African Americans from the rural South had many practical and useful traits which they transplanted to the new environment. Many of the migrant women got jobs through their personal initiative. Although their qualities were not the same as those of the middle class, they had goals that they pursued. The working class used strategies for survival that were similar to those of other ethic groups. When unexpected hardships occurred, other community members would provide help.

Black women played a significant role in creating and sustaining new social, religious, political, and economic institutions. Historian Darlene Hine concludes, "These clubs were as important as the National Urban League and the NAACP in transforming black peasants into urban proletarians."[97] These groups played a central role in the development of a working-class culture and in blending the differences between North and South to create a unified community.[98]

Victoria Matthews' death in 1907 at the age of forty-five from tuberculosis left the White Rose Home without a public voice and figure immersed in social work. Management continued under able black and white women, such as Frances Keyser and Mary Stone. Keyser was the first president of the Empire State Federation and a member of the NAACP's General Committee for fund-raising and publicity. Keyser networked with clubwomen such as Maritcha Lyons and Elizabeth Carter. She interacted with white women reformers, namely, Mary Ovington, Jane Addams, Lillian Wald, Celia Woolley, and Mary McDowell.

Clubs and self-help groups enabled African Americans to survive and also challenge institutions in society that restricted black rights. Black settlement houses modified their role, focusing on programs for community residents as the demand for segregated institutions declined and as specialized agencies, such as the National Urban League, took over the volunteer work of the clubwomen. The next chapter emphasizes the NU's work with the migrants, its assumption of the work of black clubwomen, and the professionalization of black social workers.

Chapter 7

The National Urban League and the Professionalization of Black Social Workers

Social work among Negroes has suffered not so
much from the lack of movements as from lack
of conscientious, exuberant, trained worker.
"The NUL," *Crisis*, 8 (1914).

The roots of the modern social work profession stem from the Progressive era. Two streams of social action converged to launch the social work profession: the friendly visitors of the Charity Organization Societies (COSs) and the new scholars of the urban industrial society who, after the Civil War, began to free themselves from the moralistic and deductive thinking patterns of 18th and early 19th century scholarship.[1] The new scholars turned to history, political economy, history of reform, and psychological development to understand the problems of their day and to contribute solutions.

Founded in 1877, the COS became the most widely accepted approach to social improvement. Charity Organization Societies, which developed as a response to the social ills of an industrial, urban society, used volunteers to visit, counsel, and instruct the deserving poor.[2] By the 1890s, ninety-two cities in the United States had COSs. The COSs assumed that the urban poor needed the advice and personal attention of an intelligent, kind, and friendly volunteer.[3] The COSs and similar organizations for charity and philanthropy used penny societies, friendly visitors, summer outings, playgrounds, day nurseries, and distributions of food, clothing, and medical care to teach middle-class values of thrift, cleanliness, order, efficiency, and self-denial to the lower classes.[4] Influenced by social Darwinism, many nineteenth-century Americans believed that people were poor because of personal weaknesses.

Social settlement work, which also emerged during the late nineteenth century, differed in goals and techniques from organized charity.   Efficient charity was more a process of character regeneration than social reform. Charity workers emphasized individual self-help as a means of combating poverty, while settlement workers called for changes in the social environment.[5] Charity workers attempted to lessen pauperism, whereas settlement workers sought to equalize opportunity for the working classes.   Settlement workers lived in working-class neighborhoods on the theory that dependence of classes is reciprocal.[6]

Criticism of the charity organization movement stemmed partially from the hostility of the growing professionalism of social work.   After 1900 the volunteer became subordinate to the professional in social work.[7] The transfer of leadership to professionals, such as Edward T. Devine and Mary Richmond, changed the focus from ideology to social institutions. With the development of professionalism in American social work came a shift in the intellectual orientation of social workers from social reform to individualized social casework. As early as 1897 Richmond called for the formation of a "school of applied philanthropy." Richmond brought professionalism to the field and a new expertise; her *Friendly Visiting among the Poor* (1898) was one of the earliest social work texts. In her work at the Charity Organization Department of the Russell Sage Foundation she was able to assist many of the early schools of social work.   Her book *Social Diagnosis (1917)* was a report on prevailing practice based on data collection from various fields of practice.[8] To Richmond, social work's slogan had to become, "neither alms, nor a friend nor a neighbor but a professional service."

Casework originated with the charity organizations. Group work was common during the social reform that characterized the settlement house movement. Jane Addams guided reform-minded group workers as she struggled to serve the needs of the poor and, simultaneously, to obtain humane responses to those needs from a reluctant society. Settlement house work actualized many principles that social group work practice borrowed: direct interaction among persons from diverse backgrounds, the impact of the social environment, social participation, and democratic process.[9]

The first school of social work, the New York School of Philanthropy, was established in 1898. In 1903 the Chicago School of Civics and Philanthropy was established.   Other schools of social work followed in Philadelphia, Baltimore, and St. Louis.   Julia Lathrop, Edith Abbott, and Sophonisba Breckinridge led the Chicago school in its early years. Abbott was the chief architect of a model of education for the newly developing profession of social work. In 1924 Edith Abbott became dean of the Chicago School of Social Service Administration. She and Breckinridge formulated a curriculum that included science, economics, law, medicine, immigration studies, labor problems, and governmental processes. Edith Abbott emphasized social work in which social policy was treated equally with public welfare administration.[10]

The crucial developments between 1880 and 1930 were the belief that social work was heading toward a scientific understanding and control of behavior

and clarifying its professional function. In 1915, in an address before the National
Conference of Charities and Corrections, Dr. Abraham Flexner focused on the
question, "Is Social Work a Profession?" Flexner claimed that social work lacked
a specific skill applied to a specific function. He identified criteria by which
progress toward professional status might be measured.[11] Roy Lubove asserts that
the National Association of Social Workers, founded in 1921, played a major role
in formulating professional goals and standards for the social work profession.

African Americans were not represented in social work. Edward T.
Devine, secretary of the New York Charity Organization Society, was the first white
social worker to realize the value of using trained black social workers in black
communities. Drawing from the nursing profession, the New York COS
hired a black public health nurse, Jessie Sleet, to be employed as a professional
family caseworker in 1902.[12] Historian Nancy Weiss confirmed that church
workers, clubwomen, and black settlement house workers provided the social
services in black communities, but these leaders were not professionally trained in
social work.

The October 1905 issue of the prestigious social work journal *Charities*
featured a series of articles on the problems of African Americans.[13] *Charities*
joined the settlement-derived Chicago *Commons*, founded by Graham Taylor, to
become *Charities and Commons*. It was published by the New York COS under
the direction of a publication committee headed by Edward Devine, the editor, and
Jane Addams. In 1910 the magazine became the *Survey*.

George Edmund Haynes, a founder and the first executive director of the
National Urban League (NUL), was the first black graduate of the New York
School of Philanthropy (later the Columbia University School of Social Work).
Students at the school were encouraged to study sociology and economics. The
social science students were encouraged to use their knowledge for uplift in society
by solving social problems.   Haynes acquired a strong background in social
science while studying at Yale. By the time he reached the School of Philanthropy,
the school supported social research as part of its educational curriculum.[14] He
was responsible for establishing the first recruiting and training program for African
Americans in the United States. To make the services of the NUL effective,
Haynes believed they must be provided by professional black social workers. He
maintained that social work was needed to help African American migrants from
the South adjust to an urban environment.

The NUL was one of several reform organizations begun in the
Progressive era with the assistance of white settlement workers. It originated at a
time when African Americans began migrating to the North by the hundreds of
thousands to flee discrimination and poverty, seeking higher-paying unskilled labor
jobs and a better life. The need for black social workers with training was crucial.
The motivation for the exodus to northern cities during the labor shortages of
World War I was economic, though its roots were interwoven in the entire social
system of the South. It involved a relocation of a large percentage of the black
population in the United States from the South to the North.[15]

The African American population increased significantly in major urban areas between 1910 and 1930. This was a distinct period when the Great Migration, World War I, and the conflict between blacks and whites all combined to change the traditional patterns of American life.   Migration from the South during the Great Migration added 2,000-3,000 persons a year to the black population in New York City, Chicago, Cleveland, Philadelphia, and other industrial urban areas. This movement changed the lives of the migrants and the structure of American society. It led to the emergence of large, predominantly black urban enclaves in the North. New York City's black population increased from 91,709 in 1910, to 152,467 in 1920, and 327,706 in 1930.[16]

Migration on this scale was not only a social crisis concerned with welfare problems associated with housing and jobs, but also a racial phenomenon associated with population growth. Social discord and race riots occurred over the ballot, jobs, and housing, all crucial areas in which African Americans sought self-improvement.[17] Racial prejudice and discrimination restricted employment opportunities for the migrants. The newcomers were relegated to slum housing, inadequate sanitation and health problems, and limited educational opportunities. The most serious disease among blacks was tuberculosis.   The high death rate of blacks underscored the feeling that the health of African Americans was an American problem.[18]

The National Urban League, like the NAACP, emerged during the Progressive era. Despite the denial of civil rights for African Americans during the Progressive era, the NUL was a complex of social justice movements that paid some attention to the problems of African Americans.[19]   The NUL was one of the few urban organizations that helped black urban dwellers find employment, housing, and educational opportunities, notes historian James Grossman. It was created in 1911 by black and white reformers from a consolidation of the National League for the Protection of Colored Women, the Committee for Improving the Industrial Conditions of Negroes, and the Committee on Urban Conditions among Negroes. The league would focus on questions of philanthropy and social economy in the black community.

The demand for professional black social workers exceeded the supply. Immediately after the formation of the NUL, George Haynes began to bring African Americans into the professional hierarchy of social work. He addressed the annual conference for American Social Workers and the National Conference of Charities and Corrections in 1911. Not until 1917 did the annual conference for American Social Workers address issues related to African Americans. In 1918 the NUL held its first annual meeting. In 1919 representatives from the NUL, NACW, NAACP, and YWCA sent letters to the National Conference of Social Work, resulting in the inclusion of the problems of African Americans at nearly every session. The NUL held a second conference in 1919.[20]

Women reformers were involved with the National Urban League from its inception.[21]   In 1906 the National League for the Protection of Colored Women (NLPCW) was founded by Frances Kellor, a white social worker who had studied sociology and economics at the University of Chicago and the School of

Philanthropy in New York. Like Victoria Matthews, she studied black employment agencies in attempting to suppress the importation of black women from the South under undesirable conditions.[22] Kellor conducted a major investigation of employment agencies in *Out of Work*.[23] She concluded that black women who were led into immoral habits and vice often received advice from questionable employment agencies. Black women were lured from the South on promises of "easy work, lots of money, and good times."[24] Interested in changing the environment that influenced behavioral patterns, Kellor began organizing associations to protect black women in New York City and Philadelphia.[25]

Kellor assumes that these women were alone without family or partners. She implies that they need protection. Kellor seems to be arousing moral alarm in defense of female virtue, yet she doesn't believe that they have the moral strength to defend their own interests. Thus, Kellor believes that black women become prostitutes because they are unable or unwilling to protect themselves. Hazel Carby asserts that Kellor's report makes a strong case for "the creation of an alternative set of institutions to police the actual bodies of migrating black women."[26] While Kellor blamed employment agencies that created a situation of economic dependence and exploitation to channel black women into houses of prostitution, she also identified black women's inefficiency and desire to avoid hard work as part of the problem. Kellor recommended the use of sympathetic women to guide, direct, and befriend the migrant women; a controlled system of lodging houses; and the creation of training schools to make them more efficient. This linked the social supervision of black women migrants and the control of their moral and sexual behavior. Therefore, Frances Kellor located the problem not in the lack of job opportunities for black women but in the women themselves, who, facing limited employment opportunities and the propensity to avoid hard work, chose prostitution.

In 1910 S. Willie Layten, the black field secretary of the Philadelphia association, replaced Frances Kellor as general secretary of the National League for the Protection of Colored Women. In 1912 she became the field secretary of the NUL. Evelyn Higginbotham suggests that Layten, as president of the Women's Convention of the Baptist Church, integrated her secular social work with the social service of the church.[27] The NLPCW distributed literature to women in the South through black ministers, schools, and black women's clubs.

The New York Association of the NLPCW cooperated with the Colored Mission, the White Rose Home, and the Brooklyn YWCA in providing temporary lodging for women. Frances Kellor expanded to a national scale the work begun by Victoria Matthews' White Rose Mission by hiring travelers' aid agents and placing them in Philadelphia, Baltimore, Washington, Richmond, Norfolk, and Savannah. Although the travelers' aid service of the White Rose Home and the NLPCW never merged, after 1912 Hattie Proctor became a salaried worker of the National Urban League. That year Proctor met 362 women and children in Norfolk.[28] To further complicate matters, Mary Stone, the first white president of the White Rose Home Association, was a board member also of the NLPCW. With the increasing numbers of migrant women, however, the White Rose Home continued to operate its Travelers' Aid Society.

The NLPCW conducted scientific studies to determine how to assist the women migrants and how to acculturate them into urban life. Frances Kellor and Ruth Baldwin were motivated by concern to protect newcomers to cities. Yet historian Nancy Weiss contends that their efforts also reinforced their beliefs that respectability, self-respect, and purity should be learned early.[29] It is clear that their actions were not motivated by altruism since they hoped to inculcate their values into the migrants. The idea of protection for black women, which had always been an issue, arose again in 1918 and divided the black community. Some black men attending the NUL conference that year asserted that black women did not need "protection." Speaking out a few years later, Eugene Kinckle Jones of the NUL declared that "protection was just what they needed."[30] Thus, the need to discipline the behavior of black women in urban areas was perceived as necessary not only by white organizations and institutions but also by black organizations and institutions and the black middle class. However, for poor black women, protection meant intrusion and domination over their lives.

The Committee for Improving the Industrial Conditions of Negroes (CIICN) was established by black and white reformers the same year as the NLPCW to assist blacks in finding jobs and obtaining skills and to resolve urban problems. The motivator of the committee, Dr. William Buckley, developed a model school in Harlem that offered evening lectures and courses in industrial and commercial training. Ruth Baldwin, chair of the New York CIICN, was the widow of William Baldwin, a philanthropist to black institutions in the South. She, like her husband, was influenced by Booker T. Washington. Mary E. Dreier, Verina Morton-Jones, Mary Ovington, and Fred Moore were members of the board. The CIICN cooperated with black reform agencies, and by 1908 it was sending volunteers to the docks to help migrant black women.[31]

A third group, the Committee on Urban Conditions among Negroes, soon to be known as the National Urban League, met at the New York School of Philanthropy in 1910. Among the persons present were George Haynes, Ruth Baldwin, Dr. Buckley, and Professor McCrea. Professor Seligman was elected permanent chair.[32] George Haynes, the cofounder of the Committee on Urban Conditions among Negroes, was the first African American to present a comprehensive program for training black social workers. His plan urged investigating social conditions as the foundation of social service in New York City.[33] Haynes was a graduate student at Columbia University between 1909 and 1910 completing his studies of blacks in New York City. He concluded that blacks moved to the cities for reasons similar to those of whites, to seek better educational and social advantages for themselves and their children.[34]

Investigations by George Haynes, Frances Kellor, Mary White Ovington, and Sophonisba Breckenridge were intended to provide knowledge for social work training. They were part of a series of studies conducted in the tradition of W.E.B. Du Bois. A series of studies by Du Bois on the black population in cities, first published in 1896, became the basis for his Atlanta University Publications.

Du Bois' study *Some Efforts of American Negroes For Their Own Social Betterment*, which includes black women's club work, was the first scientific documentation in social welfare.[35]

By general agreement in 1911, the National League for the Protection of Colored Women, the Committee for Improving the Industrial Conditions of Negroes, and the Committee on Urban Conditions among Negroes merged into the National League on Urban Conditions Among Negroes, later known as the National Urban League. "With the consolidation of three bodies committed to constructive social work among Negroes, a new epoch opens in the effective consideration of this phase of the American city problem." The objectives of the original social service agencies were incorporated into the purposes of the league: to develop cooperation and coordination among the agencies; to investigate the social conditions among blacks in cities; to secure and train black social workers; to establish new agencies of practical social service.[36]   Haynes was appointed executive director of the newly expanded organization. To assist the migrants, the NUL incorporated scientific social work and assistance in social service.

Haynes' ties with Columbia University and the New York School of Philanthropy brought several university professors to the NUL. Beginning in the fall of 1911, the league had fellows engaged in fieldwork in the New York School of Philanthropy, the Chicago School of Civics and Philanthropy, and Fisk University. Representation from the social work profession included Florence Kelley, Lillian Wald, and Roger Baldwin, the nephew of Ruth Baldwin.

George Haynes went to Fisk University to organize a Department of Social Science and a program of social work. He would be able to continue his research and, simultaneously, establish a training institute for black social workers.[37]   Haynes' purpose was to bring the education of the students closer to the needs of the community. There was a demand for training in the scientific methods of study of social problems and the motivation for social service among black college students. The courses offered included economics, industrial history and organization, Afro-American history, economics and labor relations, Sociology, and Social Problems.[38]   Due to the urban concentration of African Americans, students would study the conditions and develop methods of social improvement to solve social problems. Black college students trained in the social sciences and in social work would be qualified to work in urban communities. In 1913 Fisk University established a relationship with the Women's Missionary Council of the Methodist Episcopal Church, South and the Methodist Training School in conducting a social settlement.

The center will be called Bethlehem House and will be under a board of managers of seven members representing the University and the two other organizations jointly. The Director [Estelle Haskins] will have an assistant in Miss Ellie Walls to co-operate with the center in developing work in the city.[39]

The Bethlehem Center Settlement House became a laboratory for practical training for Fisk students in the social science courses. The classroom work was done at Fisk University, and the fieldwork was done at Bethlehem Settlement House in the black community in cooperation with Fisk University, the Women's Missionary Council of the Methodist Episcopal Church, South, and the Methodist Training School. The Social Work Training course, established in 1914, provided the theoretical and practical training for voluntary or salaried service, such as probation officers, settlement workers, kindergarten directors, executive secretaries in social welfare and civic organizations, church workers, charity visitors, and home and foreign missionaries. A certificate was granted to college graduates who completed the course.[40]   Seniors in Fisk's Department of Social Services were required to do four hours each week of fieldwork both in the settlement house and in the community near the campus. Six additional hours were spent studying statistics and social investigation. Community service was part of the mission of Fisk students as social workers in order to understand the needs of the African American community.[41] Each NUL fellow was required to live in residence at Bethlehem Center Settlement House; make regular visits to families in cases of illness, death, and delinquency; and cooperate with the Charity Organization Society relief work for black families.

Bethlehem Center Settlement House was valued not only for social uplift but also for improving race relations. The Nashville Urban League was initially part of the Bethlehem Center Settlement House operations. It was succeeded by the Public Welfare League, an outgrowth of the interracial relief work following a disaster in 1916. Haynes offered the services of the social work faculty, Paul Mowbray, Joseph Haskell, Helen Walker of Fisk, Estelle Haskins, supervisor of Bethlehem House, and students to conduct field investigations, and develop and maintain an orderly relief distribution.[42] A devastating fire motivated the response; the fire left 3,000 persons homeless and over $2 million of property damage in East Nashville, one of the worst slums in the state.[43] The seniors in the social work program assisted in constructing a "systematic plan for handling the relief efforts of the city." They had become familiar with the strategies of relief.[44] Thus, black students trained in social work assisted with relief in the disaster and later made personal visits to the families to survey the extent of their losses and assess their immediate needs.

The Public Welfare League, which became the Nashville Urban League, aimed to establish a spirit of cooperation among blacks and whites in order to improve the economic, social, and spiritual conditions of the black population. Its primary purpose was "to secure and train black students for social service work."[45] The motto of the Public Welfare League was "Get Together and Serve." The league cooperated with women's clubs, lodges, churches, and other organizations in a united effort to better the conditions of blacks in Nashville.

The National Urban League enlarged the social services provided by the black women's clubs, such as travelers' aid and settlement houses, and adapted the employment and social welfare services offered by charitable agencies for black communities. The NUL became the leading social service agency for African Americans in the United States. The League used many of the programs and strategies initiated by the black women's clubs to prepare the city migrants for living in urban areas. Many New York City clubwomen joined the NUL, namely, Verina Morton-Jones, Maria Coles Lawton, and Cora Horne, secretary of the Brooklyn Urban League and chair of its Big Sister Committee. Drusilla Poole, later president of the Empire State Federation of Women, worked with George Haynes, Ruth Baldwin, and Eugene Kinckle Jones. A business school graduate, Poole joined the staff of the NUL and became a part of its efforts.[46]

The NUL's social service activities prior to World War I were directly related to the efforts of black clubwomen. The National Urban League established its headquarters in New York City and developed Big Brother and Big sister work in Children's Courts, probation work in the Adults' Court, and school visiting in black schools. It cooperated with many institutions in handling various phases of social service, such as the Lincoln Settlement House in Brooklyn, the White Rose Home, the Howard Orphanage and Industrial School, the Utopia Neighborhood Club, the Sojourner Truth House, and the YWCA.[47] This kind of service before the war designated the league as an umbrella organization for welfare activities among African Americans and led to its widespread use during the war by organizations such as the Red Cross, the YWCA, the War Camp Community Service, and the Department of Labor.[48]

As part of the league's preventive measures and concern for improving the African American community, it appointed committees to conduct its welfare work. The Katy Ferguson Home for unmarried women, sponsored by the Empire State Federation of Women's Clubs, received a small annual donation for its upkeep from the women. The Sojourner Truth House was established for delinquent black girls under the age of sixteen, because the state and private institutions failed to provide the necessary services. Elizabeth Walton, vice chair of the NLPCW, headed the Sojourner Truth House Committee, which was approved by the State Board of Charities. Maria Lawton, president of the Empire State Federation, was one of the few black women on the committee.[49]

By 1913 the Utopia Neighborhood Club had given over $1,000 toward the proposed Sojourner Truth House for delinquent girls. An allied organization of the NUL, the club was founded by black women in Harlem in November 1911 for the purpose of social uplift. After the Sojourner Truth House opened in 1915, the Utopia Neighborhood Club used the house for meetings and became its primary supporter. The Utopia Neighborhood Club functioned with volunteers and the league trained social workers.[50]

To expand its membership and activities, the NUL appointed Booker T. Washington, Sophonisba Breckinridge, and Kelly Miller to its Board of Directors. The NUL complemented Washington's program of self-help by emphasizing housing and employment for urban blacks. The social work techniques incorporated by the NUL harmonized with Washington's emphasis on vocational education and persuasion to open doors for African Americans, yet Washington's rural and southern strategy was only one solution to the problems that blacks faced.[51] George Haynes believed that racial advancement required leaders of action and thought rather than leaders who promoted industrial education as the solution to the social, economic, and political problems of African Americans. Haynes did not withdraw his support from Tuskegee, and two years after Washington's death, his widow, Margaret Washington, replaced him on the board. The appointment to the Executive Board of Mary Bethune and Nannie Burroughs was influenced less by Washington's influence than by their accomplishments in interracial cooperation.[52]

League fellows were placed in leadership positions throughout the country. Prominent men trained for social service work through the league: T. Arnold Hill, Chicago; Paul F. Mowbray, Fisk University; James Hubert, New York; John T. Clark, Pittsburgh; Garry Moore, Atlanta; Forrester B. Washington, Armstrong Association and the first director of the Detroit league; John C. Dancy, Detroit; George Buckner, St. Louis; William Conners, Cleveland. These men are well known in any discussion of its history.[53]

The gendered shift in social service leadership coincided with the increased presence of African Americans in social work. Increasingly, trained scholars assumed the social service work that was done previously by black women prior to World War I. Black migration placed an enormous strain on the resources of black organizations and institutions. Black women joined the NUL as volunteers and staff members, but they were not placed in policy-making positions in the organization. Even among the early social work educators, such as Mary Richmond, Edith Abbott, and Sophonisba Breckinridge, men were disproportionately represented in the leadership ranks. Ann Tanneyhill joined the NUL as a secretary in the 1920s and did not advance to a professional post for twenty years. Some women were board members of the league, but the top echelon was male-dominated until the 1940s.[54]

The Urban League was created not only as a clearinghouse for information or an experiment in interracial cooperation, but as an agency to provide supervision for its branches and other agencies engaged in social welfare reforms among African Americans. By 1918 at least thirty cities had followed New York City's example in providing social services to black communities. Local leagues in Brooklyn, Atlanta, Chicago, and other places were providing recreation, health, and education needs to African Americans through settlement houses . Contributing to community building, several NUL branches operated settlement houses.

Several of the social settlements founded by black clubwomen or supported by their efforts were assumed by the National Urban League. The Lincoln Settlement Association merged with the Brooklyn Urban League in 1926. The united organization, which was incorporated in 1927, became the only center for relief and social services for the Brooklyn borough. The NUL social service activities consisted of Big Brother and Big Sister work in connection with the Brooklyn Juvenile Protection Association; public school visits to aid cases of truant and delinquent children; home visits and home improvement. The league first became involved with settlement work after opening its office at 185 Duffield Street in 1913. The office closed after the first year but reopened in 1916. Through the Lincoln Settlement's industrial department, which the Brooklyn

League directed, hundreds of positions were found for blacks in Brooklyn's industries.[55]   The Urban League provided services related to family problems, employment, housing, travelers' aid, and the courts.[56]   In the Fleet Street district, where the league office was located, there was a population of 120,000 persons, of whom 19 percent were African Americans from the South. Living conditions were bad, with many families living over stores in small frame houses. More than 70 percent of them worked outside the home.[57]   Among the members of the Board of Directors of the Urban League were Ruth Baldwin, Cora Horne, Rev. Henry Proctor, Laura J. Rollick, Anna Hawley, and Robert Elzy, executive director of the Brooklyn League. Along with Dr. Verina Morton-Jones, most of the women served also on the board of the Lincoln Settlement Association.[58]

The Chicago Relief and Aid Society and the Chicago Bureau of Charities merged into the United Charities of Chicago in 1908. By the outbreak of World War I, Chicago's charity and settlement workers joined together in groups such as the Chicago School of Civics and Philanthropy, the Juvenile Protective Association, the United Charities of Chicago, and the Urban League.   In Chicago black and white reformers and social workers organized the Chicago Urban League in 1916 to deal with problems arising from the rapidly growing black population.   From the beginning, social workers and social work programs dominated the Urban League agenda. Chicago social workers had begun to think about the status of blacks in their city around World War I, and their thoughts became urgent when the Chicago race riot struck the city in 1919.[59]

The Urban League was the only permanent agency in Chicago dealing exclusively with the social and economic aspects of race relations. It was a coordinating body for interracial activities of many industrial, social welfare, or religious groups. The league was not primarily a relief agency. Its activities permeated every phase of urban life in employment, home and community, self-development, and civil rights. Social workers Jane Addams, Sophonisba Breckinridge, and Mary McDowell were members of the Advisory Board.

Women in the Chicago Federation of Colored Women's Clubs, the first to endorse the Chicago Urban League, did the preliminary organizational work. Irene McCoy Gaines solicited the first memberships from the black community. Joanna Snowden-Porter represented the clubwomen on the Board of Directors. The initial meeting was held in December 1916, when a group of prominent community leaders met with Eugene Kinckle Jones and T. Arnold Hill, executive secretary from 1916 to 1925. Among the black women attending the charter session were Jennie Lawrence, superintendent of the Phillis Wheatley Home; Joanna Snowden-Porter, president of the Chicago Federation of Colored Women's Clubs and a founder of the Northwestern Association of Women's Clubs; Irene M. Gaines, president of the Illinois Federation of Colored Women and treasurer of the Phillis Wheatley Home; and Katherine Briggs of the United Charities. The welfare services included advising migrants, operating the Wendell Phillips Settlement, and working with delinquent and dependent children.[60]

The NUL assumed control of both the Wendell Phillips Settlement and the Frederick Douglass Center in Chicago. The National Urban League wrote:

For nearly two years we have been informally in cooperation with the Wendell Phillips Settlement in Chicago. Miss Breckinridge, of the Chicago School of Civics and Philanthropy, has been one of the principal people interested in that settlement. It is difficult now to guarantee the financial continuance of the Settlement. They have appealed to us for help in this crisis.[61]

The National Urban League agreed to pay one-fourth of the salary of their head worker. Strategically, this allowed the NUL to establish itself firmly in Chicago.

In 1917, upon the request of its Board of Directors, the Wendell Phillips Settlement came under the control of the local league. By taking over the supervision and support of the settlement house, the Chicago League added settlement work to its program of civic improvement. The settlement established a day nursery, provided a meeting place for clubs and organizations, and sponsored social and civic activities. The scope of such welfare services as advising migrants and operating the Wendell Phillips Settlement depended on the league's financial resources. The settlement house remained a part of the league's activities until 1923.[62]

Celia Woolley established a settlement in Chicago, the Frederick Douglass Center, through which she would instill middle-class values in the working class as a result of providing social services. Encouraging racial cooperation, she was willing to work with the NUL, a middle-class interracial organization, to achieve her goals. A wide range of settlement activities continued at the Frederick Douglass Center until February 1918. A month later Celia Parker Woolley invited the Chicago Urban League to move its headquarters into the center on South Wabash Avenue.[63] Following the death of Woolley, its founder, the Frederick Douglass Center functioned under the name of the Urban League until 1936.[64]

The city of Atlanta was a laboratory for social welfare. Atlanta had numerous social problems because of the size of its population and its identity as an industrial and economic center. The black population increased from 51,902 in 1910, to 62,796 in 1920. There were over 90,000 African Americans in Atlanta by 1930. The city also had more social agencies for both blacks and whites than any other city in the South.[65]

Morehouse College established a Department of Social Science in 1913. Upon completing his work as an Urban League fellow in 1912-1913, Garry W. Moore was appointed to teach economics and sociology at Morehouse College. While acknowledging his wife's contributions, John Hope failed to address Lugenia Hope by name as he proposed that Moore develop a department of social science and also do practical work in the city. Hope stated:

Mr. Moore and I have gone over plans for his course and for affiliation with the National League a local organization which has been doing some effective work. This organization was started by the women of the city, led by the wife of the college president [Lugenia Hope] and the circumstances are auspicious.[66]

The Atlanta Urban League was established by a group of prominent black and white leaders on 15 March 1920 to fill the pressing social and economic needs of the particular community in which it was located. They realized that "the best way to solve many of our problems was to prevent their becoming problems." [67] Led by Jessie O. Thomas, director of the Southern Regional Office, the league assumed responsibility for social services among African Americans. It worked for improved race relations, better health, better housing, more recreational facilities, less delinquency and crime, and job placement and retention.[68]

In 1921 in cooperation with the Neighborhood Union, the league assumed responsibility for, and aroused the public consciousness on the need for, community improvement. It began a free training program and placement bureau for black workers in 1923. The league was accepted as a member of the Atlanta Community Fund. The league initiated many social service efforts; helped secure black matrons at the police court; and established a maternal and baby clinic for African Americans in cooperation with the Georgia Division of the Federal Children's Bureau.[69]

TRAINING PROFESSIONAL BLACK SOCIAL WORKERS

Abraham Flexner, educator and educational reformer, influenced social work with his discussion in the National Conference of Charities and Correction in 1915. He questioned the feasibility of building a profession on volunteer or underpaid service, despite the presence of altruistic motivation. Flexner proposed criteria for profession status: the existence of formal educational training; the development of a specialized body of knowledge, techniques, and methods of procedure; establishing standards and supervision of state governments; creating professional associations; and codes of ethics and practices. Social workers, white and black, worked toward achieving these goals in the 1920s.[70]

African American students were admitted to all of the social work schools in the North. In the South, where legal segregation was enforced, African Americans created their own institutions. The earliest black institutions for training professional social workers, which are discussed in this book, were the Atlanta School of Social Work (1920) and the Bishop Tuttle School of Social Work (1925) at St. Augustine's College. The Tuttle School specialized in religious education, whereas the Atlanta School trained students for general social service. In 1935 a School of Social Work was established at Howard University.

The Atlanta University School of Social Work began as the Atlanta School of Social Service at Morehouse College in 1920 and became the most vital element in training black social workers. It was established by a group of social workers and other persons interested in solving social problems. This was especially important in the South, where only a few social welfare agencies employed blacks to work specifically with African Americans. In 1920, during the annual meeting of the National Conference of Social Workers in New Orleans, Jessie O. Thomas, southern field secretary of the National Urban League, expressed the need for solving social problems in black communities. Atlanta's delegates, including Robert Dexter, secretary of the Atlanta Associated Charities, were impressed with Thomas' speech. They called together a group of persons who were interested in exploring the possibility of establishing a social work school for African Americans. The city's social agencies, including the Atlanta Urban League, and the six black colleges of Atlanta planned the organization of the school, which opened 4 October 1920 with fourteen students.[71]

While the Atlanta School of Social Work began in 1920, its roots extended directly to the Neighborhood Union. African Americans in Atlanta needed housing, schools, jobs, medical services, day care, and recreational facilities. None of the social welfare agencies in the larger community were addressing the needs of African Americans. As a response to such conditions, Lugenia Burns Hope founded the Atlanta Neighborhood Union. The union was a comprehensive and effective social service. Members of the union conducted community surveys, collecting data and making rational decisions based on facts. The union was so successful that its techniques and methodological design were borrowed and applied by the Atlanta Board of Education, the National Tuberculosis Association, and the National Urban League.[72]

Although Lugenia Hope organized a Social Service Institute at Morehouse in September 1919 and had done much to improve conditions in Atlanta through the Neighborhood Union, a black man was appointed to head the new institution. Garry W. Moore, a graduate of the New York School of Philanthropy and chairman of the Department of Sociology and Economics at Morehouse College, was the first director of the Atlanta School of Social Service. Courses were taught by Morehouse faculty, physicians, and practitioners from local agencies, such as Robert Dexter, Associated Charities; Lugenia Hope, member of the Executive Committee and president of the Neighborhood Union; John Hope; and Jessie Thomas, chairman of the School's Executive Committee. John Hope, president of Morehouse College and later Atlanta University, offered the resources of both of those institutions. Financial support came from individuals and philanthropic organizations such as the American Red Cross and the Laura Spelman Rockefeller Foundation.[73]

The object of the Atlanta School of Social Work was to train black students in the principles and techniques of social work and to train black leaders in solving social problems of the South. Atlanta was selected as the ideal location because of its large black population, history of interracial cooperation, and several excellent black colleges and because leading social agencies in Atlanta already had strong black departments, and the Southern Headquarters of the National Urban League was in Atlanta. The school offered a one-year course in social theory and practice. Fieldwork was done at the Anti-Tuberculosis Association, Atlanta Associated Charities, Atlanta Urban League, and the Neighborhood Union. A certificate was given at the end of the year's course.

By 1922 E. Franklin Frazier, a former research fellow at the New York School of Social Work, had become director of the Atlanta School of Social Work. Under Frazier, the school developed a strong sociological and research-oriented approach. He developed a quarter system and moved the school closer to accreditation.[74] Other members of the teaching faculty were Helen B. Pendleton, teacher of Case Method and supervisor of field work and former general secretary of Associated Charities in Savannah, Georgia; Ludie Andrews, superintendent of the infirmary at Morehouse College and former superintendent of colored nurses at Grady Hospital; Alfred Jones, Atlanta physician; Ada S. Woolfolk, secretary of the Atlanta Associated Charities and former director of field service and training courses of the American Red Cross; Mary Dickinson, executive secretary of the Atlanta Anti-Tuberculosis Association and former Education Director of the Atlanta Anti-Tuberculosis Association; Beatrice Seelig, Child Welfare and Girls Work at the Jewish Educational Alliance in Atlanta.

The Atlanta School of Social Work was incorporated in 1924 and the following year   relocated to the Herndon Building on Auburn Avenue, which was also the home of the Atlanta Urban League.[75] It was also in close proximity to many of the social agencies that provided fieldwork for the students. To fill the school's emphasis on training in practical casework, each student was supervised weekly by a social agency.

The Atlanta School of Social Work prepared students for employment in associated charities, travelers' aid societies, settlement work, probation work in juvenile courts, recreation, NUL, YWCA and YMCA work, social service departments of churches, and welfare workers in industry. The Neighborhood Union, Phillis Wheatley Branch of the YWCA, the Butler Street Branch of the YMCA, and the Atlanta Community Chest offered students opportunities for community work. The Annual Negro Health Week provided similar community-wide opportunities in health programs. Students did fieldwork with the Atlanta Family Welfare Society, the Atlanta Juvenile Court, the Attendance Department of the Atlanta Public Schools, and the Grady Clinic of Grady Hospital.[76]

In 1927 Forrester B. Washington was appointed Director of the School of Social Work. Born in Salem, Massachusetts, Washington graduated from Taft College and the New York School of Philanthropy. He was the tenth NUL fellow to complete a social work program.[77]   Washington held many social work positions: the first executive director of the Detroit League; supervisor of Negro Economics of the U. S. Department of Labor for Michigan and Illinois; director of the Research Bureau of the Detroit Associated Charities; and executive secretary of the Armstrong Association of Philadelphia.   Washington had a deep understanding of the problems that African Americans faced in adjusting to urban conditions and the social planning needed to help them solve their problems. He incorporated these concerns into the social work curriculum. Under Washington's direction, the school developed closer ties to social work, to professional education, and to national social work associations.

In 1928 the Atlanta School of Social Work was accredited by the American Association of Schools of Social Work. It was the first black school to meet the requirements of membership and of accreditation. In 1930 the school divided its curriculum into four methods: casework, group work, community organization, and research. In 1933 the School of Social Work was permanently located on the Atlanta University campus. Although the school continued to use the facilities of Morehouse College and Atlanta University, it held a separate commencement, maintained a separate Board of Directors, and formulated its own admission requirements. In 1939 the school began awarding the master of social work degree. Complete affiliation with Atlanta University began in 1947, when the Atlanta School of Social Work relinquished its incorporation and became the Atlanta University School of Social Work.[78]

BISHOP TUTTLE SCHOOL OF SOCIAL WORK AND RELIGIOUS EDUCATION

It is not surprising that the Bishop Tuttle Memorial School of Social Work linked social service to the ideal of Christian evangelicalism, since most of the black schools emerged from a missionary background. In 1925 the Bishop Tuttle Memorial School of Social Work and Religious Education was established at St. Augustine's College. Located in Raleigh, North Carolina, the college was founded in 1867 for African American students by the Protestant Episcopal Church. Its School of Social Work was a national center for the training of young black women for Christian leadership in the church and community. The social service school was supported by black and white churchwomen of the Women's Auxiliary of the Episcopal Church and named in honor of Bishop Daniel Sylvester Tuttle, presiding bishop of Missouri, 1903-1923.[79]

The Bishop Tuttle Memorial School of Social Work and Religious Education trained young women for church work and social service through a two-year course in religious education and social work. The school was founded to enable its graduates to carry church teaching and social service into parochial schools and parish visiting, to lead mothers' clubs, and to provide them with an understanding of domestic science and personal hygiene. These social workers would work with children, mothers, and the unfortunate in the North and South and in rural and city parishes.[80]

The school established a unique curriculum, that viewed social work as applied Christianity. The school work covered a two-year period of class instruction and practical work. Residence was required for students in the program. It admitted students who had completed two years of college (later, four years) with a background in psychology, education, and social science.[81] The school offered a certificate in social work after a year's internship in a position. Many of its students continued to study at the Atlanta University School of Social Work. The interracial faculty consisted of Dean Bertha Richards, Bible and Church Teachings; Pearl Snodgrass, Religious Education (later librarian); Ruth L. Stevenson, Sociology and Social Work; Louise R. McKinney, Religious Education; and Cecil D. Halliburton, Social Work.

Although Dean Richards was dedicated to her work, the name most often associated with the Tuttle School of Social Work is Cecil Halliburton. A former Urban League fellow and assistant to the editor of the *Opportunity* magazine,

Halliburton was a graduate of the New York School of Social Work and the University of Pittsburgh. He eventually became a dean at the college. Special lectures were given by professors in the School of Public Welfare at the University of North Carolina. Mary Coleman Carnage was director of the Tuttle Community Center and Playground. The school cooperated with the various city, state, and county agencies: Associated Charities, County Welfare Department, Child Welfare Department, Travelers' Aid, St. Agnes Hospital, St. Ambrose Episcopal Church, Washington High School, Lucille Hunter School, and the Catholic School for Negro Children.[82]

The Tuttle Community Center, a settlement house and recreational center, provided a fieldwork area for the students of the School of Social Work and Religious Education. In the manner of Janie Porter Barrett's Locust Street Settlement at Hampton, the center became a "Paradise Castle."[83] The Tuttle Community Center originated as a community playground donated by the college president, Rev. A. B. Hunter, in 1928. It expanded to include a reading room, club room, craft room, and Sunday school. The community center hired two graduates of the School of Social Work as its first full-time workers.

The Tuttle Community Center served as a laboratory for the Tuttle School. Volunteers conducted a variety of activities in creative and recreation activities, spiritual development, handicrafts, and health improvement. During the depression, the community center featured programs emphasizing economical and savings instruction. In 1936 the Community Chest granted an allocation for the year and thereafter increased the allocation each year.

While the founding of the Tuttle School of Social Work arose from efforts to help the impoverished black community near the college, employment and placement opportunities for its graduates linked it to the National Urban League. By the late 1930s the Tuttle School had nearly 100 graduates, and two-thirds of these social workers were placed in the South. Many were employed in federal relief programs, such as the WPA and National Youth Administration. Paid workers in settlements acted as recreation and club leaders or performed clerical and maintenance tasks. Social workers were involved also with local institutions, the St. Agnes Hospital, Tuberculosis Sanitarium, Oxford Orphanage, Mary Talbert Home for Girls, Women's Prison, and County Council of Social Agencies. The Bishop Tuttle School of Social Work and Religious Education reached its height during the depression. It closed after the 1939-1940 academic year, primarily because the school revolved around its female dean, Bertha Richardson. When Richardson, who was white, relocated to St. Paul College it weakened the financial base of the social work school. College officials erroneously assumed also that the demand for social workers was diminishing.[84]

HOWARD UNIVERSITY SCHOOL OF SOCIAL WORK

The demand for black social workers from public and private agencies increased with the general demand for social workers following the passage of the Social Security Act. The awareness of the cultural contributions of all racial groups to a real democracy opened opportunities to black male and female social workers.[85]   Howard University in Washington, DC established a social work education program in 1935.   The school developed largely under two persons, E. Franklin Frazier, head of the Department of Sociology at Howard, and Inabel Burns Lindsay, the first woman to be appointed academic dean at the institution. The idea, however, evolved over a period of time. As early as 1914 the Executive Committee of the university focused on the needs and problems in society and, simultaneously, on the desire to provide courses in social service work. All appeals were turned down on the assumption that the university was not a suitable institution for training in what was regarded as a vocation closely affiliated with missionary zeal.   Lucy Diggs Slowe, Howard's first dean of women, and Inabel Lindsay, were strong advocates of social work education.

New and different programs were evolving under the New Deal to combat the disastrous effects of the depression. In 1932 a study made by the Council of Social Workers in the District of Columbia revealed that of sixty-nine persons newly hired as social workers, only five were graduates of schools of social work. Many   African Americans were recruited directly from college to meet the emergency during the New Deal.   At the time, no institution in Washington with a social work program would accept black students.[86]

Howard University School of Social Work was established: to provide professional study, including field work for persons entering social work; to provide advanced study for persons employed in social agencies; to provide opportunities for social research with the social work faculty; to provide an understanding of the cultural and economic problems of African Americans in relation to social work practice.[87]   To strengthen the Sociology Department and to introduce social work education, E. Franklin Frazier, former dean at the Atlanta School of Social Work, included a core of new courses and hired Inabel Lindsay to teach courses in the social work curriculum. Inabel Burns Lindsay, born in St. Joseph, Missouri, in 1900, was the youngest of six children.   Her great-grandparents were former slaves who had migrated from Virginia to Missouri. Inabel Burns graduated from Howard University and accepted a National Urban League Fellowship to attend the New York School of Social Work. Along with E. Franklin Frazier, Inabel Burns was one of three black students attending the institution.   She spent only one year (1920-1921) in the two-year certificate program.   Lindsay worked briefly at the Cleveland Urban League before she returned home and began teaching school in Kansas City, Missouri. After she married in 1925, Inabel gave up teaching because her husband adhered to the conventional gender rules and did not want her to work outside the home.[88]

Lindsay responded to the Urban League's request that she repay her fellowship by becoming a research assistant to Charles Johnson in Springfield, Illinois. She later worked worked in St. Louis, Missouri with the Provident Association for Child and Family Welfare as a caseworker and administrator until 1932. She played a leading role in the development of policies and programs in public welfare during the depression. Lindsay returned to school and earned a master's degree from the University of Chicago School of Social Service Administration in 1937. She joined the Howard University faculty in the fall of that year.[89]

Social work training at Howard began with a program of professional courses in the Department of Sociology. The curriculum conformed to the minimum standards of the American Association of Schools of Social Work adopted by that body in 1932. It began with a program of twelve courses that established the framework of a two-year program of graduate study. Field work practice was given in cooperation with the social agencies in the community. By the end of the 1930s, Frazier was dividing his time between the Department of Sociology and a separate Division of Social Work in the Graduate School. Lindsay became the acting director of the new division, and two full-time faculty members with masters' degrees were hired.

In 1940 the American Association of Schools of Social work accredited Howard's Graduate Division of Social Work as a one year school and the University granted it an independent status within the Graduate School. Frazier resigned in 1942, and by 1945 an autonomous professional school with a two-year curriculum awarding the master of social work degree was established. Inabel Lindsay was named acting dean of the School of Social Work, while the university continued to look for a man to take over the position. When the Association of Schools of Social Work would not accredit a school with only an acting dean, Inabel Lindsay became Howard University's designated appointee to the position of dean. She believed that it was necessary to understand the impact of racial, cultural, and social factors on human beings and their importance in shaping human behavior and development. Lindsay, like George Haynes, E. Franklin Frazier, and Forrester B. Washington, was a pioneer in advocating standards for black social workers and insisting that they should be properly trained.

PROFESSIONALIZATION OF BLACK SOCIAL WORKERS

Haynes, like other social workers, assisted in building a federation among the different ethnic and racial groups in the cities and preserving the heredity and traditions of each group. Black and white reformers confronted with social, economic, and racial problems in American cities sought solutions in a pluralistic society. Yet Haynes did not lose sight of the problems of African Americans and solutions for them. Like many black intellectuals of the Progressive era, Haynes believed that the opportunities of the few must be developed and brought to the service of the many.[90]

Many persons perceived social work to be the solution to the race problem. The NUL sought to provide the urban black population with an economic foundation, broader educational opportunities, and a greater appreciation of social values. It assisted migrant women in finding broader opportunities in the cities. It played a leading role in the pull of migrants to the North and in the development of a working-class culture. The league offered vocational training to migrants, urged businesses to hire blacks, and attempted to persuade unions to accept black members. Despite dependence on white organizations for support and patronizing attitudes by both whites and blacks, the services offered by the league were beneficial to the black community. It initiated a dialogue between white and black leaders who were concerned about community welfare.

The league was unique among social work agencies. Its publicity campaign to raise the consciousness of white communities of the benefits of hiring professional black social workers to deal with the needs of African Americans was commendable. By initiating social work education, the NUL led the way in creating opportunities for black social workers. Black social workers came to be regarded as an asset and a distinct advantage as well in many cities.

Gains in education, suffrage, and the professions created a new identity and expanded the horizon of all women in American society. The number of women in the professions increased from 11.2 percent in 1920 to 14.2 percent in 1930.[91] The emergence of a large, black middle class allowed black women to enter the professions and skilled occupations. African American women were more successful in the professions that required a college degree, mainly because there were fewer black persons working in these areas, and it was less competitive.[92] By 1940 a significant number of professionally trained women were heading the local Urban Leagues.

Historically, black women who occupied professional positions served their racial communities. Social work as a profession was new in African American communities. The NACW, having established its own Social Service Department by 1924, began encouraging the clubwomen to become interested in the departmental work. The field of social work expanded tremendously in large cities. Poverty, poor social conditions, and black migration led to serious social problems and a demand to replace volunteers with professional social workers. The professionalization of black social workers brought an increasing number of young, college-trained women into the field, particularly in large urban cities. Many African American social work students were recruited directly from college. By 1925 there were at least fifty black women engaged in social work in New York City. By 1930 black professional social workers were employed in many northern cities, such as New York, Boston, Pittsburgh, Philadelphia, and Chicago. They worked with associated charities, juvenile and women's courts, day nurseries, community service, and playground associations and as school visitors, visiting nurses, and parish visitors. Although opportunities for social work were more widespread in the North, black women in the South were also entering the profession.[93]

The Great Depression revolutionized social work and placed it among the primary functions of the government. Social work changed almost overnight during the New Deal, John Ehrenreich emphasized, from a "Cinderella that must be satisfied with the leavings" into one of the "primary functions of government."[94] The New Deal transferred the financing of social services from the private sector to the public. The new public setting for social work created an entirely new environment for the profession. Still it would be left to social workers to resist efforts to make them agents of racial segregation and division in American society. The National Urban League was very much in favor of government intervention and regulation and supported New Deal programs and the expansion of the role of the federal government.[95]

Chapter 8

A New Image: From the New Black Woman to the New Deal

The New Negro is he or she who speaks the language of the oppressed to defy the language of the oppressor.

W. A. Domingo, "The New Negro,"
Messenger (1920), 144-45.

Negro women have thrown themselves whole-heartedly into the organization of groups to direct the social uplift of their people, one of the greatest achievements of our race.

Mary McLeod Bethune, "A Century," (1933).

The urbanization of blacks, migration to the North, the Harlem Renaissance, Garveyism, and the expanding work of the Urban League were important developments in the second decade of the twentieth century. They created conditions for the emergence of a "New Negro" race consciousness that challenged uplift ideology. The New Negro combined both a concern with history and cultural origins with a concern for a racial heritage that would establish a positive public image. The Great Migration of southern blacks to northen cities provided the incentive for a resurgence of race consciousness among black intellectuals. For some intellectuals the term "New Negro" had a militant working-class meaning; for others it referred to an integrationist, middle-class cultural and artistic movement based in Harlem. Historian Kevin Gaines asserts, "Here was racial uplift ideology's old ideal of interracial cooperation, in a new setting, but still solidly bourgeois in character."[1] By promoting the contributions of black art and literature to American civilization, the intellectuals were reformulating uplift ideology by stressing an eclectic relationship between black folk culture and the black artist. The new image was defined in aggressive leaders, organizations, and black newspapers and magazines such as the *Messenger* of the Brotherhood of Sleeping Car Porters and Maids, *Opportunity* of the National Urban League, and the *Crisis* magazine of the NAACP. *Opportunity*, the magazine of social work among blacks, was an important source of New Negro information and an outlet for Harlem Renaissance men and women writers.

Jessie Fauset, the literary editor of the *Crisis*, along with Alain Locke and Charles Johnson, was a leader of the New Negro movement. Not only was she a participant, but she was fully involved with setting the Harlem literary scene. Black women expressed a deep racial and cultural identity as exemplified in the July 1926 edition of *Opportunity*. Women in literature from an earlier era continued to be recognized, namely, Alice Dunbar-Nelson, beside new writers such as Jessie Fauset, Nella Larsen, and Zora Neale Hurston.[2] Jessie Fauset and Nella Larsen were the first black women artists to depict successful, independent, single, black professional and working-class women. Ann duCille argues that not all of their characters surrendered their careers to male-dominated, bourgeois marriages, as many scholars have claimed.[3]

With the rise of the Garvey movement in the 1920s came a resurgence of race consciousness and black nationalism. Marcus Garvey brought a new conception of race to the masses of urban workers.[4] A new generation of black leaders attempted to unite the race with business and institutions of uplift to help the poor. Garvey insisted that black stood for strength, not inferiority. "Men of the Negro race, let me say to you that a greater future is in store for us. We must realize that upon ourselves depends our destiny." With its focus on a strong black manhood, Garveyism challenged activist women leaders.

In the 1920s and 1930s, some women leaders urged black women not to allow gender issues to overshadow the struggle for racial justice. Amy Jacques, Garvey's secretary, co-worker, and wife by 1922, became the associate editor of the *Negro World* and added a women's section. When Garvey was imprisoned in Atlanta in 1925, Amy worked to hold the Universal Negro Improvement Association (UNIA) together. Amy Jacques-Garvey became a vital player in the Garvey movement, the unofficial leader of the UNIA. Yet she was often critical of black men in the UNIA who prevented women members from acquiring leadership. In an editorial in *The Negro World*, she wrote that women and men leaders of the darker races were setting their own standard by which to establish a civilization:

Women of all nationalities and races have as great a part to play in the development of their particular group as the men. Do they not mold the minds of future men and women? Women are extending this holy influence outside the realms of the home, softening the ills of the world by their kindly contact.[5]

By arguing that women had special powers that could be employed toward the betterment of humanity, Amy Jacques-Garvey aligned herself with Anna Cooper, Jane Addams, and other black and white feminists who believed in women's humanizing potential.[6]

The Garvey movement, which was already in decline after Garvey's deportation in 1927, lost all support with the depression. When the movement began to fall apart, frustrated men felt that it was necessary to keep black women in their place. Amy Jacques Garvey believed that women could become worldwide leaders, replacing the men.

Black women leaders were linked by language, citizenship, and religion to a worldwide race. Influenced by the democratic rhetoric of World War I, they began to identify with people of color all over the world. In 1922 race women within the NACW formed the International Council of the Women of Darker Races to link hands with women of color worldwide. The officers were the following: Margaret Washington, president; Mary Terrell, and Lugenia Hope, vice presidents; Elizabeth Carter, secretary; and Nannie Burroughs, chair of the executive board.[7] The object of the International Council was to cooperate for the economic, social, and political interests and welfare of women of color. Women such as Bethune and Burroughs understood the role education could play in liberation struggles throughout the world. The International Council established an education committee to study the conditions under which women of color suffered because of race and gender discrimination. They extended the sisterhood to women in West Africa, Haiti, India, Ceylon (now Sri Lanka), Cuba, and the Virgin Islands.[8] By 1925 Addie Waites Hunton, who was active in the International League for Peace, was a vice president of the International Council of Women of the Darker Races.[9] The council expanded the scope of the clubwomen and broadened their focus beyond middle-class values and the quest for respectability.

The feminism of the 1920s encouraged female leadership and professionalization among black women. Elsie McDougall found that the lives of black women were changing in the public sector by the second decade of the twentieth century. They were employed in numerous occupation categories: as secretaries, administrators, probation officers, and educators and in the professions of medicine, law, dentistry, pharmacy, nursing, librarianship, and social work.[10]

African Americans used words as tools to assert their self-image. The folk tradition and working-class culture were best expressed in the lyrics of the women blues singers during the 1920s. The blueswomen were extremely popular, writing and singing about black women's autonomy and vulnerability, sexuality, and spirituality. From the Roaring Twenties to the beginning of the depression, the blueswomen reigned supreme with corsets off, hair bobbed, gin at hip, and fingers snapping.[11] Although they were admired by the public who went to hear them, they were rejected by polite, respectable society. The lyrics and the women were criticized as gut-bucket, low-down, and lower-class. Women such as Gertrude Rainey, Bessie Smith, Mamie Smith, Ida Cox, and Ethel Waters sang a gospel of dignity taken from the reality of life.[12] These singers left the boundaries of the home and took their sexuality into the public arena. Hazel Carby suggests that the cultural spaces of the blues singers-the dance halls, nightclubs, and cabarets-were the targets also of the clubwomen's reformist zeal. Carby stresses how the cultural establishments endangered the moral stability of the black middle class, thereby, producing a conflict between the emerging, black middle class and the emerging black working class.[13]

The black clubwomen were especially concerned with defending their names against charges of immorality and sexual promiscuity. Angela Davis argues that in defending black women's moral integrity and sexual purity, clubwomen such as Fannie Williams, Ida Wells, and Mary Terrell, denied sexual agency. Sexuality was one area in which the masses of black women could exercise some independence. Therefore, Davis argues, denial of sexual agency meant the denial of freedom for working-class black women. The women whom the blueswomen were singing about were those women who the clubwomen felt needed to be saved.[14] Davis suggests that the women's blues as much as clubwomen provided a cultural space for community building among the working-class black women. She contends that in this arena bourgeois notions of sexual purity and "true womanhood" were absent.

The new sexuality loosened restraints for women in other areas. The changing morality of the 1920s and the "New Woman" created the perfect environment for birth control activists.[15] The leader of the birth control movement, Margaret Sanger, finally succeeded in establishing a birth control clinic in 1923. However, the 1920s was a battle ground for legislative changes to birth control laws, mainly because of the Comstock Laws, which barred contraceptives from interstate commerce and made it illegal to send birth control information through the mail. Linda Gordon in *Woman's Body, Woman's Rights*, underscores the notion that Victorian prudery produced not only prohibition of sexual discussion but a cult of "motherhood." Progressive activists worked to amend state laws and by the 1930s more relaxed ways of interpreting the laws ushered in the legalization of birth control. Clinics, along with birth control leagues, were established all over the United States. In March 1923 the Harlem Community Forum invited Margaret Sanger to speak to it. Community centers and settlement houses, often in connection with the Urban League, became part of the referral network directing blacks to birth control services. In 1925 the New York Urban League urged the American Birth Control League to establish a clinic in the Columbus Hill community. The Henry Street Settlement House sent women to the Harlem Clinic. The Boston Urban League, Robert Gould Shaw House, and Harriet Tubman House performed referral services for clients. Excluded from the segregated clinics in the South, African Americans established their own facilities. The Bethlehem Center in Nashville integrated a birth control clinic into its public health program for African Americans in the late 1930s.[16]

In the late 1920s and 1930s, birth control was linked to the changing status of black women and the role that they could play in the survival of the race. The issue of birth control or family planning takes on a special meaning in African American communities. In 1934 at a UNIA meeting, Marcus Garvey condemned the use of birth control as a form of racial genocide. Kelly Miller, Dean at Howard University, believing that black women were having fewer children because they had strayed away from children, the kitchen, and the church, cautioned them against race genocide.[17]   Meanwhile, black scholars such as Chandler Owens, editor of the *Messenger*, E. Franklin Frazier, and W.E.B. Du Bois regarded the use of birth control as an important issue for African Americans. E. Franklin Frazier remained unconvinced that birth control would have a eugenic effect on the black population. Although he observed decreasing numbers of better educated blacks, Frazier reasoned that natural forces such as disease would cause a similar decrease in the numbers of low-income blacks.[18] W. E. B. Du Bois confirmed that blacks, like most people at the time who followed middle-class standards of morality, considered birth control immoral. Du Bois criticized persons who opposed the use of birth control methods among blacks, pointing out that they were confused by the fallacy of numbers.[19] Male and female leaders believed that birth control could be a strategy of economic survival for black women.

Fertility rates among African American women dropped during the decades prior to the depression and increased in the following decades. The changes might have been due to patterns of marriage, couples' adopting effective methods of birth control, or, most likely, fertility-inhibiting diseases, such as syphilis and tuberculosis.[20] Although sterility is not a consequence of syphilis, a pregnant woman with syphilis or another sexually transmitted disease (STD) is more likely to experience a stillbirth or spontaneous abortion. It is possible, therefore, that black men believed that black women were deliberately reducing the African American population during this period.

The clubwomen were less attuned to the new attitudes about female sexuality and more concerned about practical concerns such as black women and employment. Although many women were found in the professions, most black women did not have the resources to train for the prestigious occupations. Clubwomen were aware that black women were integral to the economic order despite working longer hours for lower salaries. The NACW supported higher wages and shorter working hours for women. It viewed economic inequality as a major oppression. The clubwomen believed that black women should be able to join the unions or organize unions of their own for protection. During the depression years, approximately 60 percent of all black women were domestic servants. Their wages were low and they worked under substandard conditions. The Depression, which brought harder times to African Americans, forced black women workers into unemployment, intensified job competition, and increased the numbers on relief. In 1930 three of every five black women were employed in domestic and personal service.[21] In New York City, of the 58,950 African Americans on relief, approximately 27,330 were domestic servants.[22]

THE DEPRESSION AND THE NEW DEAL

The severe economic crisis during the 1930s that brought large numbers of black women to the unemployment lines increased the visibility of the women and revived the negative image of African American women. African American clubwomen challenged the opinion that the presence of venereal disease fueled the racist assumption that all black women were inherently immoral. Instead, they pointed to socioeconomic factors and the exploitation of young black women in the cities as the root of the problem. Evelyn Hammonds argues that public health experts concerned about venereal disease, supplied a new scientific justification to the policy of policing black and white "dangerous" working women.[23]

Depression-like conditions were not new for the majority of African Americans, who had always managed to get by with very few material resources. Nevertheless, African American women stretched themselves further in attempting to "make ends meet" for their families. The depression brought most self-help projects to an end. Not only the National Association of Colored Women, but the clubwomen's constituencies in rural and urban communities faced disastrous situations in the 1930s. In 1930 the association modified its programmatic agenda and narrowed its functions.

ISSUE OF RACE AND CLASS

The Great Depression and the uncertain outlook of the New Deal and the administration had a profound effect on African Americans. The situation prompted many black leaders, especially the younger generation, to develop new racial ideologies and strategies. This led to an ideological division between the old and younger race leaders, such as Mary Terrell and Mary Bethune. Terrell could not accept any program that de-emphasized racial integration. She continued to advocate interracial cooperation during the depression. Terrell advocated racial integration of blacks and whites, and Bethune, who was twelve years younger, preferred economic integration of the social classes. Moreover, Terrell had refused to leave the Republican Party, while Mary Bethune became a strong leader in the Democratic Party. Many African Americans criticized the economic policies of President Herbert Hoover, and, as a result they switched to the Democratic Party of Franklin Roosevelt. Were the major problems of African Americans related more to race or class?[24] While Terrell joined older race leaders, such as Kelly Miller, in supporting integration, younger leaders like Ralph Bunche advocated that the black working class align itself with white workers to improve their economic status. He believed that under oppressive conditions identity of economic interests could overcome racial prejudices and that black and white unity was possible.[25]

In the 1930s working-class white and black women joined the International Ladies' Garment Workers Union (ILGWU). The organization was founded by men in 1900 in New York to improve conditions for employees manufacturing women's clothing. Maida Springer-Kemp, a black woman, took a job in a garment factory while in high school in the 1920s. During the Depression when her husband had to take a salary cut, she went back to work. Maida joined Local 22 of the ILGWU and participated in a strike in 1932 which won better wages and working conditions. There were nearly 4,000 black women dressmakers in Local 22 by 1933. Active on several committees, Maida became one of the ILGWU's earliest black business agents.[26] In 1933 the National

Industrial Recovery Act first gave workers the right to organize unions. In 1935, the National Labor Relations Act ensured the right of unions to organize and bargain collectively. Like Bethune, Springer-Kemp learned to lobby and work with persons in Franklin Roosevelt's administration. Maida later received recognition for her union activism when she was named Woman of the Year by the National Council of Negro Women. On becoming vice-president of the National Council of Negro Women, she brought union activism into the realm of black women's clubs. However, there is no evidence that working-class women and their activities were embraced by the clubwomen on a large scale basis.

After serving two terms as president of the National Association of Colored Women (1924-1928), Mary Bethune was convinced of the need for a united coalition of black women. Bethune had attempted to promote the association's agenda through the National Council of Women of the United States. However, she refused to be peripheral to the center of the main leadership, the position usually given African Americans. When the NACW prepared a music program for the NCW in Washington and rumors of segregated seating surfaced, Bethune led the Executive Board in canceling the program, despite the elaborate preparations the clubwomen had made.[27] The NACW was confronted with a segregated seating policy again during a meeting of the International Council of Women in 1925. When the question arose as to whether black women should support their own organizations and institutions or channel their energies into interracial groups, Bethune supported the NACW's withdrawal from the predominantly white NCW. Her actions drew criticism from the association president, Mary Waring. Waring warned black women to be aware of forming organizations that discriminated on the basis of race.

To achieve her goal of black female representation in public office, Bethune attempted to shape the indistinct National Association into a cohesive body with a comprehensive program for all the clubs. Motivated by the impact of the depression and convinced that her ideas would not materialize within the NACW, Bethune established her own organization.[28] In 1935 at the Harlem YWCA, Mary Bethune and the presidents of thirty black women's voluntary associations met to discuss the creation of a National Council of Negro Women. Mary Church Terrell accused Bethune of trying to cripple the NACW and create a political base for herself. Charlotte Hawkins Brown also hesitated to endorse the new organization. To counteract fears and criticisms, Charlotte Brown and Mary Terrell were made officers of the council.[29] Some clubwomen joined both organizations.[30] By refusing to join the National Council of Negro Women, an umbrella organization, the NACW retained its individuality as a separate organization.

By the 1930s the association was out of step ideologically and politically with the tactics and strategies of the emerging race organizations and younger leaders. Many of the welfare agencies and organizations it had created were conducted by other organizations that most often were doing it better than the association. With white financial support other groups, such as the NUL, were providing social services more efficiently.[31]

No one demonstrated the dated attitudes more than Sallie Wyatt Stewart. She succeeded Bethune as president of the National Association of Colored Women from 1928 to 1933. Stewart advocated raising moral standards, improving the home, and adult literacy of working mothers. A schoolteacher and founder of the Phillis Wheatley Home in Evansville, Indiana, Stewart headed the Indiana Federation of Women's Clubs from 1921 to 1926. Sallie Wyatt Stewart institutionalized the direction of the club movement in 1931, when she decentralized the association, decreasing its departments from thirty-eight to two: Mother, Home, and Child and Negro Women in Industry to facilitate better organization.[32]

Throughout the 1920s, and for the next decades, the National Association of Colored Women denounced female individuality and any expression of sexuality, while it supported the ideal of femininity. Instead, it was concerned with uplift, child welfare legislation, health and sanitation, and higher standards in art and literature.[33] Scholar belle hooks asserts that black male leaders did not want the American public to link their demands for civil rights with the demands for gender equality. Moreover, Deborah Gray White argues that the clubwomen's assertive leadership compromised with the masculine impulse of the New Negro movement. This ideology differed from that of women such as Anna J. Cooper and Fannie Barrier Williams.[34] Therefore, White asserts that whereas the association leaders had combined race and gender ideology so that race work and feminism did not conflict, they now defined race work within the framework of feminism.

Simultaneously, the clubwomen began to emphasize issues and the need for federal assistance in community affairs. The association's Department of Negro Women in Industry urged the employment of middle-class black women in the State Department and on the staff of the Women's Board to work for social legislation, such as old age pensions, minimum wage laws, working hours for women, child labor laws, unemployment insurance, and compensation.[35]

The Department of Negro Women in Industry encouraged the club leaders to organize working women in various fields, namely, domestic service, laundry, manufacturing, agriculture, sales, elevator operators, and menial labor. Despite good intentions, they did not appear to be working with the women according to their ability but voicing concern about what they should be doing because of their social status. The women's clubs attempted to teach the workers to be efficient, to understand their employer and working environment, to concentrate on personality development, and to be thrifty. Rural women were taught how and where to market their produce. To some extent, the socially prominent club leaders still seemed more concerned about respectable behavior than about the exploitation of working-class women.

Several black clubwomen, including Sallie Stewart and Mary Bethune, attended President Hoover's White House Conference on Children's Health and Protection in 1930. Eugene Kinckle Jones, executive secretary of the NUL, emphasized the inadequacy of housing for African Americans. Jones and other conferees called for expanding both assistance to black mothers and children as well as the use of newly trained black social workers to improve children's services. In language that seemed to be a throwback to the past, Sallie Stewart stressed that improving the lives of the children had to be "built in the Negro home and with intelligent motherhood to protect the child in the primitive and formative years of his life." The conference raised expectations that black health and social welfare concerns would receive support from the executive office, but public support for the Hoover administration dropped when this did not occur.[36]

Although the depression did affect the programs and activities of the association, there was no clear differentiation in the philosophy of middle-class women's organizations regarding race work. The ultimate goal, as they perceived it, continued to be racial uplift and equality. Thus, they believed that the economic power of the growing professional class of black women was still the means by which race progress would occur. Although the Association declined in membership, the clubwomen used old tactics and new means to survive the economic crisis. The association's membership declined for three reasons: the archaic attitudes of the clubwomen, failure to attract new and younger members, and failure to invite working-class women into the network on an equal basis.

African Americans found the early depression years, 1929-1932, to be the worst. Herbert Hoover appointed only a few African Americans to federal office and disbanded the Negro division of the Republican National Committee. The Scottsboro trial became a renowned civil liberties case that symbolized the worst in race relations in the depression era. It was against this background that African Americans began to appraise Franklin Roosevelt.

The New Deal was a new departure in American reforms, partly because the Roosevelt administration began during the worst depression in American history.[37] Some historians have considered the Franklin Roosevelt administration to be a real turning point in American race relations. It was the first time in the twentieth century that federal officials showed real concern for the plight of African Americans. Partly the concern stemmed from humanitarian interest in all the underprivileged in American society. However, the black vote, which had reached considerable numbers, was crucial in northern industrial states.[38] It was not easy for African Americans to abandon the Republican Party in 1932, but by 1936 many had shifted their votes to the Democratic Party. Although Roosevelt did not publicly associate himself with black projects or black leaders before 1935, some of his associates, such as Harry Hopkins and Will Alexander, former president of New Orleans' predominantly black Dillard University and head of the Commission on Interracial Cooperation (CIC), were more aggressively committed to making the New Deal work more generously for African Americans.[39]

Roosevelt used experts in government service and applied the new trends in social and economic thought to contemporary issues. In welfare and social legislation, the president drew heavily on the knowledge of settlement house graduates and social workers, namely, Harold Ickes, Harry Hopkins, and Frances Perkins, Grace Abbott, and Paul Kellogg, who played important roles in carrying out reform during the New Deal. In many respects, the reforms of the 1930s were partial fulfillments of the programs of preventive social work formulated before World War I. Grace Abbott, from Hull House, accepted an invitation from Julia Lathrop, the first chief of the federal Children's Bureau, to join its staff. As head of the bureau, Grace Abbott was able to maintain some independence within the Department of Labor. When Franklin Roosevelt was elected president, Abbott relied on a precedent set by Lathrop and remained in her job for an additional year to help her friend Frances Perkins, the new secretary of labor. Grace Abbott helped draft the Social Security Act, in which the Sheppard-Towner philosophy of developing programs for mothers and babies was incorporated.[40]   By charging that the Sheppard-Towner Act was intended to promote birth control, the opposition endangered not only the enactment of the act but also its existence.[41] Upon Jane Adams' illness and imminent death in 1935, Grace Abbott was asked to seriously consider becoming her successor at Hull House, but she declined.

Equally influencing on the president was the activism of the First Lady, Eleanor Roosevelt. Mrs. Roosevelt affirmed by word and deed her faith in the equality of opportunity for all. She was the vehicle for approaching, influencing, and provoking the president's conscience. Eleanor attributed her interest in helping the poor to the two years that she spent as a club leader at the University settlement.[42]   She urged the Democrats to ask respected African Americans like Mary Bethune to participate in the leadership of the party.

Mary Bethune was the leading black woman activist during the 1920s and 1930s. In 1927 Eleanor Roosevelt invited Bethune to a dinner at her home for the leaders of the National Council of Women of the United States. Bethune, then president of the NACW, was the only African American present. This event prompted the council to invite Mary Bethune, Addie Hunton, Janie Barrett, Charlotte Brown, and Cora Horne to its national meeting in 1928.[43]   Roosevelt, the future First Lady was impressed with Bethune's feminism, race pride, and compelling magnetism.[44]   Although many white women in government excluded Bethune from their support groups, Eleanor Roosevelt treated her with dignity.

MARY MCLEOD BETHUNE'S VISION OF DEMOCRACY

From 1935 to 1942 Mary McLeod, then president of the NCNW, held two positions in the administration of Franklin Roosevelt, as president of a specially created Division of Minority Affairs of the National Youth Administration and as a member of the Federal Council on Negro Affairs. A race woman, Mary Bethune adhered to a strategy through her NYA work that promoted her race leadership. Bethune believed that opportunities for such leadership were essential for American democracy.[45]   At the time of her appointment to the National Youth Administration, 5 million youths were out of school and jobless and two million were on relief.[46]   Sensitive to the status of black youth and oriented toward public service, Bethune accepted the position in order to fulfill her vision. The object of the NYA was to find jobs for unemployed youth in private industry. The NYA provided aid to high school, college, and graduate students.

Its major objective was to find employment for white and black youth in private industry or provide work relief and vocational training projects. The NYA kept thousands of black students in school and more than 120 colleges participated in the student aid programs.[47]

In agencies like the National Youth Administration (NYA), the New Deal's policy was acceptance of separate, but equal consideration of blacks in the programs of the southern and border states.[48] Through Bethune's influence, the NACW and the NYA conducted a special project: the grounds of the Douglass Home were landscaped by the boys, and the girls were employed as clerks and nurses' aides at Freedmen's Hospital. In another case, thirty-one youths assisted recreation leaders at the Robert Gould Shaw House in Boston. Since Bethune refused to allow racial segregation to set limits for her in the 1930s, she was criticized for accepting segregated projects and vocational employment as the only means of assisting black youth.[49] In the NYA program, Bethune interpreted "separate but equal" as meaning black supervisors for black projects; black participation in the policy-making phase of the program; and NYA activities for black youth to enhanced their training beyond menial jobs as janitors and maids.[50]

Known as the Black Cabinet or Roosevelt's advisory committee, the Federal Council on Negro Affairs was composed of educators, lawyers, journalists, and experts on housing, labor, and social welfare. Among its members were Mary Bethune, Robert C. Weaver, Eugene Kinckle Jones, executive director of the NUL, and Lawrence Oxley, a professional social worker. Since all of the cabinet members held administrative posts, we may ask to what degree or perspective the appointees were able to influence the policies of their respective agencies toward African Americans. Leaders placed in high positions, other than the NYA, did not necessarily voice the sentiments of the mainstream black community. Historian B. Joyce Ross declares that Bethune held both public and private views that differed considerably: presenting one opinion to interracial groups and another in her privately expressed attitudes.[51] More importantly, Ross argues, was the failure of Bethune to use the prestige of her Division of Negro Affairs to challenge the reluctance of the Roosevelt's administration to demand a desegregated society. Bethune, the only woman, emerged as the leader of the unofficial black advisers, holding informal weekly meetings to unite a campaign for civil rights in employment and government facilities.

Mary Bethune's vision of black empowerment stemmed from appropriating opportunities in education and public life. In spite of racism, her vision reflected an optimistic belief that the American principles of democracy and equality would triumph over its discriminatory practices based on class, race, and gender. Bethune played a key role in empowering black women nationally with respectability when she became the NYA director. Although it was not a key post, it was the highest position ever held by an African American woman. Bethune served in this capacity from 1936 to 1944. Bethune believed that neither black men nor the black press recognized the significance of the appointment. However, her position as a black leader and thousands of potential votes from the clubwomen were important to the FDR administration. Mary McLeod Bethune was an advocate for African Americans.[52]

The clubwomen in the 1930s and 1940s focused on matters related to race rather than gender. Mary McLeod Bethune continued the tradition of female race leadership. Unlike Mary Church Terrell, Ida Wells-Barnett, or Anna Julia Cooper, she did not challenge black men. One observer concluded that a tremendous amount of intelligence, insight, and knowledge was distributed among African American women. Graduates from college, law and medical schools headed church groups, women's clubs, sororities, and professional groups. However, most women avoided politics, leaving campaigning to black men. As Deborah White asserts, black women knew the harsh price they paid for helping the race.[53] Bethune was concerned about the economic security of black women.

While gender tension eased somewhat during the 1930s, ambition and fierce competition among the women continued. When Sallie Stewart was elected president, Charlotte Hawkins Brown won the vice presidency over Janie Porter Barrett after a vigorous contest. Mary F. Waring, a physician, was elected president of the association in 1933. She received support from the large membership of Illinois, her adopted state, and Kentucky, her native state. Both Waring and Charlotte Brown had been NACW vice presidents, and each expected to win. Brown withdrew but reentered because of pressure from supporters Jennie Moton and Nannie Burroughs. Brown eventually withdrew from the election and supported Waring for the good of the organization. Thus, Waring was reelected in 1935 over Charlotte Hawkins Brown, the choice in twenty states. Nevertheless, Brown, with support from Bethune, Daisy Lampkin, and Sallie Stewart, led a spirited campaign for the presidency. Lampkin was appointed vice president.[54]

Despite a permanent decrease in national visibility, the Association continued to protest and seek social justice. The clubwomen, supporting higher wages and shorter working hours for women, joined the NUL and NAACP in exposing the unequal wage rates provided in the National Industrial Recovery Act (NIRA), which launched both the National Recovery Administration and the Public Works Administration. Nannie Burroughs represented the association at a Washington conference related to the act. Alonzo Thayer, industrial secretary of the Chicago Urban League, urged the clubwomen to secure copies of the NIRA for their own benefit.[55] Sallie Stewart, Hallie Brown, Nannie Burroughs, and Daisy Lampkin sent a telegram to President Franklin Roosevelt urging him to use his executive power under the National Industrial Recovery Act to prevent discrimination in public works.[56] They requested qualified African Americans in administrative posts to ensure just treatment of the workers. The clubwomen joined the National Council of Women of the United States and the International Congress of Women in establishing a "united front" for women workers.[57]

Middle-class clubwomen continued their dedication to uplifting the race at a time when most African Americans were thwarted by race prejudice and economic depression. Black women lobbied local governments and voluntary agencies to provide health services for the poor in black communities. The Georgia

Federation of Colored Women's Clubs created the Cuyler Children's Free Clinic in Savannah. Throughout the 1930s, the clinic provided free health services to poor children and women, many of whom were domestics. Black and white physicians donated their services.[58]

Between 1935 and 1942 Dorothy Boulding Ferebee, a graduate of Tufts Medical School in 1924, headed a medical project in Bolivar County, Mound Bayou, Mississippi. Unable to rent space for a clinic because plantation owners opposed the project, she and members of the Alpha Kappa Alpha Sorority used their cars as mobile health vans and immunized over 15,000 children for diphtheria, smallpox, and other infectious diseases. The project evolved into the first black hospital in Mississippi.[59] In the 1930s Dorothy Ferebee, who later succeeded Mary Bethune as president of the NCNW, joined Mabel Staupers and a few black women in the birth control movement.

Although the clubwomen held conferences in Washington to develop federal policies and programs for African Americans, their approach to social problems remained the same. Mary Bethune called upon government officials to appoint black women to the various departments that dealt with the welfare of women and children. By elevating black middle-class women in policy-making positions and management- level employment in government, Bethune anticipated benefitting all African Americans.[60]

The demand for jobs, relief, and higher wages recognized the social needs of African Americans and focused black efforts on the government. Racial politics became the basis for community organization. Black leaders spoke less about the culture of African Americans and more about the social programs for farmers, workers, or the unemployed.[61] Mary McLeod Bethune as well as Jennie Moton, the association president, developed a close relationship with the federal administration. With the influence of both the council and the association, black women were appointed to the Children's Bureau, the Farm Security Administration, the U.S. Housing Authority, the Office of Civilian Defense, and several positions in the NYA.[62]

Although for African Americans the New Deal was psychologically encouraging, most blacks were ignored by the New Deal programs. While many were tenant farmers, farm laborers, domestic workers, or migrants, they did not qualify for unemployment insurance, minimum wages, social security, or farm subsidies.[63] Social service agencies followed the same pattern as society in general. Custom and laws restricted African Americans civil service employees to lower positions. They seldom won promotions and the administrative positions were held by whites. Relief agencies refused to assign black caseworkers to visit white persons and justified their actions by claiming that the clients would object. This policy stereotyped African Americans as inferior and unable to visit superior whites. Thus the relief agencies were perpetuating Jim Crow segregation. Black professional social service workers would have to unite to protest and fight this effort to keep them in a subordinate position.[64]

Historian Jacquelyn Jones states that officials used federal funds provided by the Relief Emergency Administration (FERA) and the WPA to reinforce class, race, and gender divisions. Although black women were hired in jobs other than domestic service and agriculture, less than 20 percent of all WPA workers were female, and only about 3 percent of all WPA workers received employment.[65] Many black women who, in desperation had exhaused the regular channels for help, turned to the federal government. Mosell Brinson , a widow in Georgia with seven children, wanted to farm, but she had no mule, no wagon, no feed, and no groceries. She asked the government to help her make a crop that year. In Mississippi, Pinkie Pilcher wondered what would happen to the many black women who were widows with or without children. When they went to the PWA office looking for work, the white women heading the agencies steered them to laundry (washing) work. A Louisiana woman about 25 years old claimed she had been sick for 4 months and needed food and clothes. She had worked for the NYA for 10 months before she was laid off for being sick. These black women insisted upon their civil rights despite the overwhelming circumstances against them.[66]

While race relations appeared to change during the depression and New Deal, fundamentally things remained the same. Racial problems during this period, such as the Unity Farm incident, exposed the racially liberal veneer of the National Federation of Settlements and the depth of Jim Crow segregation in public facilities. In May 1934 the National Federation of Settlements (NFS) held its annual conference at Unity Farm which was located near Kansas City, Missouri. Although the facility was owned by the Unity School of Christianity and willing to open its facilities to both blacks and whites, it refused to admit African Americans for overnight accommodations. The Kansas City Urban League was notified and expected to arrange housing for the delegates but they were not informed of the situation prior to arriving at the farm. Lea Taylor, the executive secretary of the NFS, and another white delegate offered to share their rooms with the few African American delegates but this request was denied by the management.[67]

The African American delegates protested not only against the Unity Farm arrangements but also the white leaders of the NFS, who failed to carry out their policy of racial equality. The white delegates hesitated in their response and some wanted to "cover-up" the incident.[68] Much of the protest from the black delegates came from Gertrude Brown, head resident of the Phyllis Weatley Settlement House in Minneapolis.[69] The African American delegates appealed to the National Conference of Social Work that was meeting in Kansas City around the same time. Meanwhile, the downtown hotel in Kansas City voluntarily suspended its Jim Crow policy for the meeting. In the aftermath of the incident, the 200 participants of the National Conference of Social Work officially endorsed the black delegates and criticized the white delegates at the settlement conference for not joining the African Americans in leaving the conference.[70]

Despite the "New Deal reforms," African Americans and their communities remained the same. When the Great Migration brought hundreds of blacks into the northern communities, white hostility and job competition led to a wave of race riots in 1918 and 1919.   While the proliferation of nationalist movements seemed to fade during the 1920s, economic nationalism persisted as a solution to black economic problems. Between 1929 and 1941 African Americans were involved in boycotts and active campaigns to break down employment barriers.   Black women, especially those in the NAACP such as Daisy Bates in Little Rock, Arkansas, and Ella Baker in New York City, campaigned for social change. African American women activists led Don't Buy Where You Can't Work campaigns.[71] The boycott for jobs, which exploded in black communities, were part of the efforts of the black community to grapple with hard times. In the 1930s, Mary Bethune created a grassroots organization in Washington, the New Negro Alliance, that boycotted discriminatory stores. She personally picketed a drugstore in Washington, DC that refused to hire black workers.[72]

In New York, under the slogan, "Don't buy where you can't work," intense educational and political work was carried on and a large-scale boycott movement developed. In Harlem, for example, overcrowding was prevalent, tuberculosis was common, and more than half of the married women worked as domestics. In 1931, from ten to twenty evictions a day were reported to the Urban League. In March 1935 the anger of Harlem residents exploded into a riot.   It was triggered by emotions that had been building up from the hardships of the depression. The riot began when a rumor spread through the black community that a teenager had been beaten to death in a department store on 125th Street, where he had been caught stealing a $.10 pocket knife.   Nannie Burroughs blamed the Harlem riot on America's age-old attitude on the race question.[73]

Thus, as historian Howard Zinn asserts, the belief in equal rights held by Eleanor Roosevelt as well as FDR, the appointment of Mary Bethune and others to important secondary positions in the government, the distribution of relief and WPA jobs, did not alter the fundamental injustice of being black in America. Zinn emphasizes the limitations of the New Deal's program of reform. The nature of the New Deal to experiment could have led to significant accomplishments, but the reform neither ended segregation nor accomplished economic objectives.[74] Thus, the greatest shortcoming of the New Deal was its failure to link inextricably the principle of federal sponsorship of racial equality with the concept of a desegregated society.[75]

Chapter 9

Epilogue

> What was needed was to build a social
> democracy, for that we needed new formulas,
> new inspirations.
>   L. T. Hobhouse, *Democracy and Reaction*,
>   (1905).

African American women in organized clubs and leagues struggled to work out their own destiny during the latter quarter of the nineteenth and early twentieth centuries. Black woman, like most nineteenth-century Americans, had faith in the expansive possibilities of the future. Black clubwomen were optimistic despite disappointments. Their speeches and writings were designed to motivate African Americans toward progress and achievement. They were optimistic in feeling that the possibilities of what they could do were immeasurable. They believed in the power of self-help organizations, especially women's clubs, to initiate social change in black communities.

African American women organized club networks to carry out social reform, although they had strong feelings of trepidation about the magnitude of the endeavor. The clubwomen justified their activism not on white provocation but on broader philanthropic impulses. African American women created successful communities: encouraged persons to take responsibility for their own lives; provided help to small communities; and provided moral uplift. Their basic vkeues never changed. For women who were just one generation out of slavery, there was an exhilarating sense of possibility. They were convinced that spiritual and social uplift could be attained through sheer force of will. Yet this was not enough. Race, class, and gender inequality remained a main feature of American life.

The NACW was the dream of a few black women who felt that the time had come to band together as a group to advance the cause of the race and to vindicate national sentiment and comments that black women were of low moral character. Middle-class black women with a keen sense of social consciousness found expression in the National Association of Colored Women. This was the distinguishing feature of black women's club work: from the beginning, every member was encouraged to improve conditions and standards among the black population. The clubwomen attempted to improve themselves and others by offering examples of self-help and persistent community service.

The clubwomen who organized the first national conference of black women and launched a women's club network realized that it would take collective leadership to eliminate ignorance, poverty, racial discrimination, and political inequality. It was a tremendous task that only "superwomen" would be able to accomplish.[1] These middle-class "superwomen" combined work in the domestic arena with social action outside the home. The clubwomen performed multiple roles in their domestic responsibilities and community affairs.[2] Black women's tendency to encompass seemingly contradictory roles as worker, homemaker, mother, and activist has contributed to the confusion in understanding black womanhood. It has led to the assumption also of the "myth of the strong black woman" or the "superwoman," a black woman who is expected to work endlessly for the black community without any personal compensation and without complaining.[3] She must cope with race and gender oppression in silence. Although the black women's club network began during the technological revolution in American society, black women planned their first national conference without the convenience of the telephone, typewriter, or automobile. Yet the clubwomen, as did other middle-class women, utilized the new technological time saving inventions from factory produced clothing to processed foods to provide time for uplifting activities.[4] Many also had the help of paid household workers, and a family support network that facilitated their activism.

The early black women's association was successful partially because of the stability and ability of its leadership. Between 1900 and 1928 the Association was best known by its presidents: Mary Terrell, Lucy Thurman, Elizabeth Carter, Margaret Washington, Mary Talbert, Hallie Q. Brown, and Mary McLeod Bethune. They required collective efforts to build a strong association. Of these early national presidents, three were born in the North, three were from the South, and one was born in Ontario, Canada. Rather than regional in ideology, the association represented diverse ideas.

All women's clubs, religious and secular, were invited to send representatives to the black women's conference in 1896. Mary Terrell indicated that there had long been a complex network of black women organized in the church, but in the early years of the 1890s, secular organizations among them were rare. There appears to be a link, however tenuous, between the previous local activities of black women and the work of the national association. The continuity of the women's clubs is revealed in the names of the societies, clubs, and circles attending the conference: the Woman's Mutual Benefit Society, Woman's Mutual

Improvement Club,   F.E.W. Harper Reading Circle,   Lend-a-Hand Circle, Woman's Suffrage Association, Sojourner Truth Club, Hooks School Association, headed by the clubwoman Julia Hooks.[5] Another Memphis group, the Daughters of Zion, apparently did not send a delegation.[6] Several religious organizations attended the founding meeting from New York City: the Cleave Circle King's Daughters, Christian League, Mount Tabor Club, and Young People's Society of Christian Endeavor were recruited by Victoria Matthews as affiliates of the Woman's Loyal Union; churches sent delegations from Washington, DC Although the black women's clubs emerging in the early twentieth century were secular in ideology, the Christian concept of agape manifested itself through these secular clubs.

The black women's club activities were valuable because of the efficacy of their work. The outcome of their club work was explicit in the number of institutions and social agencies that the women established. The clubwomen sought assistance from state legislatures for many of their projects, especially reform institutions. Black clubwomen, in conjunction with state and regional Federations of Colored Women's Clubs, establish industrial training schools and juvenile reform institutions for youth who had already succumbed to the pitfalls of the environment. Janie Porter Barrett, Cornelia Bowen, Selena Sloan Butler, and Charlotte Hawkins Brown led financial campaigns to build institutions. The Empire State Federation adopted the White Rose Home for Working Women and the Katy Ferguson Home for unwed mothers as federation projects. Club women organized efforts to bring playgrounds, recreational facilities, and community centers to black communities. They led the kindergarten movement in local areas. Thus, the public activism of the club women brought social services and programs to African American communities.

Communitywide United Fund agencies, and state and federal agencies later provided funds for some of the social service activities of the NACW. The Virginia Home School for Girls became a state-controlled institution. Funds for the Neighborhood Union Settlement were provided by the Community Chest. The Colored Settlement in Washington, DC, was taken over by the federal government during World War I. Clubwomen struggled for decades to maintain the Frederick Douglass Home, which became a part of the National Park Service in 1964. Some of the clubwomen's experiences became a permanent part of our society, such as the Mt. Meigs Social Settlement and School, later the Montgomery County Training School, the Alabama Industrial School for Negro Children, and now the Alabama State Department of Youth Services.

At the turn of the century large numbers of African American club women, motivated by charitable impulses, devised a strategy of personal service to ameliorate social problems. The clubwomen sought, in their speeches and projects, to promote a specific approach to social problems. The voluntary work of black clubwomen was part personal charity and part professional social work. They believed that they were Americans and accepted American standards and values. The goals of the clubwomen focused on uplift and contained the overtones of social Darwinism that were prevalent in the charity organization movement.[7] I contend, however, that the clubwomen never believed that African Americans were inferior. Some black women, such as Mary Terrell and Fannie Williams, carved out a special role for themselves as public speakers. Other women, namely, Victoria Matthews, Lugenia Hope, and Janie Barrett, turned their voluntary efforts toward settlement activities.

Voluntary social service efforts initiated by black clubwomen, from travelers' aid to settlement houses, were incorporated into the ideological stance of the National Urban League. The clubwomen's individualistic approach to solving social problems was eventually replaced by black professional social workers who were more concerned about getting the job done. However, if the value of an organization is measured by the projects and programs that it instituted and was able to turn over to other agencies as a continuing responsibility, then black women's clubs of the National Association of Colored Women left a strong legacy of service. Beginning with the NUL and transferred to other organizations and institutions, social agencies, schools, employers, and local and national government agencies are now carrying on many projects that originated with the clubwomen.

Even as the clubwomen labored in pursuit of their goals, the great disparity in economic conditions among African Americans continued. Most persons in the small black upper class and middle class were not concerned with philanthropy. Many clubwomen focused more on debutante balls and similar social affairs. The image of the clubwomen found in E. Franklin Frazier's study of the black bourgeoisie revealed the tendency of many black society women during the late forties and fifties to be more concerned with their personal status than with the welfare of others.[8] W.E.B. Du Bois eventually posited a definition for a new talented tenth, a concept of group leadership that would not be based on education and self-sacrifice alone, but with a vision of world conditions connecting African Americans in the United States with cultural groups worldwide.[9]

Settlement workers played a major role in the Progressive era reform. Settlement workers regarded themselves as social reformers rather than charity workers. Settlement workers fought for better housing, promoted playgrounds and neighborhood parks, public health, college extension courses, vocational guidance, and kindergartens. Settlements became laboratories for developing new techniques and offering training in the developing profession of social work. With World War I, some of the idealism and faith in progress faded from the Progressive movement. The increasing dominance of social work schools diverted the profession from its interest in reform. During the New Deal some social workers, such as Edith Abbott, continued to envision the role of settlements as the initiator of experiments. Overall, the reduced budgets of the settlements probably prohibited most new experimental efforts. The New Deal emphasis on large scale reform originating with the federal government altered the role of the settlements .

Race, along with class, gender, and professionalism, is a major theme in this book. As late as the 1930s, most settlement workers perceived their movement as being primarily for whites. Most black settlement workers in African American communities have been overlooked by historians because they appeared different from mainstream settlements. Before World War II only a few settlements were established for African Americans. There were few attempts at integration and some settlements closed their doors in order not to serve African Americans. Judith Trolander believes the problem stemmed partially from the lack of leadership and discriminatory policies of joint funding agencies such as the Community Chest. The chest controlled the budget, standardized the level of funding among settlements in the NFS as well as other aspects of their operations. Most settlement houses founded by African Americans did not meet the strigent requirements for funding by the community chests. Due to pressure from the Urban League, some black settlements, namely Atlanta's Neighborhood Union and the Colored Settlement in Washington, DC, received support from local chests and agencies for playgrounds, kindergartens, and adult education.

Despite the close similarity between the National Urban League's method and those of the settlement house movement, the league was reluctant to identify with the movement. The Lincoln Settlement House Association, under the auspices of the NUL and a member of the city federation of settlements, dropped its membership in the United Neighborhood Houses of New York City in 1940. More typical were black settlements that never received funding from any city, state, or federal agency. The White Rose Home and Industrial Association, for example, struggled to survive on small donations from the Empire State Federation of Colored Women's Clubs, the Northeastern Federation of Women's Clubs, and rent from an occasional lodger when individual philanthropy ceased.

The growing importance of the settlements' national organization, the NFS, coincided with the advent of the New Deal and the shifting of action in welfare reform in Washington. Although the New Dealers faced more difficult problems in reform than their predecessors, like the Progressives, they were confident that the economic and environmental causes of poverty could be eradicated.[10] The idea of voluntary responsibility for relief was not as actively asserted in the 1920s as earlier, but it was not challenged seriously before 1930. By the time Franklin Roosevelt became president, the question of federal participation in relief was not an issue. In a speech in 1935, the president proposed the establishment of the Works Progress Administration (WPA) and denounced public assistance in the form of money and food.[11] The New Deal changed the "Negro problem" from civil rights, education, and charity, to housing, nutrition, medicine, education, relief, Social Security, wages, working conditions, children, and women's labor. In establishing the welfare state pattern of reform, the New Deal set the standards of social policy for the following quarter of a century.

The New Deal programs were aimed at industrial and commercial workers in a society where most African Americans were locked into agricultural poverty. By providing a disproportionate share of benefits to whites, John Ehrenreich argues it helped to sustain and increase disparities. Far from being color-blind during the New Deal, the Civilian Conservation Corps used a racial quota to limit black participation; the National Recovery Administration approved discriminatory hiring practices and segregated office facilities in government buildings. Roosevelt refused to support either anti-lynching legislation, a civil rights act, or economic programs aimed at the problems of African Americans. Most African Americans had to leave the farms and find employment as urban commercial and industrial workers in order to benefit even minimally from the new welfare state.[12]

Thus, during the Progressive era the conflict between the individual approach of the Charity Organization Society and the social reform approach of the settlement was resolved by the collapse of liberal social policy and the rise of case workers in the twenties. The revival of social action in the thirties set off a new period of ferment and the limited social reforms of the early New Deal gave way to the creation of the modern welfare state. Scholar John Ehrenreich believes that the reforms in the 1930s and 1960s do not support the conservative conclusion that government can do nothing directly to alleviate poverty and other social programs. Ehrenreich also challenges the argument that we cannot afford such programs.[13]

After World II, integration increasingly came to be the goal of the settlements. Influenced by the civil rights movement and brought under pressure by African Americans, the renamed National Federation of Settlements and Neighborhood Centers made a commitment to race and economic justice. In the 1940s the number of black staff members increased in settlement houses. During the late forties, Hull House served as home base for Robert Weaver, the director of Community Services in Chicago for the American Council on Race Relations. In 1960 USES (United South End Settlements) was formed in Boston. By the 1960s the Methodist had sixteen Bethlehem Centers in the South, but did not plan to build anymore because they were embarrassed by the racial configuration.

In 1966, with funds from the Board of Missions of the Methodist Church and other funds, the National Federation of Settlements (NFS) published a study by St. Clair Drake. The scholar Drake praised the settlements' attempt at interracial programing and interracial staffs and boards, but deplored predominantly black settlement houses, most likely viewing them as institutions that had served their time and were now an obstruction to integration.[14] Consequently, he viewed settlements as the means of becoming a democratic society. In 1969, the New Direction Committee of the National Federation of Settlements and Neighborhood Centers reaffirmed the settlements' old commitment to social reform. Still things moved slowly in the South. While the Bethlehem Houses had mixed staffs by the 1940s with white directors, not until 1970 did Wesley House, Centenary Center, and Bethlehem Center merge to form the United Methodist Neighborhood Centers of Nashville.

African American clubwomen created successful communities: encouraged persons to take responsibility for their own lives; provided help to small localities; and provided moral uplift. Black women, who were overwhelmingly descendants of slaves, assumed they could make a difference. They sought to effect moral and social uplift for all African Americans through dedicated collective work. They failed to attack the root of social problems in American society. Along with a small, fragile, black middle class came an economic polarization among African Americans. The black underclass increased as race, class, and gender discrimination limited access to jobs, housing, education, and good salaries.[15]

The critical issue is whether settlement houses should work toward a goal of social change or community service. One theory emphasizes the problems of the individual and sees casework as the solution. The other theory emphasizes the problems of society and sees social reform or social policy as the solution. One scholar argues that transforming society was never the goal of settlement workers.[16] In African American communities social change and community service have been interchangeable concepts. The Neighborhood Union, which Lugenia Hope headed from 1908 to 1933, began with the idea of servicing the poor and developed into a vehicle for self-help and a training ground for grassroots community organizing.[17]

In the 1930s and again in the 1960s African American women banned together in grassroots protest. The grassroots community mobilization of the clubwomen laid the foundation for the civil rights movement of the 1960s. In the civil rights movement of the 1960s, black women took the place they customarily had in social movements, in the vanguard but not as policy-makers. Sociologist Belinda Robinett states that "gender was a defining construct of power relations and shaped the structure of the movement." African American women were "bridge leaders" engaged in the vital functions of recruitment, mobilization, and sustenance in the civil rights movement.[18] Women played a crucial role in the civil rights movement. The clubwomen were the predecessors of black women activists who were interested in the poor and unfortunate in urban ghettos and rural communities. Thus, concomitant with the new emphasis on collective social action to achieve goals, a feminist ideology reemerged among African American women.

Women, black and white, who entered settlement house work adhered to a gendered ideology of reform. The future direction and strategy of community centers and settlement houses in black communities will depend on women. The Harriet Tubman Community Center in New York has played a leading role in community building and race relations for the past seventy years. The community center provided opportunities for African Americans when options were scare or non-existent. When viewing the innovative role of women in the processes of social change and community survival, clearly, without women these racially oppressed communities would not have institutions, organizations, strategies, and ethics that enabled the collective group not only to survive but to challenge the oppressive environment. Through creating their own self-help institutions and organizations, black women generated a set of values that challenged and changed American society. Nevertheless, we should not romanticize black culture and communal solidarity but explore the diversity and complexities of African American women and their historical experiences.

African American clubwomen were motivated by a dual consciousness of racial identity and a sense of American nationhood that led them to accept rather than reject the idea of cultural diversity and a commitment to its ideology of democracy. Can we restructure society to ensure egalitarian pluralism for everyone?   Most African Americans were structurally separated but did not participate on an equal basis in society's political and economic institutions. Among the best means of affecting a social democracy is through the revitalization of community institutions.

This book challenges feminist leaders to organize to realistically pursue egalitarian goals and to meet the diverse social needs dealing with poverty, AIDS, the environment, and other issues in American society. A continuing evolution of social action is needed to effect a pluralistic democratic America. In *Women, Culture, and Politics*, Angela Davis asserts that "We must climb in such a way to guarantee that all of our sisters, regardless of social class, and all of our brothers, climb with us."[19] She feels that we must create a multiracial women's movement that addresses the main issues affecting poor and working-class women. Often to improve local communities and conditions, it is necessary to reach beyond that level to a broader perspective. In this century, the collaborative action of women and some men will direct and pursue a strategy of humanitarian efforts for universal improvement, a common good that is the foundation of our national and global destinies.

Notes

PREFACE

1. Ida Mae Hiram was part of a husband-and-wife dental team in Athens. Her husband was Lace Hiram. The first woman to pass the Georgia Dental Board, she practiced dentistry for fifty-five years. See Frances T. Thomas, *A Portrait of Historic Athens and Clarke County* (Athens: University of Georgia Press, 1992), 161-62. Lace Hiram's sister, Sara "Dee" Hill, did laundry work in her home while helping her brother attend dental school. Sarah Hill was my stepfather's mother. Lace Hiram sent his wife to school after they were married.

2. Dr. Hiram's daughter, Alice Mae Hiram-Wimberly directed a nursery school and kindergarten from their home prior to teaching at the local high school.

3. United States Census and oral history: Daisy Stroud (1891-1981) and Andrew Stroud (1886-1972), married in 1912, were the parents of six children: Thomas, McWhorter, Nellie, Lillie, Mable, and Fannie. Daisy was the daughter of James "Gene" Adams ((1869-1945) and Fannie Middlebrooks (1873-1948). Her paternal and maternal grandparents were Joseph "Joe" Adams and Sibbe "Sybil" Adams; Aaron Middlebrooks and Silla (Middlebrooks). Andrew was the son of Anthony "Andy" Stroud (1844-1915) and Catherine Dean Stroud (1854-1889).

4. Sarah A. Delany, Elizabeth Delany, and Amy Hill Hearth, *Having Our Say; The Delany Sisters' First 100 Years* (New York: Kodansha, 1993), 48.

5. Alice Walker, *In Search of Our Mothers' Garden* (New York: Harcourt Brace Jovanovich, 1983), 17.

CHAPTER 1

1. Anne Firor Scott, "Most Invisible of All: Black Women's Voluntary Associations," *The Journal of Southern History* 56. 1 (February 1990): 3-22.

2. Quoted in Judith P. Zinsser, *History and Feminism: A Glass Half Full* (New York: Twayne, 1993), 81-82.

3. Hazel Carby, *Reconstructring Womanhood: The Emergence of the Afro-American Woman Novelist* (New York: Oxford University Press, 1987), 7.

4. See Anne Firor Scott, *Natural Allies, Women's Associations In American History* (Urbana: University of Illinois Press, 1991).

5. See Robert Weibe, *The Search for Order* (New York: Oxford University Press, 1968).

6. Evelyn Higginbotham, *Righteous Discontent: The Women's Movement in the Black Baptist Church, 1880-1920* (Cambridge: Harvard University Press, 1993), 19-46.

7. Kevin Gaines, *Uplifting the Race: Black Leadership, Politics, and Culture in the Twentieth Century* (Chapel Hill: University of North Carolina Press, 1996).

8. Rayford Logan, *The Negro in the U.S.* (Princeton: D. Van Nostran, 1957), 39.

9. Richard Hofstadter, *Social Darwinism in American Thought* (Boston: Beacon Press, 1955).

10. C. Vann Woodward, *The Strange Career of Jim Crow* (NY: Oxford University Press, 1957).

11. Lee D. Baker, *From Savage to Negro, Anthropology and the Construction of Race, 1896-1954* (Berkeley: University of California Press 1998), 29.

12. Marvin Olasky, *The Tragedy of American Compassion* (Washington, DC: Regnery, 1992), 16.

13. Ralph Luker, *The Social Gospel in Black and White, American Racial Reform, 1885-1912* (Chapel Hill: The University of North Carolina Press, 1991). Church denominations organized the Federal Council of Churches in 1909. Black and white social reformers organized the National Association of Colored People and the National Urban League in 1909 and 1911, respectively. Luker states that a half century later, these and allied organizations formed the institutional core of America's civil rights movement.

14. Mary Terrell, "The Progress of Colored Women," *Voice of the Negro* I (July 1904): 291-94.

15. Ida B. Wells, *Southern Horrors, Lynch Law in all its Phases*, ed. and Introduction by Trudier Harris, *Selected Works by Ida B. Wells*, (New York, Oxford University Press, 1991), 14-45.

16. See Tullia Hamilton's "The National Association of Colored Women, 1896-1920," diss. at Emory University (1978) and Gerda Lerna's *The Majority Finds Its Past: Placing Women in History* (New York: Oxford University Press, 1979).

17. See W. E. B. Du Bois, *Some Efforts of American Negroes for Their Own Social Betterment* (Atlanta, GA: Atlanta University Publications, 1898).

18. Mamie Garvin Fields, *Lemon Swamp and Other Places* (New York: Free Press, 1983), 198.

19. August Meier, "Negro Class Structure and Ideology in the Age of Booker T. Washington," *Phylon* 23 (1962): 259-66. Sharon Harley, "The Middle Class," in *Black Women in America: An Historical Encyclopedia*, ed. Darlene Clark Hine, Elsa Barkley Brown, and Rosalyn Terborg-Penn (Brooklyn, NY: Carlson, 1993), 786-89.

20. Willard Gatewood, *Aristocrats of Color, the Black Elite, 1880-1920* (Bloomington: Indiana University Press, 1990).

21. Stephanie Shaw, *What A Woman Ought to Be and To Do: Black Professional Women Workers during the Jim Crow Era* (Chicago: University of Chicago Press, 1996), 2.

22. Bettye Collier Thomas, "Annie Turnbo Malone," in *Notable Black Women*, ed. Jessie Carney Smith (Detroit: Gale Research, 1992), 727-34. Founder of Poro Beauty College in 1902 and active in the St. Louis club Federation, Thomas maintains that Malone was the first black millionairess.

23. Linda K. Kerber and Jane DeHart, ed., *Women's America: Refocusing the Past* (New York: Oxford University Press, 2000), 265.

24. Barbara Harris, *Beyond Her Sphere: Women and the Professions in American History* (Westport, CT: Greenwood Press, 1978).

25. Glenna Matthews, *The Rise of Public Woman: Woman's Power and Woman's Place in the United States, 1630-1970* (New York: Oxford University Press, 1992), 9.

26. Karen Blair, *The Clubwoman as Feminist: True Womanhood Redefined, 1898-1914* (New York: Holmes and Meier, Inc., 1980).

27. G. M. Young, *Victorian England, Portrait of an Age* (London: Oxford University Press, 1960), 11-17. Davis Harris Wilson, *A History of England* (Hinsdale, Il: The Drysden Press, 1972), 628.

28. Barbara Christian, *Black Feminist Criticism: Perspectives on Black Women Writers* (New York: Pergamon Press, 1985).

29. Elsa Barkley Brown, "Womanist Consciousness: Maggie Lena Walker and the Independent Order of Saint Luke," *Signs* 14.3 (Summer 1989): 610-33.

30. Mary Church Terrell, *A Colored Woman in a White World* (1940; Washington, DC: NACWC, 1968).

31. Patricia Hill Collins, *Black Feminist Thought: Knowledge, Consciousness, and the Politics of Empowerment* (New York: HarperCollins, 1990), 30.

32. Paula Giddings, *When and Where I Enter, The Impact of Black Women on Race and Sex in America* (New York: William Morrow, 1984).

33. belle hooks, *Ain't I a Woman: Black Women and Feminism* (Boston: South End Press, 1981), 7.

34. Deborah Gray White, *Too Heavy a Load, Black Women in Defense of Themselves 1894-1994* (New York: W. W. Norton, 1999).

35. Shaw, *What a Woman Ought to Be and to Do,* 140.

36. Ibid.

37. Cynthia Neverdon-Morton, *Afro-American Women of the South and the Advancement of the Race, 1895-1925* (Knoxville: University of Tennessee Press, 1989), 9.

38. Judith Trolander, *Professionalism and Social Change, from the Settlement House Movement to Neighborhood Centers 1886 to the Present* (New York: Columbia University Press, 1987).

39. Glenda Gilmore, *Gender and Jim Crow: Women and the Politics of White Supremacy in North Carolina, 1895-1920* (Chapel Hill: University of North Carolina Press, 1996).

40. Allen F. Davis, *Spearheads for Reform: The Social Settlements and the Progressive Movement, 1890-1914* (New York: Oxford University Press, 1967). 41. Rivka Shpak Lissak, *Pluralism and Progressives: Hull House and the New Immigrants, 1890-1919* (Chicago: University of Chicago Press, 1989), 4-5.

42. Elizabeth Lasch-Quinn, *Black Neighbors: Race and the Limits of Reform in the Settlement House Movement, 1890-1945* (Chapel Hill: University of North Carolina Press, 1993) 2.

43. Milton Gordon, *Assimilation in American Life: The Role of Race, Religion, and National Origin* (New York: Oxford University Press, 1964.

44. Judith Stein, "Defining the Race, 1890-1930," in *The Invention of Ethnicity*, ed. Werner Sollors (New York: Oxford University Press, 1989), 77-104.

45. "The Conservation of the Races," in *W.E.B. Du Bois: Writings*, ed. Nathan Huggins (1897; New York: Library of America, 1986).

46. Cornel West, *Race Matters* (Boston: Beacon Press, 1993).

47. Evelyn Higginbotham, "African American's Women's History and the Metalanguage of Race," in *"We Specialize in the Wholly Impossible": A Reader in Black Women's History*, ed., Darlene Clark Hine, Wilma King, Linda Reed (Brooklyn, NY: Carlson, 1995): 3-24.

48. See William E. Leuchtenburg, ed., *Franklin D. Roosevelt: A Profile* (New

York: Hill and Wang) 1967. Carl Degler, *Out of Our Past, The Forces that Shaped Modern America* (New York: Harper and Row, 1962). Howard Zinn, *New Deal Thought* (New York: Bobbs-Merrill, 1966).

49. August Meier and Rudwick Elliott, *From Plantation to Ghetto* (New York: Hill and Wang, 1965), 212.

50. Clarke A. Chambers, *Seedtime of Reform: American Social Service and Social Action, 1918-1933* (Minneapolis: University of Minnesota Press, 1963).

CHAPTER 2

1. Inabel Burns Lindsay, "Some Contributions of Negroes to Welfare Services, 1865-1900," *Journal of Negro Education* 25 (Winter 1956): 15-24.

2. Dorothy Porter, "The Organized Educational Activities of Negro Literary Societies, 1828-1846," *Journal of Negro Education*, 5 (October 1936): 556-66.

3. Darlene Clark Hine and Kathleen Thompson, *A Shining Thread of Hope: A History of Black Women in America* (New York: Broadway Books, 1998).

4. Leonard Curry, *The Free Black in Urban America, 1800-1850: The Shadow of a Dream* (Chicago: The University of Chicago Press, 1981), 110.

5. Paula Giddings, *When and Where I Enter, the Impact of Black Women on Race and Sex in America* (New York: William Morrow, 1986).

6. Ann M. Boylan, "Benevolence and Antislavery Activity Among African American Women in New York and Boston 1820-1840," in *The Abolitionist Sisterhood: Women's Political Culture in Antebellum America*, ed. Jean Fagan Yellin and John Van Horne (New York: Cornell University Press, 1994), 119-38.

7. James Horton, *Free People of Color: Inside the African American Community* (Washington, DC, Smithsonian Press, 1993).

8. Linda Perkins, "Black Women and Racial Uplift prior to Emancipation," in *The Black Woman Cross Culturally*, ed. Filomina Steady, (Cambridge: Schenkman, 1981), 317-34.

9. Curry, *The Free Black in Urban America*.

10. Benjamin Quarles, *Black Abolitionists* (New York: Collier Macmillan, 1987), 101-2.

11. *New York Freedman's Journal* (February 1828).

12. Ann Firor Scott, *Natural Allies, Women's Associations in American History* (Urbana: University of Illinois Press, 1991), 14.

13. Constitution of the Abyssinian Benevolent Daughters of Esther Association, New York City.

14. Horton, *Free People of Color*.

15. Porter, "The Organized Educational Activities of Negro Literary Societies, 1828-1846," 555-76.

16. Maria W. Stewart, "Religion and the Pure Principles of Morality, the Sure Foundation on Which We Must Build" (1831), 22 pages. Marilyn Richardson, *Maria W. Stewart, America's First Black Woman Political Writer* (Bloomington: Indiana University Press, 1987), 22.

17. Ruth Bogin and Bert James Lowenberg, eds., *Black Women in Nineteenth-Century American Life: Their Words, Their Thoughts, Their Feelings* (University Park: Pennsylvania State University Press, 1976), 183-84. Perkins, "Black Women and Racial Uplift prior to Emancipation."

18. Horton, *Free People of Color*, 109.

19. Audrey Johnson, "Catherine (Katy) Ferguson," in *Black Women in America:*

An Historical Encyclopedia, ed. Darlene Clark Hine, Elsa Barkley Brown, Rosalyn Terborg-Penn (Brooklyn, New York: Carlson, 1993), 426. Catherine A. Latimer, "Catherine Ferguson, Black Founder of a Sunday School," *Negro History Bulletin* 5 (November 1941): 38-9. Allen Hartnick, "Catherine Ferguson," *Negro History Bulletin* 35 (December 1977): 176-77.

20. Eugene Kinckle Jones, " Social Work Among Negroes," *The Annals of Political and Social Science* 140 (November 1928): 287-93.

21. Ibid.

22. Robert Bremner, *The Public Good: Philanthropy and Welfare in the Civil War Era* (New York: Alfred K. Knopf, 1980).

23. Marable Manning, *Race, Reform, and Rebellion: The Second Reconstruction in Black America, 1945-1990* (Jackson: University of Mississippi Press, 1991), 11-12.

24. Walter Trattner, *From Poor Law to Welfare State: A History of Social Welfare in America* (New York: Free Press, 1974).

25. William S. McFeely, "Unfinished Business: The Freedmen's Bureau and Federal Action in Race Relations," in *Key Issues in the Afro-American Experience*, ed. Nathan Huggins, Martin Kilson, and Daniel Fox (New York: Harcourt Brace Jovanovich, 1971), 5-25.

26. "The Howard Orphan Asylum," *The Colored American Magazine* 10 (April 1906): 238-43.

27. Gussie Mims Logan, "The Carrie Steel Orphanage," *The Voice of the Negro* 1:11 (November 1904): 538-40. Cynthia Neverdon-Morton, *Afro-American Women of the South and the Advancement of the Race, 1895-1925* (Knoxville: University of Tennessee Press, 1996), 143-44.

28. "Charitable Institutions," in *Progress of a Race*, ed. William H. Crogman and John Gibson (Naperville, Il: J. L. Nicholas, 1929), 43-46. "Negro Women and Their Work," in *The Story of the Negro*, Booker T. Washington, II (1909; Gloucester, MA: Peter Smith, 1969), 309.

29. Neverdon-Morton, *Afro-American Women,* 144-45. Herman Mason, ed., *Going against the Wind* (Marietta, GA: Longstreet Press, 1992), 27.

30. "Amanda Smith-Negro Woman Evangelist," in *Great Women of Christian Faith*, Edith Deen (Chappaqua, NY: Christian Herald Books, 1959), 232-39. William Andrews, ed., *Sisters of the Spirit: Three Black Women Autobiographies of the Nineteenth Century* (Bloomington: Indiana University Press, 1986), 3.

31. Wanda A. Hendricks, *Gender, Race, and Politics in the Midwest, Black Club Women in Illinois* (Bloomington: Indiana University Press, 1998), 45-46.

32. Elizabeth L. Davis, *The Story of the Illinois Federation of Colored Women's Clubs,* 1900-1912 (Washington, D.C., 1922) 102-3.

33. Howard Rabinowitz, *Race Relations in the Urban South, 1865-1890* (Urbana: University of Illinois Press, 1980), 125-26.

34. Bettina Aptheker, *Woman's Legacy, Essays on Race, Sex, and Class in American History* (Amherst: University of Massachusetts Press, 1982), 104.

35. Interview by the author with Allen Garcia, grandson of Mary Bailey, 1991.

36. Aptheker, *Woman's Legacy*, 30.

37. William Seraile, "Susan McKinney Stewart: New York State's First African American Woman Physician," *Afro-Americans in New York Life and History* 9.2 (July 1985): 27-44.

38. Sarah W. Brown, "Colored Women Physicians," *The Southern Workman* 52.12 (December 1923): 580-89.

39. Aptheker, *Woman's Legacy*, 104-5.

40. "Death of Mrs. Peake," *American Missionary* (April 1862): 83. John Hope Franklin and Alfred A. Moss, *From Slavery to Freedom*, 6th ed. (New York: McGraw-Hill, 1988), 184. Carter G. Woodson, *The Education of the Negro Prior to 1861* (New York: G. P. Putnam's Sons, 1915).

41. Bettye Collier-Thomas, "Frances Ellen Watkins Harper: Abolitionist and Feminist Reformer, 1825-1911," in *African American Women and the Vote, 1837-1965*, ed. Ann Gordon et al. (Amherst: University of Massachusetts Press, 1997), 41-65.

42. Francis Ellen Watkins Harper, "Colored Women of America," *Englishmen's Review* (15 January 1878): 10-15. Bogin and Lowenberg, *Black Women in Nineteenth-Century American Life*, 243-44.

43. Glenna Matthews, *The Rise of Public Woman: Woman's Power and Woman's Place in the United States, 1630-1970* (New York, Oxford University Press, 1992), 116.

44. Giddings, *When and Where I Enter*, 72.

45. Linda Perkins, *Fanny Jackson Coppin and the Institute for Colored Youth, 1865-1902* (New York: Garland Press, 1987).

46. Leonard G. Davis, "Issues on Survival Techniques," in *The Politics of Black Self-help in the United States: A Historical Overview in Black Organizations*, ed., Lennox Yearwood (Washington, DC: University, 1980), 37-50.

47. See Jacqueline Jones, *Soldiers of Light and Love, Northern Teachers and Georgia Blacks, 1865-1873* (Chapel Hill: The University of North Carolina Press, 1980).

48. Daniel C. Thompson, *A Black Elite: A Profile of Graduates of UNCF Colleges* (Westport, CT: Greenwood Press, 1986), 5. Samuel Du Bois Cook, "The Socio-Ethical Role and Responsibility of Black College Graduates," in ed. Charles Willie and Edmonds, *Black Colleges in America: Challenge, Development, Survival (New York: Teachers College Press, 1978)*, 54-55.

49. Herbert Gutman, *The Black Family in Slavery and Freedom, 1750-1925* (New York: Vintage, 1976), 34. Higginbotham, *Righteous Discontent*, 42-6.

50. Charles Valentine, *Culture and Poverty: Critique and CounterProposals* (Chicago: University of Illinois Press, 1968).

51. Lawrence Levine, *Black Culture and Black Consciousness Afro-American Folk Thought from Slavery to Freedom* (New York: Oxford University Press, 1977).

52. Higginbotham, *Righteous Discontent*, 31-40. See Florence Read, *The Story of Spelman College* (Princeton, NJ: Princeton University Press, 1961). Beverly Guy-Sheftall and Jo Moore Stewart, *Spelman: Centennial Celebration, 1881-1981* (Atlanta, GA: Spelman College, 1981).

53. Bremner, *The Public Good: Philanthropy and Welfare*, 212.

54. John A. Fisher, *The John F. Slater Fund: A Nineteenth Century Affirmative Action for Negro Education* (New York: University Press of America, 1986).

55. Elizabeth Jacoway, *Yankee Missionaries in the South, the Penn School Experiment* (Baton Rouge: Louisiana State University Press, 1980).

56. W. E. B. Du Bois, *The Souls of Black Folk* (New York: Fawcett, 1961).

57. Higginbotham, *Righteous Discontent*, 19-46.

58. Kathleen C. Berkeley, "Colored Ladies also Contributed: Black Women's Activities from Benevolence to Social Welfare, 1866-1896," in *The Web of Southern Relations: Women, Family, and Education, ed. Walter J. Fraser, R. Frank Saunders, and Jon Wakelyn* (Athens: University of Georgia Press, 1985).

59. Pauline Parker (president, Concord Baptist Church of Christ) "The Dorcas History," three-page typescript.

60. Edyth Ross, ed., *Black Heritage in Social Welfare*, 1860-1930 (Metuchen, NJ: Scarecrow Press, 1978).

61. Elsa Barkley Brown, "Womanist Consciousness: Maggie Lena Walker and the Independent Order of Saint Luke," *Signs* 14.3 (Summer 1989): 610-33.

62. Ralph E. Luker, "Missions, Institutional Churches, and Settlement Houses: The Black Experience, 1885-1910," *Journal of Negro History* 69:3,4 (Summer/Fall 1984): 101-113.

63. "The Colored Mission," *Charities: A Weekly Review of Local and General Philanthropy* (18 January 1902): 67. Gilbert Osofsky, *Harlem: The Making of a Ghetto, Negro New York, 1890-1930* (New York: Harper and Row, 1971), 54-55.

64. Inabel Burns Lindsay, "Some Contributions of Negroes," *Journal of Negro History*, (1956): 15-24.

65. Dorothy Salem, "To Better Our World, Black Women in Organized Reform, 1890-1920," (diss., Kent State University, 1986), 12.

CHAPTER 3

1. William H. Crogman and John Gibson, eds., *Progress of a Race* (Naperville, IL: J. L. Nicholas, 1929), 190.

2. *The National Association Notes* (July 1904).

3. Fannie Barrier Williams, "The Club Movement Among Colored Women of America," in *A New Negro for a New Century,* ed. Booker T. Washington, (Chicago: American Publishing House, 1900).

4. Josephine Silone Yates, "The National Association of Colored Women," *The Voice of the Negro* I (July 1904): 283-87.

5. Mary Terrell, "The Progress of Colored Women," *The Voice of the Negro* I (July 1904): 291-94.

6. Willard Gatewood, *Aristocrats of Color: The Black Elite, 1880-1920* (Bloomington: Indiana University Press, 1990).

7. Interview by the author with Daisy Lee Shaw, retired elementary schoolteacher and and piano teacher, age ninety-one, assisted by A. Mildred Hill, Athens, GA, March 1997.

8. Stephanie Shaw, *What a Woman Ought to Be and to Do: Black Professional Women workers during the Jim Crow Era* (Chicago: The University of Chicago Press, 1996), 124.

9. Paula Giddings, *When and Where I Enter: The Impact of Black Women on Race and Sex in America* (New York: William Morrow, 1984) 113.

10. Christine Smith, "The Larger Life for Women," *National Association Notes* (May/June 1915).

11. "The David T. Howard Family," *The Negro History Bulletin* 17.3 (December 1953): 51-5.

12. John Cromwell, " Bethel Literary and Historical Association," Paper read before the association, 24 February 1896, Washington, DC..

13. Mary Helen Washington, *Invented Lives: Narratives of Black Women, 1860-1960* (New York: Doubleday, 1987), 74-5.

14. Anna Julia Cooper, "The American Negro Academy," *Southern Workman* 27 (1910): 11-12. Alfred A. Moss, *The American Negro Academy, Voice of the Talented Tenth* (Baton Rouge: Louisiana University Press, 1981), 78-79.

15. Monroe Majors, *Noted Negro Women: Their Triumphs and Activities* (1893; Salem: Ayer, 1986).

16. See Alfreda Duster, *Crusade for Justice: The Autobiography of Ida B. Wells* (Chicago: University of Chicago Press, 1970).

17. *The Woman's Era,* (December 1894).

18. Interview by the author with Elizabeth Bowers, granddaughter of Carrie Fortune, Sag Harbor, 1995. Fortune, who married at sixteen, supported herself and her two children through her sewing after she and her husband separated in 1906 due to his severe depression and alcoholism. See Emma Lou Thornbrough, *T. Thomas Fortune: Militant Journalist* (Chicago: University of Chicago Press, 1972).

19. *The Woman's Era,* (March 1898).

20. Hallie Q. Brown, *Homespun Heroines and Other Women of Distinction* (1926; New York: Oxford University Press, 1988), 110-14.

21. Dorothy Sterling, ed., *We Are Your Sisters: Black Women in the Nineteenth Century* (New York: Norton Press, 1984). The Harry A.Williamson Papers, Schomburg Center for Research in Black Culture, New York Public Library.

22. "The Woman's Era Club," *The Woman's Era*, (March 1894).

23. Wilson Jeremiah Moses, *The Golden Age of Black Nationalism, 1850-1925* (New York: Oxford University Press, 1978), 107-108.

24. Elizabeth Davis, *Lifting As They Climb* (Washington, DC: NACW, 1933). Adelaide Hill, "Josephine St. Pierre Ruffin," in *Notable American Women, 1607-1950,* ed. Edward James, Janet James, and Paul Boyer, vol. 3 (Cambridge: Belknap Press of Harvard, 1971).

25. *The Woman's Era,* (March 1894).

26. Inabel Burns Lindsay, "Some Contributions of Negroes," *Journal of Negro History* 25 (Winter 1956): 15-24.

27. Louise Daniel Hutchinson, "Anna J. Cooper," in *A Voice From the South* (Washington, DC: Smithsonian Institute Press, 1981), 85-101.

28. Duster, *Crusade for Justice,* 48.

29. *The National Association Notes,* (July 1904). Anne Meis Knupfer, *Toward A Tenderer Humanity and A Nobler Womanhood: African American Women's Clubs in Turn-of-the-Century Chicago* (New York: New York University Press, 1996).

30. Miriam De Costa-Willis, ed., *The Memphis Diary of Ida B. Wells* (Boston: Beacon Press, 1995), 21.

31. Giddings, *When and Where I Enter*, 17-34.

32. De Costa-Willis, *The Memphis Diary of Ida B. Wells*.

33. *A History of the Club Movement Among the Colored Women of the United States of America* (1902; Washington, DC: NACW, 1978), 13.

34. Ibid., 15-27.

35. "Preamble, Constitution, Act of Incorporation-Colored Woman's League of Washington, DC," Mary Church Terrell Papers.

36. Richard T. Greener, "Greener Paper" This paper consists of notes taken at the Boston Conference of 1895 by Greener, Manuscript Collection, Boston Public Library.

37. Eleanor Flexner and Ellen Fitzpatrick, *Century of Struggle, The Woman's Rights Movement in the United States* (Cambridge: Harvard University Press, 1996), 179.

38. See Bert Loewenberg and Ruth Bogin, *Black Women in Nineteenth-Century American Life* (University Park: Pennsylvania State University Press, 1976).

39. Charlotte E. Martin, *The Story of Brockport for One Hundred Years, 1829-1929,* (Brockport, New York: Brockport Historical Society, 1962), Seymour Library. Wanda Hendricks, *Gender, Race, and Politics in the Midwest, Black Club Women in Illinois* (Bloomington: University of Indiana Press, 1998), 4-7. Charles Lemert and Esme Bhan, ed. *The Voice of Anna Julia Cooper* (Lanham, MD: Rowman and Littlefield, 1998), 201.

40. Fannie Williams, "The Intellectual Progress of Colored Women Since

Emancipation," World's Congress Auxiliary of the World's Columbian Exposition, 1893, in *The World's Congress of Representative Women*, ed. May Wright Sewall   (New York: Rand, McNally, 1894).

41. Anna Julia Cooper, "The Needs and Status of Black Women," in *The World's Congress of Representative Women*, 700-2.

42. Nancie Caraway, *Segregated Sisterhood: Racism and the Politics of American Feminism* (Knoxville: University of Tennessee Press, 1991), 164.

43. Hazel Carby, *Reconstructing Womanhood: The Emergence of the Afro-American Woman Novelist* (New York: Oxford University Press, 1987), 69-70.

44. "Address of Josephine St. Pierre Ruffin," *The Woman's Era*, (August 1895): 13-15.

45. Carby, *Reconstructing Womanhood*, 117.

46. *A History of the Club Movement*, 11-29.

47. "A Call, Let Us Confer Together." *A History the Club Movement*, 3-5.

48. Rayford Logan, *The Betrayal of the Negro* (New York: Collier Books, 1963), 250.

49. See Patricia Hill Collins, *Black Feminist Thought* (New York: HarperCollins, 1990).

50. Henry Louis Gates, "The Face and Voice of Blackness," in *Facing History: The Black Image in American Art, 1710-1940*, ed. Guy C. McElroy (Washington, DC: Bedford Art and the Corcoran Gallery of Art, 1990).

51. Darlene Clark Hine, "Rape and the Inner Lives of Black Women in the Middle West: Preliminary Thoughts on the Culture of Dissemblance." *Signs* 14 (Summer 1989): 912-20.

52. Josephine Ruffin, "Address before the Conference of Colored Women," in *A History of the Club Movement*, 31-34.

53. *The Woman's Era*, (August 1896). "The Boston Convention of 1895," Boston Public Library.

54. Greener, "Greener Paper."

55. "Call to the National Federation of Afro-American Women," *The Woman's Era* (November 1895).

56. Mrs. Booker T. Washington, "The New Negro Woman," *Lend-a- Hand* 15 (October 1895): 254-60 (paper read).

57. *A History of the Club Movement.*

58. Victoria Earle Matthews, "Value of Race Literature," an Address before the first Convention of African American Women, Boston, 1895.

59. Davis, *Lifting As They Climb*, 23-4. Alice Bacon, *The Negro and the Atlanta Exposition*, Occasional Papers, No. 7, Hampton Institution, 1896, 10-2.

60. See James H. Timberlake, *Prohibition and the Progressive Movement, 1900-1920* (New York: Atheneum Press, 1970), 120-21.

61. Flexner and Fitzpatrick, 176-77.

62. "The Woman's Christian Temperance Union and the Colored Woman," *AME Church Review* (1888). Pauline Hopkins, "Famous women of the Negro Race," *Crisis Magazine* (April 1902): 366-71.

63. Ruth Bordin, *Women and Temperance: The Quest for Power, 1873-1900* (Philadelphia: Temple University Press, 1981), 83.

64. Duster, *Crusade for Justice*, 209. Editorial, *Woman's Era*, (July 1895): 12.

65. Lee Baker, *From Savage to Negro: Anthropology and the Construction of Race, 1896-1954* (Berkeley: University of California Press, 1998), 60-62.

66. Mrs. Arthur S. Gray, "The Negro at the Atlanta Exposition," *The Woman's*

Era (January 1896): 7-10.

66. 67. Nancie Caraway, *Segregated Sisterhood, Racism and the Politics of American Feminism* (Knoxville: The University of Tennessee Press 1991), 164.

68. Samuel Spencer, *Booker T. Washington and the Negro's Place in American Life* (Boston: Little, Brown , 1955), 93.

69. See E. Merton Coulter, *Georgia, A Short History* (Chapel Hill: University of North Carolina Press, 1960), 410-411.

70. "The First Annual Convention of the National Federation of Afro-American Women," *Bulletin*, Boston Public Library.

71. *The Woman's Era*, (June 1896): 7.

72. Emma Lou Thornbrough, *T. Thomas Fortune: Militant Journalist* (Chicago: University of Chicago Press, 1972), 107.

73. Editorial, "Our Women," *Washington Bee*, July 1896.

74. *The Woman's Era* (August/September, 1896): 3.

75. Editorial, "Report to the Association," *National Association Notes*, (January 1903): 5.

76. *A History of the Club Movement*, 31-33.

77. Greener, " Greener Paper"

78. Richard Hofstadter, *The Age of Reform* (New York: Vintage Books, 1955), 135-36. "Jane Addams: The College Woman and the Family Claim," in *The New Radicalism in America, 1889-1963, ed.* Christopher Lasch (New York: Vintage Books, 1965), 3-37.

79. Flexner and Fitzpatrick, *Century of Struggle*, 178.

80. Williams, "The Club Movement among Colored Women of America," 379-428.

81. Williams, Fannie Barrier, "Club Movement among Negro Women." 197-231.

CHAPTER 4

1. Mary Church Terrell, First Address as President of the NACW. *The Woman's Era* (August/September 1896): 3.

2. Mary Church Terrell, Address as President of the NACW, Nashville, TN, September 1897, Terrell Papers, Library of Congress.

3. Patricia Hill Collins, *Black Feminist Thought* (NY: HarperCollins, 1990), 96. Gerda Lerner, *The Creation of Feminist Consciousness* (New York: Oxford University Press, 1993), 232.

4. Anna H. Jones, "How We as Women Can Advance the Standing of the Race," *The National Association Notes* (July 1904).

5. Anna H. Jones, "The American Colored Woman," *The Voice of the Negro* (October 1905): 692-94.

6. Mary Parrish, *Fourth Statistical Report of the National Association of Colored Women* (Louisville, KY: American Baptist Press, 1914), 62 pp.

7. Gerda Lerner, *The Majority Finds Its Past: Placing Women in History* (NY: Oxford University Press, 1979) 86.

8. St. Clair Drake and Horace R. Clayton, *Black Metropolis, A Study of Negro Life in a Northern City* (Chicago: The University of Chicago Press, Chicago: the University of Chicago Press, 1970), 394-95.

9. Cheryl Townsend Gilkes, "If It Wasn't for the Women: African American Women, Community Work, and Social Change," in *Women of Color in U.S. Society*, ed. Maxine Baca Zinn and Bonnie Thornton Dill (Philadelphia: Temple University Press, 1994),

229-46.

10. Elizabeth Davis, *Lifting As They Climb* (Washington, DC: NACW, Inc., 1933). Tullia Hamilton, "The National Association of Colored Women, 1896-1920 " (diss., Emory University, 1972).

11. "A Club Model," *The Woman's Era* (November 1895), 10.

12. Margaret Washington, "Synopsis of the Lecture on the Organization of Women's Clubs," 22 June 1910, Mary Murray Washington Papers, Hollis Burke Frissell Library, Tuskegee University.

13. Letter to Mrs. H. R. Halloway, Plainfield, NJ, from Mrs. Booker T. Washington, 6 December 1895, Margaret Murray Washington Papers.

14. Victoria Earle Matthews, "Work before Our Women: Appeal by the National Organization of Colored Women," 1-4, Moorland-Spingarn Collection, Howard University Library.

15. Davis, *Lifting As They Climb*, 22.

16. Mary Terrell, "What Role Is the Educated Negro Woman to Play in the Uplifting of Her Race" In *Twentieth Century Negro Literature*, D. W. Culp (1902: Miami, FL: Mnemosyne, 1969), 172-77.

17. Josephine Silone Yates, *The National Association of Colored Women* 1.7 (July 1904): 283-87. Emily Williams, "The National Association of Colored Women," *Southern Workman* 43 (December 1914): 481-93.

18. Harold Courlander, *Negro Folk Music, U.S.A.* (New York: Columbia University Press, 1963; Dover Books, 1991). Eileen Southern, *The Music of Black Americans: A History* (New York: W. W. Norton, 1971), 225-28.

19. W.E.B. Du Bois, "Women's Clubs," in *Efforts for Social Betterment Among Negro Americans* (Atlanta, GA: Atlanta University Publications, 1909), 47-8.

20. Mattie Ford, "The Atlanta Woman's Club," *The National Association Notes* (April/May 1917).

21. *The National Association Notes*, (July 1904).

22. Rosa Bowser, "What Role Is the Educated Negro Woman To Play in the Uplifting of Her Race?," in *Twentieth Century Negro Literature*, ed. D. W. Culp (1902: Miami, FL: Mnemosyne, 1969), 177-82.

23. *The National Association Notes* (1915).

24. Addie Hunton, "The National Association of Colored Women," *Crisis Magazine* 1 (May 1911): 16-7.

25. *Atlanta Daily World*, 26 September 1941.

26. "Club Notes," *National Notes* (February 1900).

27. Convention of the Southern Federation, *National Association Notes* (February 1902).

28. *The National Association Notes* (June 1912).

29. E. W. A. Brooks, "Tribute for Harriet Tubman," Schomburg Center for Research and Black Culture, New York Public Library. Al Cohn, "Money Woes Revisit an Ex-Slave's Church," New York *Newsday,* 23 October 1983, 8.

30. Obituary, "Harriet Tubman Dies Monday at Auburn, New York" *New York Age*, 13 March 1913. "Report of the Empire State Federation of Women's Clubs," *The National Association Notes* (March/April 1915).

31. The Empire State Federation of Women's Clubs, Inc. designated 11 July 1974 Harriet Tubman Day. The clubwomen made a pilgrimage to the historic site, planted a tree, placed a wreath on her grave, and dedicated themselves to her philosophy. "Women's Clubs Pay Homage," *Syracuse Gazette*, 12 July 1974, 12.

32. *The National Association Notes* (February 1912): 16. Josephine Washington, "Some Things Our Women Are Doing," *The National Association Notes* (November 1913).

33. Davis, *Lifting As They Climb*, 338. J. E. Davis, "Fertilizing Barren Souls, the Industrial Home School for Delinquent Colored Girls of Virginia," *The Southern Workman* (1914), 463-73.

34. Hamilton, "The National Association of Colored Women," 72.

35. "Convention Minutes and Program," National Association of Colored Women, 1914, Biennial Convention, Mary Church Terrell Papers, Howard University.

36. Davis, *Lifting As They Climb*, 56.

37. Mrs. Arthur S. Gray, "The Negro at the Atlanta Exposition," *The Woman's Era* (1895), 7-10.

38. See, Gladys-Marie Fry, "Harriet Powers: Portrait of a Black Quilter," in *Missing Pieces: Georgia Folk Art 1776-1976* (Georgia: Georgia Council for the Arts, 1976), 16-23. Marie Jeanne Adams, "The Harriet Powers Pictorial Quilts," *Black Arts* 3.4 (1979):12-28.

39. Charles Cuthberth Hall, *The Bulletin of Atlanta University* (April 1908). Robert T. Handy, *A History of Union Theological Seminary in New York* (New York: Columbia University Press, 1987).

40. *National Association Notes* (5 August 1914).

41. "Financial Considerations and Facts," Moorland-Spingarn Collection.

42. "Many Attend Dedication of the Douglass Home," *Washington Tribune*, 17 August 1922.

43. August Meier and Elliot Rudwick, *From Plantation to Ghetto. An Interpretive History of American Negroes* (New York: Hill and Wang, 1966), 176.

44. A'Lelia Bundles, *Madam C. J. Walker: Entrepreneur* (New York: Chelsea House, 1991. Walter Fisher, *Notable American Women*, ed. Edward James, Janet James, and Paul Boyer 3 (Cambridge: Belknap Press of Harvard University, 1971), 533-35; "Madam C.J. Walker to Her Daughter A'Lelia Walker-the Last Letter," *Sage* (Fall 1984):45-55. A'Lelia Bundles, "Madam C.J. Walker," *Ms. Magazine* (July 1983): 91-4.

45. Beverly Washington Jones, *Quest for Equality, The Life and Writings of Mary Church Terrell, 1863-1954* (New York: Carlson, 1990), 22.

46. "Negro Club Women Meet," Chicago *Tribune*, 15 August 1899. "To Aid the Negro," Chicago *Times Herald*, 15 August 1899. *The National Association Notes*, December 1911.

47. *The National Association Notes* (July 1918).

48. Alfreda Duster, ed., *Crusade for Justice: The Autobiography of Ida B. Wells* (Chicago: University of Chicago Press, 1970) 258. "Fannie Barrier Williams," in *Dictionary of American Negro Biography*, ed. Rayford Logan and Michael R. Winston (New York: W. W. Norton, 1983), 656.

49. Davis, *Lifting As They Climb*, 46-7.

50. Allan Spear, *Black Chicago: The Making of a Negro Ghetto, 1890-1920* (Chicago: University of Chicago Press, 1967), 66-69.

51. August Meier, *Negro Thought in America 1880-1915* (Ann Arbor:University of Michigan Press, 1978), 100-18.

52. Vincent P. Franklin, *Living Our Stories, Telling Our Truths: Autobiography and the Making of the African-American Intellectual Tradition* (New York: Scribner Press, 1995), 79.

53. Meier, *Negro Thought*, 239-40. Spear, *Black Chicago*, 59.

54. "Colored Women in a Row," Chicago *Chronicle*, 17 August 1899.

55. "Election in Colored Women's Convention Breeds Trouble," *Chicago Tribune*, 17 August 1899.

56. "Negro Club Women Meet," *Chicago Tribune*, 15 August 1899. "To Aid the Negro," *Chicago Times Herald*, 15 August 1899.

57. "The Colored Women's Clubs," *Chicago Tribune*, 16 August 1899. *Chicago InterOcean*, 18 August 1899. *Chicago Sunday Times*, 21 August 1899.

58. Kathy Russell, Midge Wilson, and Ronald Hall, *The Color Complex: The Politics of Skin Color among African Americans* (New York: Harcourt Brace Jovanovich, 1992), 24-40.

59. Nannie Burroughs, "Not Color but Character," *Voice of the Negro* 1. 7 (July 1904): 277-79.

60. "Colored Women's Convention," *Detroit Journal*, 1906.

61. Wilson Jeremiah Moses, *The Golden Age of Black Nationalism, 1850-1925* (New York: Oxford University Press, 1978), 125.

62. Paula Giddings, *When and Where I Enter, the Impact of Black Women on Race and Sex in America* (New York: William Morrow, 1984), 95.

63. Anne Meis Knupfer, Toward a Tenderer Humanity and a Nobler Womanhood, African American Women's Clubs in Turn-of-the-Century Chicago (New York: New York University Press, 1996), 12-13.

64. Mary Terrell, "What Role Is the Educated Woman to Play in the Uplifting of Her Race?" in *Twentieth Century Negro Literature*, ed. D. W. Culp (1902; Miami, FL: Mnemosyne, 1969), 172-77.

65. See Nancy A. Hewitt, "Beyond the Search for Sisterhood: American Women's History in the 1980s," *Social History* 10 (March 1985): 299-321.

66. Sharon Harley, "For the Good of Family and Race: Gender, Work, and Domestic Roles in the Black Community, 1888-1930," in *Black Women in America: Social Science Perspectives*, ed. Micheline R. Malson, Elisabeth Mudimbe-Boyi, Jean F. O'Barr, and Mary Wyer (Chicago: University of Chicago Press, 1988): 159-72.

67. Mary Church Terrell, *A Colored Woman in a White World* (1940; Washington, DC: NACWC, 1968), 157-58.

68. Fannie Barrier Williams, "Club Movement among Negro Women," *Progress of a Race*, ed. Gibson, 216-8.

69. "Ruffin Incident at the Fifth Biennial of the General Federation," *National Association Notes* (November 1900). "Ruffin Incident," *Milwaukee Daily News*, 6 June 1900, 1. *Milwaukee Daily News*, 8 June 1900, 1. *Milwaukee Daily News*, 5 June 1900, 4.

70. Mary Church Terrell, "What Colored Women Want," *The National Association Notes* (November 1900).

71. The National Council of Women of the United States, NCW Papers, New York Public Library.

72. Adella Hunt Logan, "Why the National Association of Colored Women Should Become a Part of the National Council of Women," *The National Association Notes* (December 1899). *The National Association Notes* (November 1900). Josephine Silone Yates, "A Personal Letter from Our President," *National Association Notes* (January 1901).

73. *The National Association Notes* (July 1918).

74. Alice Dunbar-Nelson's biographer, Gloria T. Hull notes that she was fired from her position in the high school because of her independent lifestyle and political activities. See Gloria Hull, ed., *Give Us Each Day: The Diary of Alice Dunbar-Nelson*, New Yori: W. W. Norton, 1984.

75. "Woman's Club Notes," *Half-Century Magazine* (September/October 1918): 11.

76. Letter from Laura Jean Williamson Rollicks to Mrs. Bertram Baker, n.d. Courtesy of Mrs. Bertram Baker, New York, 12 September 1985.

77. Elizabeth L. Davis, *The Story of the Illinois Federation of Colored Women's Clubs, 1900-1922* (Chicago: Illinois Writers Project, 1922).

78. "A Conference of Negro Women," *The Survey* 40 (3 August 1918): 513-4.

79. "An Appeal to Colored Women," *Brooklyn Standard Union,* 19 October 1917.

80. "Negro Women Entering Trades and Business," *New York Post,* 1917.

81. "Negro Women in New York Industry," *New York Post,* 21 March 1919.

82. Glenda Gilmore, *Gender and Jim Crow, Women and the Politics of White Supremacy in North Carolina, 1896-1920* (Chapel Hill: University of North Carolina Press, 1996), 199.

83. L. H. Hammond, *Southern Women Racial Adjustment* (1917; 2d ed., Lynchburg, VA: J. P. Bell, 1920), 1-6, 9-27, CIC Papers, Atlanta University Center.

84. Ann Firor Scott, *The Southern Lady, from Pedestal to Politics, 1830-1930* (Chicago: University of Chicago Press, 1970), 195.

85. Jacqueline Dowd Hall, *Revolt Against Chivalry, Jessie Daniel Ames and the Campaign Against Lynching* (New York: Columbia University Press, 1979), 70.

86. Mrs. W. A. Newell, *Handbook for Interracial Committees* (Nashville, TN: Woman's Department, Board of Missions M.E. Church South), CIC Papers.

87. Minutes of the Twelfth Convention of the NACW, 12-16 July, 1920, Tuskegee Institute, AL, Mary Church Terrell Papers, Howard University.

88. *The National Association Notes* (October, November, December 1920.

89. Margaret Washington, "The Negro Home," address at the Interracial Conference, Memphis, TN, 1-7 October 1920, Margaret Murray Washington Papers, Hollis Frissell Library, Tuskegee University, AL.

90. "A Biography of Charlotte Hawkins Brown," n. d. Charlotte Hawkins Brown Papers. Edna Arter, "Biographical Sketch of Mrs. C. H. Brown," *The Woman's Missionary Magazine of the United Presbyterian Church* 64.1 (August 1930), Charlotte Hawkins Brown Papers, Schlesinger Library, Radcliffe College, Cambridge, MA.

91. "What the Negro Woman Asks of the White Women of North Carolina," May 1920, excerpts of address delivered by Mrs. Charlotte Hawkins Brown, 2, Charlotte Hawkins Brown Papers.

92. Monroe Work, *The Negro Year Book* (Tuskegee: Negro Year Book, 1921/1922), 125.

93. Hall, *Revolt Against Chivalry*, 100-02.

94. Gerda Lerner, "Early Community Work of Black Club Women," *The Journal of Negro History* 59.2 (April 1974): 158-67. Robert Moton, "Negro Women in America, a Study in Inter-racial Co-operation," *Southern Workman* (December 1922): 573-81.

95. Judia C. Jackson Harris, *Race Relations* (Athens: GA, June 1925), 1-16.

96. *Thirty Years of Lynching in the United States, 1889-1918* (1919; New York: Arno Press, 1969), 7.

97. Glenda Elizabeth Gilmore, *Gender and Jim Crow: Women and the Politics of White Supremacy in North Carolina, 1896-1920* (Chapel Hill: University of North Carolina Press, 1996), 202-04.

98. *The National Association Notes* (1912).

99. Rosalyn Terborg-Penn, "Discrimination against Afro-American Women In The Woman's Movement, 1830-1920," in *The Afro-American Woman: Struggles and Images,* ed. Rosalyn Terborg-Penn and Sharon Harley (Port Washington, NY: Choanocyte Press, 1978), 17-27.

100. Giddings, *When and Where I Enter*, 166.

101. Rosalyn Terborg-Penn, *"African American and the Vote: An Overview,"* in *African American Women and the Vote, 1837-1965*, ed. Ann Gordon et al. (Amherst: University of Massachusetts Press, 1997), 14.

102. Giddings, *When and Where I Enter*, 166-68.

103. Bobby L. Lovett, *The African American History of Nashville, Tennessee, 1780-1930, Elites and Dilemmas* (Fayetteville: University of Arkansas Press, 1999), 231-36.

104. Jessie Fauset, "The Thirteenth Biennial of the N.A.C.W." *Crisis Magazine* 24 (October 1922): 257-60.

105. "A Call to Action to Colored Voters of America," Mary Church Terrell papers. Evelyn Higginbotham, "Club Women and Electoral Politics in the 1920s," in *African American Women and the Vote, 1837-1965*, ed. Ann D. Gordon, Bettye Collier-Thomas, John H. Bracy, Arlene Vesca Avakian, and Joyce Averech Berkman (Amherst: University of Massachusetts Press, 1997), 134-55.

106. Florette Henri, *Black Migration, Movement North 1900-1920* (Garden City, NY: Anchor Press/Doubleday 1975), 49-80. Carole Marks, *Farewell-We're Good and Gone: The Great Black Migration* (Bloomington: Indiana University Press, 1989), 139-43.

107. Wanda Hendricks, *Gender, Race, and Politics in the Midwest, Black Club Women in Illinois* (Bloomington: University of Illinois Press, 1998), 110, 119-120.

108. Wilma Peebles-Wilkins and E. Aracelis Francis, "Two Outstanding Black Women in Social Welfare History: Mary Church Terrell and Ida B. Wells-Barnett, *Affilia: Journal of Women and Social Work* 5:4 (Winter 1990): 87-100.

109. Mary McLeod Bethune, "President's Monthly Message," The *National Association Notes*, (September 1927).

CHAPTER 5

1. Mary Ryan, *Womanhood in America, from Colonial Times to the Present* (New York: New Viewpoints, 1979), 143.

2. See Cynthia Neverdon-Morton, *Afro-American Women of the South and the Advancement of the Race, 1895-1925* (Knoxville: University of Tennessee Press, 1996).

3. Julius Nimmons, "Social Reform and Moral Uplift in the Black Community 1890-1910 Social Settlements, Temperance, and Social Purity," (diss., Howard University, 1987). belle hooks, *Ain't I A Woman: Black Women and Feminism* (Boston: South End Press, 1981).

4. Ann duCille, *The Coupling Convention: Sex, Text, and Tradition in Black Women's Fiction* (New York: Oxford University Press, 1993).

5. Jacqueline Jones, "A Bridge of Bent Backs and Laboring Muscles: The Rural South, 1880-1915," in *Labor of Love, Labor of Sorrow: Black Women, Work, and the Family from Slavery to the Present* (New York: Basic Books, 1985), 79-109. For a historical context, see Robert H. Abzug, "The Black Family During Reconstruction," in *Key Issues in the Afro-American Experience*, eds. Nathan I. Huggins, Martin Kilson, Daniel M. Fox vol. I (New York: Harcourt Brace Jovanovich, 1971), 26-41.

6. Leslie A. Schwalm, "Sweet Dreams of Freedom: Freedwomen's Reconstruction of Life and Labor in Lowcountry South Carolina," *Journal of Women's History* (1997): 9-38.

7. Susan Mann, "Slavery, Sharecropping, and Sexual Inequality," *Signs* (1989): 792-98.

8. John Blassingame, *Black New Orleans, 1860-1880* (Chicago: University of

Chicago Press, 1973).

9. Arnold Taylor, *Travail and Triumph: Black Life and Culture in the South Since the Civil War* (Westport, CT: Greenwood Press, 1976), 161-63.

10. Gertrude Mossell, *The Work of the Afro-American Woman* (1894; New York: Oxford University Press, 1988).

11. Ibid., 15-125.

12. Gerda Lerner, ed., *The Female Experience, an American Documentary* (New York: Oxford University Press, 1977), 266-67.

13. Neverdon-Morton, *Afro-American Women of the South and the Advancement of the Race*.

14. Pitt Dillingham, "Black Belt Settlement Work: I. The Settlement," *Southern Workman* 31.7 (July 1902): 382-88.

15. G. F. Richings, *Evidence of Progress among Colored People* (Philadelphia: George S. Ferguson, 1897).

16. Emmett J. Scott, "Mrs. Booker T. Washington's Part in Her Husband's Work," *Ladies Home Journal* (24 May 1907): 42.

17. Robert Bremner, *The Public Good: Philanthropy and Welfare in the Civil War Era* (New York: Alfred A. Knopf, 1980), 213.

18. August Meier, *Negro Thought in America, 1880-1915* (Ann Arbor: University of Michigan Press, 1978), 88.

19. Meier, *Negro Thought in America*, 89.

20. Margaret Murray Washington, "What Girls Are Taught and How," *Tuskegee and Its People*, ed. Booker T. Washington (New York: D. Appleton, 1905), 68-83.

21. Max Thrasher, "Women and Their Work," *New York Evening Post*, 23 August 1900, 8.

22. Margaret Murray Washington, "The Organization of Women's Clubs," 22 June 1910, Margaret Washington Papers, Hollis Burke Frissell Library, Tuskegee University Archives.

23. Margaret Murray Washington, "The Tuskegee Woman's Club," *The Southern Workman* 49, (August 1920): 365-69.

24. Margaret Murray Washington, "Social Improvement of the Plantation Woman," *Voice of the Negro* 1 (July 1904): 288-90.

25. "Training Dusky Griseldas: Mrs. Booker Washington's Missionary Work among Negro House-Wives," *San Francisco Bulletin*, 2 August 1903, also in *The Booker T. Washington Papers*, ed. Louis Harlan vol. 7 (Urbana: University of Illinois Press, 1974), 208-51.

26. See James Jones, *Bad Blood: The Tuskegee Syphilis Experiment* (New York: Free Press, 1981).

27. "Two Earnest Addresses Delivered by Professor Washington and His Wife," Charleston, SC, 12 September 1898, in Booker T. Washington Papers, ed. Louis Harlan vol. 4, 461-69.

28. Mary White Ovington, *Portraits In Color* (New York: Viking Press, 1927). Herbert Gutman looked at the composition of Afro-American families between 1850 and 1880 using state, federal, and Freedmen's Bureau censuses. He calculated percentages for thirty types of black families ranging from augmented-extended to subfamilies living in either white or black homes; Herbert Gutman, "Persistent Myths about the Afro-American Family," in *The American Family in Social-Historical Perspective*, ed. Michael Gordon (New York: St. Martin's Press, 1978), 467-89.

29. Stephanie Shaw, *What a Woman Ought to Be and to Do: Black Professional Women Workers during the Jim Crow Era* (Chicago: University of Chicago Press, 1996), 69.

30. *Crisis*, 15 November 1915): 13-14.

31. "Locust Street Social Settlement," in *Handbook of Settlements*, ed. Robert A. Woods and Albert J. Kennedy (New York: Charities Publication Committee, 1911; rpt. New York: Arno Press, 1970), 298. Florence Lattimore, *A Palace of Delight: The Locust Street Social Settlement for Negroes at Hampton*, (University Archives, Hampton University, 1915.

32. "Settlement at Hampton, Virginia," *The Commons* 9 (September 1904): 438.

33. Allen Davis, *Spearheads for Reform: The Social Settlement and the Progressive Movement, 1890-1914* (New York: Oxford University Press, 1967), 40-59.

34. Mrs. Harris Barrett, "Negro Women's Clubs and the Community," *The Southern Workman* 39.1 (January 1910): 33-34.

35. "Mrs. Barrett Entertained at Tea by Jane Addams," *Chicago Defender*, 22 April 1910.

36. "Industrial Home for Wayward Girls," *New York Age*, 3 July 1915.

37. Minutes, Thirteenth Biennial Convention, August 1922, 36. "School for Wayward Girls," *Chicago Defender*, 6 February 1916. Sadie Daniel St. Clair, "Janie Porter Barrett," in *Notable American Women: A Biographical Dictionary*, ed. Edward T. James, Janet W. James, and Paul Boyer I (Cambridge: Belknap Press of Harvard University, 1971).

38. Cynthia Neverdon-Morton, "Self-help Programs as Educative Activities of Black Women in the South, 1895-1925," 51 *Journal of Negro History* (Summer 1982): 207-21.

39. Mary Beard, *Woman's Work in Municipalities* (New York: D. Appleton, 1915), 208-10.

40. Charles F. Weller, "Neglected Neighbors: In the Alleys, Shacks, and Tenements of the National Capitol," *Charities and The Commons* 15.22 (3 May 1906).

41. Anna Julia Cooper, *The Social Settlement, What It Is and What It Does*, (Washington, DC: Murray Brothers Press, 1913).

42. "Philanthropy as a Calling," *Charities and the Commons* 21 (1908-1909): 323.

43. Charles Lemert and Esme Bhan, eds., *The Voice of Anna Julia Cooper* (New York: Rowman and Littlefield, 1998).

44. Sharon Harley, "Anna J. Cooper: A Voice for Black Women," in *The Afro-American Woman: Struggle and Images*, ed. Sharon Harley and Rosalyn Terborg-Penn, (New York: Choanocyte Press, 1978), 87-96. *Washington Post*, 10 August 1958. At the age of sixty-six, Cooper received her Ph.D. from the Sorbonne. She was inaugurated as the second president of Frelinghuysen University, which was founded in Washington by Jesse Lawson in 1907.

45. Lemert and Bhan, *The Voice of Anna Julia Cooper*, 35.

46. Cooper, "The Social Settlement, What It Is and What It Does" (1913).

47. Rose Hunter Moore, "A Pioneer Settlement Worker," *The Southern Workman* 52.7 (July 1923).

48. K. Miller, "For Charity's Sake," *Evening Star*, 27 August 1904. Sarah Collins Fernandis, "A Social Settlement in South Washington," *Charities and Commons* 15 (7 October 1905): 64-66. Cooper, *The Social Settlement*.

49. Washington, DC *Evening Star*, 27 August 1904, 8.

50. Sarah Collins Fernandis, "A Colored Social Settlement," *Southern Workman* (June 1904): 346-50.

51. "A Biographical Sketch of Mrs. John Hope," in *A Report of Results Gained Through Cooperative Efforts of College Neighbors*, Walter R. Chivers, Neighborhood Union Papers, Special Collection, Woodruff Library, Atlanta, GA.

52. Walter R. Chivers, "A Report of Results Gained through Cooperative Efforts of College Neighbors" (n.p., n.d.,), Neighborhood Union Papers.

53. Jacqueline Rouse, *Lugenia Burns Hope: Black Southern Reformer* (Athens: University of Georgia Press, 1989).

54. Walter Chivers, "Neighborhood Union: An Effort of Community," *Opportunity* (June 1925): 178-79. "Morehouse Holds Memorial Service for Mrs. John Hope," *The Morehouse Alumnus* (March/April 1948): 10.

55. "Social Work through Social Science," in *W.E.B. Du Bois, Propagandist of the Negro*, ed. Elliot M. Rudwick (New York: Atheneum, 1969), 39-53.

56. "Our New Teachers," *The Bulletin of Atlanta University* (October 1904).

57. Rouse, *Lugenia Burns Hope*, 3.

58. "The Constitution of the Neighborhood Union," (n.p., n.d.).

59. "Work of the Neighborhood Union," *Spelman Messenger*, (November 1916). Neighborhood Union Papers, Robert Woodruff Library, Atlanta University Center.

60. "Annual Report of the Neighborhood Union, 1913-4," *Spelman Messenger*, (1913/1914) 7, Neighborhood Union Papers.

61. Rouse, *Lugenia Burns Hope*, 46.

62. "Anti-Tuberculosis Campaign Among Negroes Is Discussed," *Atlanta Constitution*, 21 June 1914.

63. "Social Service Institute." "Announcement: Atlanta School of Social Service," Morehouse College, Atlanta, GA (September 1920).

64. "Announcement: Atlanta School of Social Service."

65. Cornelia Bowen, "A Woman's Work," in *Tuskegee and Its People*, 211-18.

66. Louis Harlan, ed. "Cornelia Bowen," The Booker T. Washington Papers 2 (Urbana: University of Illinois Press).

67. "Miss Cornelia Bowen," in *The National Cyclopedia of the Colored Race*, ed. Clement Richardson (Montgomery, AL: National, 1919), 22-23.

68. Minutes, NACW Biennial Convention, July 1904.

69. Bowen, "A Woman's Work," 211-18.

70. Mable W. Dillingham, "Calhoun Colored School," *Lend-a-Hand* 13 (July 1894): 52-55.

71. Mary White Ovington, "A Woman Who Answered a Prayer," *The Woman Citizen* (March 1927), 21-25.

72. "The Calhoun Land Company," *What Our Graduates Are Doing, 1868-1904*, Hampton, VA: Hampton Institute, 8.

73. "Black-Belt Settlement Work: The Community," *The Southern Workman* 31.7 (July 1902): 437-45.

74. Fifteenth Annual Report of the Principal, The Calhoun School, 1906-1907, Special Collection, Robert Woodruff Library, Atlanta, GA.

75. Ibid.

76. Thirty-eighth Annual Report of the Principal of the Calhoun Colored School, 1929, Robert Woodruff Library, Atlanta University Center, Atlanta, GA.

77. Robert Woods and Albert Kennedy, eds., *Handbook of Settlements* (Charities Publication Committee, 1911; rpt: New York: Arno Press, 1970), 6.

78. Butler Wilson, "What I Saw at Calhoun," *The Southern Workman* (January 1932): 1-10.

79. Elizabeth Lasch-Quinn, *Black Neighbors: Race and the Limits of Reform in the American Settlement House Movement, 1890-1945* (Chapel Hill: University of North Carolina Press, 1993), 95-99.

80. "The Work before Mrs. Judia Jackson Harris," *The Atlanta University Bulletin* (March 1928): 4-6.

81. Thomas J. Woofter, "The Negroes in Athens, Georgia," *Bulletin of the University of Georgia* 14.4 (December 1913): 5-41.

82. Michael Thurman, *A Story Untold: Black Men and Women in Athens, Georgia* (Athens: Clark County School District, 1978).

83. Interview by the author with Helen Neal Joseph, August, 1999.

84. Interview by the author with Roberta Glenn Barnett, February 1999. Barnett grew up in the area and attended the Judia Jackson Harris School through the ninth grade, its highest grade at the time.

85. Thurman, *A Story Untold.*

86. Ibid., 82.

87. U. S., Department of Commerce Bureau of the Census, Twelfth Census of the U. S.: Population, Census Microfilm, Annapolis Junction, MD.

88. Judith Trolander, *Professionalism and Social Change, from the Settlement House Movement to Neighborhood Centers, 1886 to the Present* (New York: Columbia University Press, 1987), 107.

89. *Bethlehem Centers of Nashville, Profile of Services* (Nashville, TN: Bethlehem Centers of Nashville, A United Methodist Mission Agency.

90. "Social Service Survey of the Bethlehem House Community," Nashville, TA, December 1920, Methodist Episcopal Church, South, Bethlehem House, Fisk University, Nashville.

91. "Social Service Survey of the Bethlehem House Community."

92. Jessie Carney Smith, *Notable Black American Women Book 2* (Detroit: Gale Research, 1996), 126-28.

93. Ibid.

94. Gerda Lerner, *The Female Experience: An American Documentary History* (New York: Oxford University Press, 1977), 245-47.

95. Gerda Lerner, *The Majority Finds Its Past: Placing Women in History* (New York: Oxford University Press, 1979) 84.

96. Tera Hunter, "The Correct Thing, Charlotte Hawkins Brown and the Palmer Institute," *Southern Exposure* 11.5 (September/October, 1983): 37-43.

97. *The National Association Notes*, (July 1928), 12.

98. Elaine Smith, "Mary McLeod Bethune," in *Notable American Women, The Modern Period*, ed. Barbara Sickerman and Carol Hurd Green (Cambridge: Belknap Press of Harvard University Press, 1980), 76-80.

99. Frances Reynolds Keyser, "What One Woman Has Done for the Young Girls of Florida," *Competitor* (March 1920): 55-7.

100. See Sheila Flemming, *The Answered Prayer to a Dream, Bethune Cookman College, 1904-1994* (Virginia Beach, VA: Donning, 1995).

101. Evelyn Higginbotham, "Nannie Helen Burroughs (1879-1961)," *Black Women in America,* ed. Darlene C. Hine et al. (New York: Carlson, 1993): 201-15.

102. Sharon Harley, "Beyond the Classroom: The Organizational Lives of Black Female Educators in the District of Columbia, 1890-1930," *Journal of Negro Education* 51 (Summer 1982): 254-65.

103. Nancy Schom Dye, "Creating a Feminist Alliance: Sisterhood and Class Conflict in the New York Women's Trade Union League, 1903-1914," *Feminist Studies* 2.2-

3 (1975): 24-37. Although the WTUL went further than any other women's organization in establishing sustained relations with working women, it had only limited success in achieving its goal of egalitarian, cross-class alliance.

104. "National Association of Wage Earners," *Competitor Magazine*, (21 June 1928): 399-402. "Constitution," National Association of Wage Earners, Washington, DC, Nannie Burroughs Papers, Library of Congress.

105. Higginbotham, *Righteous Discontent*, 212..

106. Elizabeth Davis, *Lifting As They Climb* (Washington, DC: NACW, 1933), 51-53.

CHAPTER 6

1. Ruth H. Crocker, *Social Work and Social Order: The Settlement Movement in Two Industrial Cities, 1889-1930* (Urbana: University of Illinois Press, 1992).

2. Katheryn Kish Sklar, *Florence Kelly and the Nation's Work: The Rise of Women's Political Culture, 1830-1900* (New Haven, CT: Yale University Press, 1995).

3. Patricia Hill Collins, *Black Feminist Thought: Knowledge, Consciousness, and the Politics of Empowerment* (New York: HarperCollins, 1990), 95.

4. Cynthia Neverdon-Morton, "Advancement of the Race through African American Women's Organizations in the South, 1895-1925," in *African American Women and the Vote, 1837-1965*, ed. Ann D. Gordon, et al. (Amherst: University of Massachusetts Press, 1997), 120-33.

5. Nathan Glazer and Daniel P. Moynihan, *Beyond the Melting Pot, A Study of Blacks and Other Ethnic Groups in New York City* (Cambridge: Massachusetts Institute of Technology Press, 1963), 53.

6. Allen F. Davis, *Spearheads for Reform: The Social Settlement and the Progressive Movement, 1890-1914* (New York: Oxford University Press, 1967), 11, 25, 43.

7. Jill Conway, "Women Reformers and American Culture, 1890-1930," *Journal of Social History* 5 (Winter 1971-72): 164-67.

8. Rivka Shpak Lissak, *Pluralism and Progressives: Hull House and the New Immigrants, 1890-1919* (Chicago: University of Chicago Press, 1989). Jane Addams, *Democracy and Social Ethics* (Cambridge: Harvard University Press, 1902).

9. Gilbert Osofsky, *Harlem: The Making of a Ghetto, Negro New York, 1890-1930* (New York: Harper and Row, 1971), 54-55.

10. August Meier, *Negro Thought in America, 1880-1915* (Ann Harbor: University of Michigan Press, 1978), 134.

11. Hallie Q. Brown, *Homespun Heroines and Other Women of Distinction* (1926; New York: Oxford University Press, 1988), 210-11. L. A. Scruggs, *Women of Distinction* (Raleigh, NC: L. A. Scruggs, 1893), 202.

12. Jean Blackwell Hutson, "Victoria Earle Matthews," *Notable American Women, 1607-1950*, vol. 3 (Cambridge: Harvard University Press, 1971), 510-11.

13. Irving Garland Penn, *The Afro-American Press and Its Editors* (1891; Salem, NH: Ayer, 1988).

14. Fannie Barrier Williams, "The Intellectual Progress of the Colored Woman of the United States since Emancipation," in *World's Congress of Representative Women*, ed. May Wright Sewall (Chicago: Rand McNally,1893: 696-711. Also Bert Loewenberg and Ruth Bogin, eds., *Black Women in Nineteenth-Century American Life: Their Words, Their Thoughts, Their Feelings*, (University Park: Pennsylvania State University Press, 1975), 272.

15. Mary Helen Washington, *Invented Lives: Narratives of Black Women, 1860-1960* (New York: Doubleday, 1987), 74.

16. Victoria Earle Matthews, "The Awakening of the Afro-American Woman," address at the Annual Convention of the Society of Christian Endeavor, San Francisco, July 1897.

17. Fannie Barrier Williams,"Colored Women of Chicago," *The Southern Workman* 43 (October 1914): 565.

18. In a study of black women domestics, Elizabeth Clark-Lewis found that the transition from live-in servitude to day work brought the women greater freedom. See Clark-Lewis, "'This Work Had an End': African-American Workers in Washington, DC, 1910-1940," in *'Toil the Livelong Day' America's Women at Work, 1780-1980*, ed. Carol Groneman and Mary Beth Norton (Ithaca, New York: Cornell University Press, 1987), 196-212.

19. Florette Henri, *Black Migration: Movement North, 1900-1920* (Garden City, New York: Anchor Press/Doubleday 1975), 88-89. Carol Marks, F*arewell-We're Good and Gone, the Great Black Migration* (Bloomington: Indiana University Press, 1989).

20. Osofsky, *Harlem: The Making of a Ghetto*, 9-15.

21. David Pivar, *Purity Crusade: Sexual Morality and Social Morality, 1868-1900* (Westport, CT: Greenwood Press, 1973).

22. Ruth Rosen, *The Lost Sisterhood: Prostitution in America, 1900-1918* (Baltimore: Johns Hopkins University Press, 1982), 12.

23. Letter from Victoria Matthews to Booker T. Washington, 8 January 1898, in *The Booker T. Washington Papers*, ed. Louis Harlan vol. 7 (Urbana: University of Illinois Press, 1974), 36.

24. Brown, *Homespun Heroines*, 211.

25. Mary Lewis, "The White Rose Home and Industrial Association; the Friend of the Strange Girl in New York," *Messenger* 7 (April 1925), 158.

26. Lasalle Best, "History of the White Rose Mission and Industrial Association," WPA Research Paper, n.d., Schomburg Center for Research and Black Culture, New York Public Library.

27. "Partial History of the White Rose Home and Industrial Association, 1911," n.d., Board of Directors, White Rose Home and Industrial Association, typescript.

28. *Annual Report*, White Rose Home Industrial Association, 1911.

29. Osofsky, *Harlem: The Making of a Ghetto*, 16.

30. "White Rose Mission Settlement," *New York Age*, 6 July 1905.

31. Ruth Crocker, *Social Work and Social Order:* The Settlement Movement in Two Industrial Cities, 1889-1930 (Urbana: University of Illinois Press, 1992).

32. *New York Age*, 25 May 1905.

33. Brown, *Homespun Heroines*, 212.

34. "Travelers' Aid," *Annual Report*, White Rose Home Industrial Association, 1912, Schomburg Center for Research in Black Culture, New York Public Library.

35. Robert D. Cross, "Grace Hoadley Dodge," in *Notable American Women*, ed. Edward James, Janet James, and Paul Boyer, vol. 1 (Cambridge: Belknap Press of Harvard University , 1971), 489-92.

36. "Partial History of the White Rose Home and Industrial Association, 1911," n.d., Board of Directors, White Rose Home Association and Industrial Association, typescript.

37. Victoria Matthews, "Dangers Encountered by Southern Girls in Northern Cities," Hampton Negro Conference, Proceedings, July 1898, Hampton Archives, Hampton University.

38. Herbert Gutman, *The Black Family in Slavery and Freedom, 1750-1925* (New York: Vintage Books, 1976), 453. George E. Haynes, "Negro Migration,"

Opportunity (October 1924): 273.

39. Frances A. Kellor, "Southern Colored Girls in the North: The Problem of their Protection," *Charities* (18 March 1905): .

40. Haynes, "Negro Migration," 273.

41. Darlene Clark Hine, "Rape and the Inner Lives of Black Women in the Middle West: Preliminary Thoughts on the Culture of Dissemblance," *Signs* 14:4 (Summer 1989): 912-20. Evelyn Brooks Higginbotham, *Righteous Discontent* (Cambridge: Harvard University Press, 1993), 13.

42. Thomas Lee Philpott, *The Slum and the Ghetto, Neighborhood Deterioration and Middle-class Reform, Chicago, 1880-1910* (New York: Oxford University Press, 1978), 299.

43. See Addams, *Democracy and Social Ethics*.

44. John Daniels, *In Freedom's Birthplace: A Study of the Boston Negroes* (Boston: Houghton Mifflin, 1914). Lee Baker, *From Savage to Negro*, (Berkeley: University of California Press, 1998), 22-23.

45. Frantz Fanon, *Black Skin, White Masks* (New York: Grove Press, 1967). Steve Diner, "Chicago Social Workers and Blacks in the Progressive Era," *Social Service Review* 44 (12 December 1970): 393-410.

46. Elizabeth L. Davis, *The Story of the Illinois Federation of Colored Women's Clubs* (Chicago: Illinois Writers Project, 1922).

47. Louise de Koven, "The Colored People of Chicago," *Survey* (1 November 1913): 117-120. See Allen F. Davis and Mary Lynn Bryan, eds. *100 Years at Hull-House* (1969; rpt. Bloomington, Indiana University Press, 1990.

48. Anne Meis Knupfer, *Toward A Tenderer Humanity and A Nobler Woman-hood*: African American Women's Clubs in Turn-of-the- Century Chicago (New York: New York University Press, 1996), 99.

49. *New York Age*, January 1913. "The Social Settlement: Its Work Among Colored Americans," 4. "To Our Audience," 2, n.d., Lillian Wald Papers, Rare Books and Manuscript Collection, Columbia University.

50. Birdye Haynes, "Lincoln House: Its Work For Colored Americans," *The Standard, American Ethical Society* (1918), 122-24. Lillian Wald Papers, Rare Books and Manuscript Collection, Columbia University.

51. "Columbus Hill Branch of the National Urban League on Urban Conditions among Negroes," Eugene Kinckle Jones, Letter to Lillian Wald, 21 May 1918, Lillian Wald Papers, Columbia University.

52. Minutes of the Board of Directors of Lincoln House, 6 November 1919, Report of Lincoln House Settlement, 20 May 1922.

53. Letter to Olivia C. Holt, chair of the Lincoln House Committee, from Mrs. L. Emmett, 10 March 1922, Lillian Wald Papers, Columbia University.

54. Letter to the directors of Henry Street Settlement House, from Olivia C. Holt, 28 March 1922. Letter to Rev. George H. Sims, pastor, Union Baptist Church, from the Lncoln Settlement House, 24 December 1923, Lillian Wald Papers, Columbia University.

55. South End House (Boston: South End House Association, 1910). John Daniels, *In Freedom's Birthplace: A Study of Boston Negroes* (Boston: Houghton Mifflin, 1914), 193-5.

56. Robert Woods and Albert J. Kennedy, *Handbook of Settlements*, (Charities Publication Committee, 1911; rpt. New York: Arno Press, 1970), 121-22.

57. Isabel Eaton, "Robert Gould Shaw House and Its Work," *Crisis* 6.3 (July 1913): 142. Florida Ruffin Ridley, "The Negro in Boston," *Our Boston* 2 (January 1927): 1-20. Robert Gould Shaw House, *Annual Reports*, Social Welfare History Archives,

University of Minnesota.

58. Robert Gould Shaw House, Inc., *Annual Reports*, Social Welfare History Archives, University of Minnesota.

59. Robert C. Hayden, *African-Americans in Boston: More Than 350 Years* (Boston, MA: Boston Urban League, 1971).

60. Albert Boer, *The Development of USES: A Chronology of the United South End Settlements, 1891-1966* (Boston, MA: United South End Settlements). Boer, a social worker, was a member of the Federation of the United South End Settlements staff from 1954 to 1964.

61. Charles Flint Kellogg, *NAACP: A History of the National Association for the Advancement of Colored People, 1909-1920* (Baltimore: Johns Hopkins Press, 1967), 71-72.

62. Interview with Judge Franklin W. Morton, grandson of Verina Morton-Jones, and his wife Mrs. Gwendolyn Morton (now deceased), 1986; October 1998.

63. Harold X. Connolly, *A Ghetto Grows in Brooklyn* (New York: New York University Press), 83-5.

64. Woods, *Handbook of Settlements*, 178-9.

65. Robert L. Elzy, "Social Work in Brooklyn," *Opportunity* 5 (August 1927): 238-39.

66. Interview by the author with Mrs. Virginia Williams, a retired Brooklyn schoolteacher who joined the Lincoln Settlement and Association during the 1930s. She died in 1995 at the age of ninety-six.

67. "Lincoln Settlement," Brooklyn, NY, 8.

68. Verina Morton-Jones, letter to Carlotta Stewart (Lai), Hawaii, Box 97-103, Folder 33, Stewart Flippin Family Papers, Moorland-Spingarn Collection, Howard University. Carlotta was the daughter of T. McCants and Charlotte Harris Stewart.

69. "History of the Brooklyn Urban League," WPA Papers, Schomburg Center for Research in Black Culture, New York Public Library.

70. Interview by the author with Mrs. Fay C. Latimer, Hempstead, New York, September 1995. Dr. Verina Morton-Jones delivered Mrs. Latimer's youngest brother more than sixty years ago. Floris B. Cash, "Gender and Race Consciousness: Verina Morton-Jones Inspires a Settlement house in Suburbia," in *Long Island Women Activists and Innovators*, ed. Natalie A. Naylor and Maureen O. Murphy (Hempstead, New York: Long Island Studies Institute, 1998): 133-45.

71. Anne Firor Scott, "Most Invisible of All: Black Women's Voluntary Associations," *The Journal of Southern History* 56: 1 (February 1990): 3-22.

72. "Brief History of the Harriet Tubman Community Club, Inc. of Hempstead," one-page unpublished typescript, Courtesy of Mrs. Fay C. Latimer.

73. Ibid.

74. Al Cohn, "Money Woes Revisit an Ex-Slave's Church," *Newsday*, 13 October 1983, 8. For a recent secondary source, see Darlene Clark Hine, "Harriet Ross Tubman," in *Black Women in America: An Historical Encyclopedia*, ed. Darlene Clark Hine, Elsa Barkley Brown, and Rosalyn Terborg-Penn, 2 vols. (Brooklyn, NY: Carlson, 1993), 176-80.

75. Interview by the author with Reda Ezell (Mrs. Frederick) Williams, November 1995. Raised in Harlem, Reda Williams recalls that her grandmother, Margaret Banks, and Lucy Henson attended Abyssinian Baptist Church and sang in the choir. As a youth, Williams was unaware of Henson's historical contributions, since black history was not emphasized in the school curriculum.

76. Darlene Clark Hine, "Black Migration to the Urban Midwest: The Gender

Dimension, 1915-1945," in *The Great Migration In Historical Perspective: New Dimensions of Race*, Class, and Gender, ed. Joe William Trotter (Bloomington: Indiana University Press, 1991).

77. Inez, Frederick, and their older sister Helen (died, c. 1992) were raised by their parents, Pope and Hattie Williams in Hempstead. They attended meetings and activities in the Harriet Tubman Community Center. (Interview by the author with Hattie Williams, assisted by her daughter, Inez Williams, November 1995. Hattie Williams died in June 1997.

78. "Brief History of the Harriet Tubman Community Club of Hempstead."

79. The Harriet Tubman Community Club of Hempstead, *Biennial Dinner and Debutante Cotillion Program*, 1994.

80. As African Americans settled in the area, they established their own institutions. The churches associated with the Harriet Tubman Community House are the Jackson Memorial African Methodist Episcopal Zion, 1827; St. John Episcopal Church, 1904; Union Baptist Church, 1922; and Antioch Baptist Church, 1929. Shirley Small used the Community Center's library for homework assignments. The Small family lived next door to Dr. Verina Morton-Jones when she first went to Hempstead. In 1921 McDonald and Rosetta Small, natives of Barbados, helped establish a Baptist Church in their home for the increasing number of persons migrating from the South of that denomination. (Interview by the author with Shirley White, April 1997.) Fay Latimer is the daughter of the Reverend S.M.B. Usry. Under his pastorate, the Union Baptist Church was built, and he founded Antioch Baptist Church. Prior to 1925, he lived in Atlanta, Georgia.

81. Harriet Tubman Community Club, *Biennial Dinner and Debutante Cotillion Program*, 1994.

82. "Harriet Tubman Community Center," in *Hempstead Then and Now* (Hempstead: League of Women Voters, 1959, 1968).

83. Inez Marie Williams graduated from high school in Hempstead, New York, in 1948. A black youth growing up in the 1940s, she looked forward to the programs and activities provided by the Harriet Tubman Community Center. Williams believes that it was a vital community organization. Interview by the author with Inez Williams, November 1995.

84. *The Phillis Wheatley Christmas Annual* 1.1 (December 1929): 3, Chicago Historical Society. Many black institutions and organizations were named in honor of Phillis Wheatley, the first black poet. Black women adopted her name in order to identify their institutions with a famous black woman. Hereafter spelled Phillis Wheatley to correspond with the poet's name.

85. Obituary, Elizabeth Davis, *Chicago Defender*, 29 July 1944.

86. Anne Meis Knupfer, "If You Can't Push, Pull, If You Can't Pull, Please Get Out of the Way: The Phillis Wheatley Club and Home in Chicago, 1896 to 1920," *The Journal of Negro History* 82:2 (Spring 1997): 22-31.

87. "Saving the Girl Who Comes to Chicago," *The Negro in Chicago, 1779-1927* (Chicago: Chicago Washington Intercollegiate Club, 1922), 154-55.

88. Knupfer, "The Phillis Wheatley Club and Home in Chicago."

89. *Phillis Wheatley Home Association*, Chicago Historical Society.

90. Bylaws of the Phillis Wheatley Association, 1-8, Chicago Historical Society.

91. Letter to the Editor, *Record-Herald*, 26 January 1912.

92. St. Clair Drake and Horace A. Clayton, *Black Metropolis: A Study of Negro Life in a Northern City* (1945; Chicago: University of Chicago Press, 1993), 77.

93. Davis, *The Story of the Illinois Federation of Colored Women's Clubs*, 95.

94. John Rousmaniere, "Cultural Hybrid in the Slums: The College Woman and

and the Settlement House, 1889-1894," *American Quarterly* 22 (1970): 45-66.

95. Steven J. Diner, "Chicago Social Workers and Blacks in the Progressive Era," *Social Service Review* 44 (12 December 1970): 393-409.

96. James Grossman, *Land of Hope: Chicago Black Southerners and the Great Migration* (Chicago: University of Chicago Press, 1989).

97. Darlene Clark Hine, "Black Migration to the Urban Midwest: The Gender Dimension, 1915-1945," in *The Great Migration in Historical Perspective: New Dimensions of Race, Class, and Gender*, 127-146.

98. Grossman, *Land of Hope: Chicago Black Southerners*.

CHAPTER 7

1. Miriam Potocky-Tripodi and Tony Tipodi, *New Directions for Social Work Practice Research* (Washington, DC: NASW Press, 1999).

2. Robert Bremner, *From the Depths, The Discovery of Poverty in the United States* (New York: New York University Press, 1972), 52.

3. Roy Lubove, *The Professional Altruist: The Emergence of Social Work as a Career, 1880-1930* (Cambridge: Harvard University Press, 1965), 7.

4. Dorothy Salem, "To Better My World: Black Women in Organized Reform, 1890-1920" (diss., Kent State University, 1986), 126-27.

5. Lubove, *The Professional Altruist*, 12.

6. Allen F. Davis, "Settlements: History," in *Encyclopedia of Social Work* (16th ed.) Washington, DC: National Association of Social Workers, 1971), 1175-80.

7. Bremner, *From The Depths*, 54. Lubove, *The Professional Altruist*, 18.

8. Clarke A. Chambers, *Seedtime of Reform: American Social Service and Social Action, 1918-1933* (Minneapolis: University of Minnesota Press, (1963), 97. "Mary E. Richmond, Social Worker," *Family* 9.2 (February 1929): 319-59.

9. Scott Briar, "The Origins of Social Group Work," *Encyclopedia of Social Work*, 1240-45.

10. Lela B. Costin, *Two Sisters for Social Justice: A Biography of Grace and Edith Abbott* (Urbana: University of Illinois Press, 1983), 58-59.

11. Lubove, *The Professional Altruist*, 106.

12. For the profession of social work, the "charity organization" view of history is the most frequent choice. Historical data can be found to support the proposed "nursing" perspective of the profession's development. Sandra Taylor-Owen, "The History of the Profession of Social Work: A Second Look" (diss., Brandeis University, 1986).

13. Nancy Weiss, *National Urban League* (New York: Oxford University Press, 1974), 71-73.

14. Iris Carlton-La Ney, "Notes on a Forgotten Black Social Worker and Sociologist: Geoge E. Haynes," *Journal of Sociology and Social Welfare (September* 1983): 330-31.

15. George E. Haynes, "Negro Migration" *Opportunity* (October 1924): 273.

16. E. Franklin Frazier, *The Negro in the United States* (New York: Macmillan, 1966), 230. Daniel Johnson and Rex Campbell, *Black Migration in America, a Social Demographic History* (Durham, NC: Duke University Press, 1981).

17. Charles Johnson, "The Urban League's Responsibility to the Future," National Urban League Papers.

18. Walter Chivers, "Northward Migration and the Health of Negroes," *Journal of Negro Education* 8.1 (January 1939): 34-43.

19. L. Hollingworth Wood, "The Urban League Movement," *Journal of Negro History* 9. 2 (April 1924): 117-26.

20. Guichard Parris and Lester Brooks, *Blacks in the City* (Boston: Little, Brown, 1971), 118.

21. "Women of Vision," *Opportunity* (August 1996): 63-65.

22. Parris and Brooks, *Blacks in the City*, 187.

23. Frances A. Kellor, *Out of Work* (New York: G. P. Putnam's Sons, 1905).

24. Frances A. Kellor, "Southern Colored Girls in the North: The Problem of their Protection," *Charities* (18 March 1905): 584-85.

25. Frances A. Kellor, "Associations for the Protection of Colored Women," *The Colored American Magazine* (December 1905): 695-99.

26. Hazel Carby, "Policing the Black Woman's Body in an Urban Context," *Critical Inquiry* 18.4 (Summer 1992): 738-55.

27. Evelyn Higginbotham, *Righteous Discontent*, (Cambridge: Harvard University Press, 1993), 180-81.

28. Minutes of the Norfolk Association for the Protection of Colored Women, September 1912, George E. Haynes Papers, Fisk University.

29. Weiss, *National Urban League*, 1910-40.

30. Eugene Kinckle Jones, "The National Urban League," *Opportunity* 3 (January 1925): 12-15, address delivered at Urban League Annual Conference, Cleveland, OH, 4 December 1924.

31. Gilbert Osofsky, *Harlem: The Making of a Ghetto, Negro New York* (New York: Harper and Row, 1971), 63-66.

32. Minutes of the Committee on Urban Conditions among Negroes, 7 November 1910, George E. Haynes Papers, Box 4, Fisk University.

33. Eugene K. Jones, "Social Work among Negroes," *The Annals of the American Academy of Political and Social Science* 140 (November 1928): 2 93.

34. George Haynes, *The Negro in New York City: A Study in Economic Progress* (New York: Longmans, Green, 1912).

35. Edyth Ross, ed., *Black Heritage in Social Welfare, 1860-1930* (Metuchen, NJ: Scarecrow Press, 1978), 152-55. Carlton-La Ney, " Notes on a Forgotten Black Social Worker."

36. Jones, "Social Work among Negroes." Weiss, *National Urban League*. Parris and Brooks, *Blacks in the City*.

37. Robert C. Dexter, "The Negro in Social Work," *Survey* 46 (25 June 1921): 440.

38. Preston Valien, "History of the Department of Social Science, Fisk University, 1911-1948," (August 1950), unpublished paper, Charles Johnson Papers, Fisk University, Box 14.

39. "A Social Survey of the Bethlehem House Community," Nashville, TN, 1920, Methodist Episcopal Church, South, Methodist Training School, Fisk University.

40. "National League on Urban Conditions among Negroes." extract from the report of the director, June, July, August and September 1913. Minutes of the NUL, October 1913, George E. Haynes Papers, Fisk University.

41. Carlton-La Ney, "Notes on a Forgotten Black Social Worker."

42. Parris and Brooks, *Blacks in the City*, 78.

43. Lester Lamon, *Black Tennesseans, 1900-1930* (Knoxville, TN, 1977) 212.

44. Carlton-La Ney, "Notes on a Forgotten Black Social Worker."

45. The Public Welfare League, Nashville, 11 February 1918, Box 4, George E. Haynes Papers, Fisk University.

46. "Our Guest of Honor," Testimonial Luncheon Honoring Mrs. Drusilla W. Poole, president, Empire State Federation of Women's Clubs, Inc., 1953, New York City.

47. *National Urban League Bulletin* (1915-1916). "Advantages of Cooperation," *Southern Workman* (November 1918): 2.

48. "Advantages of Cooperation" 2.

49. "Home for Negro Girls Planned," *New York Evening Post,* 27 November 1912, 21. Letter to the Members of the "Sojourner Truth" House Committee, Sojourner Truth House for Delinquent Colored Girls, 26 March 1914, Lillian Wald Papers, Columbia University.

50. "The Utopian Neighborhood Club," *Crisis Magazine* 25 (1923): 208-10.

51. Jessie Thomas Moore, *A Search for Equality: The National Urban League* (University Park: Pennsylvania State University Press, 1981).

52. Ibid.

53. Wood, "The Urban League Movement." "Secretariat," *Opportunity* (March 1928): 84-89.

54. Paula Giddings, *When and Where I Enter: The Impact of Black Women on Race and Sex in America* (New York: William Morrow, 1984), 258.

55. Robert L. Elzy, "Social Work in Brooklyn" *Opportunity* 5 (August 1927): 238-39. *Annual Report,* Brooklyn Urban League, 1919, 17.

56. "Brooklyn Urban League" *Urban League Bulletin,* 1921, 10.

57. *Annual Report,* Brooklyn Urban League and Lincoln Settlement Association, 1925, Social Welfare History Archives, University of Minnesota.

58. Ibid.

59. *Annual Report,* Chicago Urban League, 1916.

60. Arvarh E. Strickland, *A History of the Chicago Urban League* (Urbana: University of Illinois Press, 1966), 18, 36, 46.

61. *Annual Report,* Chicago Urban League.

62. Strickland, *A History of the Chicago Urban League,* 47.

63. Ibid.

64. Celia Parker Woolley, "The Frederick Douglass Center, Chicago," *The Commons* 9 (July 1904): 329.

65. *Bulletin,* Atlanta University School of Social Work, 1926-1927. Frazier, *The Negro in the United States.*

66. "The Atlanta Urban League, Analysis of Its Functions," 1-14, National Urban League Papers. *Bulletin,* Atlanta School of Social Work, 1926-1927, Library of Congress, Washington, DC.

67. See *Annual Reports,* Atlanta Urban League, Library of Congress, Washington, DC.

68. *Timeless, 40th Annual Report,* Atlanta Urban League, Social Welfare History Archives, University of Minnesota.

69. Annual Report, Atlanta Urban League, 1920, Library of Congress, Washington, DC.

70. Chambers, *Seedtime of Reform,* 92. "Abraham Flexner (1866-1959)," in *Encyclopedia of Social Work,* 451.

71. *Bulletin,* Atlanta School of Social Work, 1920-1947. Jessie O. Thomas, *My Story in Black and White,* (New York: Exposition Press, 1967).

72. Louie D. Shivery, "The History of Organized Social Work among Atlanta Negroes, 1890-1935" (M.A. thesis, Department of Sociology, Atlanta University, 1936).

73. *Bulletin,* Atlanta School of Social Work, 1924, 1926-1927. Jacqueline Rouse, *Lugenia Burns Hope, A Black Southern Reformer* (Athens: University of Georgia

Press, 1989), 82-84.

74. Charles L. Sanders, ed., "Crossing Over," *Proceedings, 50th Anniversary*, The Atlanta University School of Social Work (1970), 2, Robert Woodruff Library, Atlanta University Center, Atlanta, GA.

75. Rouse, *Lugenia Burns Hope, A Black Southern Reformer*, 84.

76. *Bulletin*, Atlanta School of Social Work, 1926-1927.

77. Parris and Brooks, *Blacks in the City*.

78. Sanders, "Crossing Over," 2-4. *Bulletin*, Atlanta School of Social Work, 1929-1930, 1930-1931.

79. *Annual Catalogue of the Saint Augustine's College, 1927-1928*. Arthur Ben Chitty, *A Brief History of St. Augustine's College*, n.d., 15 pages.
Interview by the author with medical social worker Frances Cutchin Miller, Philadelphia, May 1998. Miller's grandmother, a matron at the Tuttle School of Social Work, raised her on the campus.

80. *St. Augustine's Record* 36 (October-November 1930), Special Collections, St. Augustine University, Raleigh, NC.

81. *Annual Catalogue, 1924-1925, 1927*.

82. Cecil D. Halliburton, *A History of St. Augustine's College, 1867-1937* (Raleigh, 1937), 67; *St. Augustine's Record, 39. 1* (September 1935). *Annual Catalogue, Saint Augustine's College*, 1936-1937. Interview by the author with Mrs. Mary Jane Halliburton, of St. Louis, Missouri, in June 1997. She graduated from the Bishop Tuttle School of Social Work in 1932.

83. *Annual Catalogue, Saint Augustine's College*, 1939-1940. *Parents' Handbook*, Tuttle Community Center, 1994, 12 pages. See Linda Simmons Henry and Linda Harris Edmisten, *Culture Town, Life in Raleigh's African American Communities-Architectural History* (Raleigh, NC: Raleigh Historic Districts Commission, 1993), 119-20.

84. *St. Augustine's Record* 61 (October-November 1935).

85. "The School of Social Work," Howard University, Social Welfare Archives, University of Minnesota.

86. Kathleen Hill, Evelyn Greene, and Marcela W. Daniels, "Breaking Barriers in Pursuit of Excellence-Howard University School of Social Work-A Force for Change," *50th Anniversary Brochure*, Howard University School of Social Work, 1987.

87. School of Social Work," Howard University.

88. Ruth Hill, "Inabel Burns Lindsay (1900-1983)," *Notable American Black Women*, ed. Jessie Smith (Detroit: Gale Research, 1992), 678-80. Black Women Oral History Project Interview with Inabel Lindsay, Cambridge: Radcliffe College, Schlesinger Library, 1980.

89. Hill, et al., "Breaking Barriers in Pursuit of Excellence."

90. Moore, *A Search for Equality*.

91. William H. Chafe, *The American Woman, Her Changing Social, Economic, and Political Role, 1920-1970* (New York: Oxford University Press, 1972), 89-90.

92. Giddings, *When and Where I Enter*.

93. Eva Bowles, "Opportunities for the Educated Colored Woman," *Opportunity* 1.3 (March 1923): 8-10.

94. John H. Ehrenreich, *The Altruistic Imagination, A History of Social Work and Social Policy in the United States* (Ithaca, New York: Cornell University Press, 1985), 106-07.

95. Donna Cooper Hamilton, "The National Urban League During the Depression, 1930-1939: The Quest for Jobs for Black Workers" (diss., Columbia University, 1982).

CHAPTER 8

1. Kevin Gaines, *Uplifting the Race: Black Leadership, Politics, and Culture in the Twentieth Century* (Chapel Hill: University of North Carolina Press, 1996), 224.

2. Gloria T. Hull, *Color, Sex, and Poetry: Three Women Writers of the Harlem Renaissance* (Bloomington: Indiana University Press, 1987), 2-5.

3. Ann duCille, *The Coupling Convention: Sex, Text, and Tradition in Black Women's Fiction* (New York: Oxford University Press, 1993), 87.

4. Robert Hill, ed., *The Marcus Garvey and Universal Improvement Papers*, vol. 2 (Berkeley: University of California Press, 1983).

5. Amy Jacques Garvey, Editorial, *The Negro World*, (October 24, 1925), in *Black Women in White America, a Documentary History*, ed. Gerda Lerner (New York: Vintage Books, 1973), 576-79.

6. Karen S. Adler, "Always Leading Our Men in Service and Sacrifice: Amy Jacque Garvey, Feminist Black Nationalist," *in Race, Class, and Gender, Common Bonds, Different Voices*, ed. Esther Ngan-Ling Chow, Doris Wilkinson, and Maxine Baca Zinn (Thousand Oaks, CA: Sage, 1996), 5-31.

7. "International Organization of Colored Women Formed, Mrs. Booker T. Washington Elected President," *Philadelphia Advocate*, 22 August 1922. *Crisis*, (October 1923): 274.

8. "International Council Holds Public Meeting," *Chicago Defender*, 16 August 1924.

9. "Addie Waites Hunton," *Opportunity* (August 1925): 255.

10. Elsie McDougal, "The Task of Negro Womanhood," in *The New Negro*, ed. Alain Locke (New York: Atheneum; 1992), 369-382. Hull, *Color, Sex, and Poetry.*

11. Linda Dahl, *Stormy Weather, The Music and Lives of a Century of Jazzwomen* (New York: Limelight Editions, 1984), 120.

12. Ibid., 104-6.

13. Hazel Carby, "Policing the Black Woman's Body in an Urban Context," *Critical Inquiry* 18.4 (Summer 1992): 754.

14. Angela Davis, *Blues Legacies and Black Feminism, Gertrude Ma Rainey, Bessie Smith, and Billie Holiday* (New York: Pantheon Books, 1998), 44.

15. David Kennedy, *Birth Control in America: the Career of Margaret Sanger* (New Haven, CT: Yale University Press, 1970).

16. Jessie M. Rodrique, "The Black Community and the Birth Control Movement," in eds., Kathy Peiss and Christina Simmons, *Passion and Power: Sexuality in History* (Philadelphia: Temple University Press, 1989) 138-54

17. J. A. Roger, "The Critic," *The Messenger* (April 1925).

18. E. Franklin Frazier, " The Negro and Birth Control," *Birth Control Review* 17 (March 1933): 8, 68-70.

19. W.E.B. Du Bois, "Black Folk and Birth Control," *Birth Control Review* 17 (May 1938): 8, 90.

20. Reynolds Farley and Walter Allen, *The Color Line and the Quality of Life* (New York: Oxford University Press, 1989), 18.

21. Charles Wesley, *The History of the National Association of Colored Women's Clubs* (Washington, DC: NACWC, 1984), 102.

22. Ibid., 108.

23. Evelyn Hammonds, "Missing Persons: African American Women and the History of Disease," *Radical America* 24 (1987): 8-13.

24. See Beverly Washington Jones, *Quest for Equality, The Life and Writings of Mary Eliza Church Terrell, 1863-1954* (New York: Carlson, 1990). Paula Giddings, *When and Where I Enter, the Impact of Black Women on Race and Sex in America* (New York: William Morrow, 1984), 233.

25. Ralph Bunche, "The Programs of Organizations Devoted to the Improvement of the Status of the American Negro," *Journal of Negro Education* 8 (July 1939): 539-50.

26. Brigid O'Farrell and Joyce L. Kornbluh, "We Did Change Some Attitudes: Maida Springer-Kemp and the International Ladies's Garment Workers Union," *Women's Studies Quarterly* 23.1,2 (Spring/Summer 1995): 41-70.

27. "Statement from the Executive Board of the National Association of Colored Women," Mary Church Terrell Papers, Library of Congress.

28. "Mrs. Bethune Asks Race Women to a Conference," *New York Age*, 21 December 1929, 3.

29. Bettye Collier Thomas, *The National Council of Negro Women*, Mary McLeod Bethune Archives, Washington, DC.

30. Interview by the author with Mattie Kelley Daniels, President of the White Rose Home and Industrial Association (1952-1985) and President of the Empire State Federation of Women's Clubs (1965-1969), in 1984. Mrs. Daniels, who often contributed personally to the maintenance of the White Rose home, died in 1985.

31. Giddings, *When and Where I Enter*, 203.

32. Charles Wesley, *The History of the National Association of Colored Women's Clubs* (Washington, DC: NACWC, 1984), 105.

33. "Negro Womanhood's Greatest Needs, a Symposium," *The Messenger* (June 1927).

34. Deborah Gray White, *Too Heavy a Load* (New York: W. W. Norton, 1999), 130.

35. *The National Association Notes* (March 1929).

36. David McBride, *From TB to AIDS: Epidemics among Urban Blacks since 1900* (New York: SUNY Press, 1991), 94.

37. Robert Bremner, *From the Depths: The Discovery of Poverty in the United States* (New York: New York University Press, 1967), 261.

38. Leslie H. Fishel, "The Negro in the New Deal Era," in *America's Black Past*, ed. Eric Foner (New York: Harper and Row, 1970), 388-413.

39. Ibid. Raymond Wolters, "The New Deal and the Negro," in *The New Deal: The National Level*, ed. Robert Bremner, John Braeman, and David Brody (Columbus: Ohio State University Press, 1975), 170-217.

40. Clarke Chambers, *Seedtime of Reform: American Social Service and Social Action, 1918-1933* (Minneapolis: University of Minnesota Press, 1963), 250.

41. Lela B. Costin, *Two Sisters for Social Justice: A Biography of Grace and Edith Abbott* (Urbana: University of Illinois Press, 1983), 126-130.

42. Chambers, *Seedtime of Reform*, 256.

43. "Colored Women at Waldorf Astoria Meet," *National Association Notes* (January 1928).

44. Blanche Wiesen Cook, *Eleanor Roosevelt, 1933-1938*, 159-60.

45. Elaine Smith, "Mary McLeod Bethune, 1875-1955," in *Notable Black American Women*, ed. Jessie Carney Smith (Detroit: Gale Research, 1992), 86-92.

46. Mary Berry, "Twentieth-Century Black Women in Education," *Journal of Negro Education* 51 (Summer 1982): 288-300.

47. Maxine Jones and Joe Richardson, *Talladega College* (Tuscaloosa: The University of Alabama Press, 1990), 125.

48. B. Joyce Ross, "Mary McLeod Bethune and the National Youth Administration: A Case Study of Power Relationships in the Black Cabinet of Franklin D. Roosevelt," *Black Leaders of the Twentieth Century*, eds. John Hope Franklin and August Meier (Urbana: University of Illinois, 1982): 191-219.

49. Wolters, "The New Deal and the Negro."

50. Ross, "Mary McLeod Bethune," 201.

51. Ibid., 193.

52. See Elaine Smith, "Mary McLeod Bethune and the National Youth Administration," in *Clio Was a Woman: Studies in the History of American Women,* ed. Mable E. Deutrich and Virginia Purdy (Washington, DC: Howard University Press, 1980), 149-77.

53. See Deborah Gray White, "The Cost of Club Work, the Price of Black Feminism," in *Visible Women: New Essays on American Activism*, ed. Nancy Hewitt and Suzanne Lebsock (Urbana: University of Illinois Press, 1993), 243-46.

54. "Mary F. Waring to Head Women," *Baltimore Afro-American*, 3 August 1935.

55. *The National Association Notes* (October 1933).

56. Ibid.

57. Ibid.

58. Susan Smith, *Sick and Tired of Being Sick and Tired: Black Women's Health Activism in America, 1915-1950* (Philadelphia: Temple University Press, 1995). "Social Welfare Movement," *in Black Women in America*, ed. Darlene Clark Hine et al. (New York: Carlson, 1993), 1086-88.

59. "Dorothy Boulding Ferebee, M.D.," *Journal of the National Medical Association* 62 (March 1970): 177.

60. Elaine Smith, "Mary McLeod Bethune," in *Black Women in America*, 113-27.

61. Judith Stein, "Defining the Race, 1890-1930," in *The Invention of Ethnicity*, ed. Werner Sollors (New York: Oxford University Press, 1989), 77-104.

62. Wesley, *The History of the National Association of Colored Women's Clubs*, 101.

63. Howard Zinn, *The Twentieth Century, a People's History* (New York: Harper and Row, 1980), 105.

64. Loren Miller, "Jim Crow in Relief," *Social Work Today* 2 (May 1935): 28.

65. Jacquelyn Jones, *Labor of Love, Labor of Sorrow* (New York: Basic Books, 1985), 217.

66. Gerda Lerner, *Black Women in White America: A Documentary History* (New York: Vintage Books), 398-405.

67. Trolander, *Settlement Houses and the Great Depression* (Detroit: Wayne State University), 135.

68. Ibid., 136.

69. Howard Jacob Karger, "Phyllis Wheatley House: A History of the Minneapolis Black Settlement House, 1924-1940," *Phylon* 47.1 (1986): 76-90.

70. "Settlement Workers are Segregated: Negro Delegates Withdraw from Meeting When Jim Crowed," *Kansas City Call*, 1934, 25.

71. Giddings, *When and Where I Enter*, 257.

72. Blanche Wiesen Cook, *Eleanor Roosevelt, 1933-1938*, vol. 2 (New York: Viking Press, 1999), 160.

73. Nannie Burroughs, "Declaration of 1776 Is Cause of Harlem Riot," *The Afro-American* (13 April 1935) in *Black Women in White America*, 407-10.

74. Zinn, *The New Deal* (New York; Bobbs-Merrill, 1966), xxxvi.

75. B. Joyce Ross, "Mary McLeod Bethune and the National Youth Administration," 191-215.

CHAPTER 9

1. Florida Ruffin Ridley, "Memorial to Josephine St. Pierre Ruffin," *National Association Notes (*September/October 1928), 18.

2. Patricia Hill Collins, *Black Feminist Thought* (New York: HarperCollins, 1990).

3. Marcia Ann Gillespie, "Myth of the Strong Black Woman," in *Feminist Frameworks: Alternative Theoretical Accounts of the Relations Between Women and Men*, ed. Allison Jaggar and Paula Rothenberg (New York: McGraw Hill, 1984), 32-35.

4. Robert Wiebe, *The Search for Order* (New York: Oxford University Press, 1968).

5. *A History of the Club Movement among the Colored Women in the United States of America* (1902; Washington, DC: NACWC, 1978), 30-31.

6. Kathleen C. Berkeley, "Colored Ladies Also Contributed: Black Women's Activities from Benevolence to Social Welfare, 1866-1896," in *The Web of Southern Relations: Women, Family, and Education*, ed. Walter J. Fraser, R. Frank Saunders, and Jon Wakelyn (Athens: University of Georgia Press, 1985).

7. Wilma Peebles-Wilkins and E. Aracelis Francis, "Two Outstanding Black Women in Social Welfare History: Mary Church Terrell and Ida B. Wells-Barnett," *Affilia* 5.4 (Winter 1990): 87-100.

8. E. Franklin Frazier, *Black Bourgeoisie* (New York: Free Press, 1957).

9. W.E.B. Du Bois, "The Talented Tenth Memorial Address" (1948), in *The Future of the Race*, Henry Louis Gates and Cornel West (New York: Alfred A. Knopf, 1996), 159-77.

10. Robert Bremner, *From the Depths, the Discovery of Poverty in the United States* (New York: New York University Press, 1967), 265.

11. Ibid., 262.

12. John H. Ehrenreich, *The Altruistic Imagination: A History of Social Work and Social Policy in the United States* (New York: Cornell University Press, 1985) 100.

13. Ibid., 222-27.

14. Elisabeth Lasch-Quinn, *Black Neighbors, Race and the Limits of Reform in the American Settlement House Movement, 1890-1945* (Chapel Hill: University of North Carolina Press, 1993), 51. Judith Trolander, *Professionalism and Social Change, From the Settlement House Movement to Neighborhood Centers 1886 to the Present* (New York: Columbia University Press, 1987), 116.

15. William Julius Wilson, *The Truly Disadvantaged: The Inner City, The Underclass, and Public Policy* (Chicago: University of Chicago Press, 1987).

16. Ruth H. Crocker, *Social Work and Social Order: The Settlement House Movement in Two Industrial Cities, 1889-1930* (Urbana: University of Illinois Press, 1992).

17. Gerda Lerner, *The Majority Finds Its Past: Placing Women in History* (New York: Oxford University Press, 1979).

18. Belinda Robinett, *How Long? How Long? African American Women in the Struggle for Civil Rights* (New York: Oxford University Press, 1997).

19. Angela Davis, *Women, Culture, and Politics* (New York: Random House, 1989).

Bibliography

MANUSCRIPT COLLECTIONS

Archival and Manuscript Collections, Fisk University Library, Nashville, TN
  George E. Haynes Papers
Archives and Special Collections, Robert Woodruff Library, Atlanta University Center
  Neighborhood Union Papers
Arthur and Elizabeth Schlesinger Library on the History of Women in America
Radcliffe College, Cambridge, MA
  Charlotte Hawkins Brown Papers
Beineke Rare Books and Manuscript Library , Yale University, New Haven, CT
Bethune Museums and Archives, Washington, DC
Chicago Historical Society, Chicago
  Irene McCoy Gaines Papers
Hampton Archives, Hampton University, Hampton, VA
  Janie Porter Barrett Papers
Manuscript Division, Library of Congress, Washington, DC
  Mary Church Terrell Papers
  Nannie Helen Burroughs Papers
Manuscript Collection, New York Public Library, New York
Moorland-Spingarn Research Center, Howard University, Washington, DC
  Mary Church Terrell Papers
  Stewart Flippin Family Papers
Rare Books and Manuscript Department, Boston Public Library, Boston
  The Woman's Era (also available on microfilm)
Rare Books and Manuscript Collection, Columbia University, New York
  Lillian Wald Papers (also available on microfilm)
Schomburg Center for Research and Black Culture, New York Public Library
  WPA Papers
  Harry A. Williamson Papers
Social Welfare History Archives, University of Minnesota, Minneapolis
  National Federation of Settlements Papers
Special Collections, St. Augustine University, Raleigh, NC
Tuskegee Archives, Tuskegee University, Tuskegee, AL
  Margaret James Murray Washington Papers
  The National Association Notes (also available on microfilm)

Primary Sources

Abbott, Edith. *Public Assistance*. Chicago: University of Chicago Press, 1940.

Abbott, Grace. *The Child and the State*. 2 vols. Chicago: University of Chicago Press, 1938.

Adams, Jane. *Democracy and Social Ethics*. Cambridge: Harvard University Press, 1902.

Address of Josephine St. Pierre Ruffin." *The Woman's Era*, August 1895.

"An Appeal to Colored Women," *Brooklyn Standard Union* 19 October 1917.

Annual Report of the White Rose Home and Industrial Association, 1911. Schomburg Center for Research and Black Culture, New York Public Library.

"Anti-tuberculosis Campaign Among Negroes is Discussed." *Atlanta Constitution*, 21 June 1914.

Bacon, Alice. *The Negro and the Atlanta Exposition*, Hampton Archives, Occasional Papers, No. 7 Hampton Institution, 1896. 10-2.

_____."Negro Women's Clubs and the Community." *The Southern Workman* 39.1 (January 1910), 33-34.

Beard, Mary. *Woman's Work in Municipalities*. New York: D. Appleton, 1915.

Bethune, Mary McLeod. "A Century of Progress of Negro Women." Speech delivered to the Chicago Federation of Colored Women's Clubs, 30 June 1933. In *Black Women in White America, A Documentary History*. ed. Gerda Lerner. New York: Vintage Books, 1973, 579-84.

_____. "President's Monthly Message." *The National Association Notes* (September 1927).

_____. "A Tribute to my Friend and Co-Worker Frances Reynolds Keyser." In *Lifting As They Climb*, Elizabeth Davis. Washington, DC: NACW, 1933, 213-15.

Bowen, Cornelia. "A Woman's Work." in *Tuskegee and Its People*, ed. Booker T. Washington. New York: D. Appleton, 1905, 63-83.

Bowles, Eva. "Opportunities for the Educated Colored Woman." Opportunity 1.3 (March 1923): 8-10.

Bowser, Rosa. "What Role Is the Educated Negro Woman to Play in the Uplifting of Her Race?" In *Twentieth Century Negro Literature*, ed. D. W. Culp, 1902; Miami, FL: Mnemosyne, 1969.

Brown, Charlotte Hawkins. "What the Negro Woman Asks of the White Women of North Carolina," May 1920, excerpts of address, 2, Charlotte Hawkins Brown Papers.

Brown, Hallie Q. *Homespun Heroines and other Women of Distinction. 1926;* New York: Oxford University Press, 1988.

Brown, Sarah W. "Colored Women Physicians." *The Southern Workman* 52.12 (December 1923): 580-89.

Burroughs, Nannie. "Declaration of 1776 is the Cause of the Harlem Riot." *The Afro-American* (13 April 1935) in *Black Women in White America: A Documentary History*. ed. Gerda Lerner. New York: Vintage Books, 1972, 407-10.

_____. "Not Color but Character." *Voice of the Negro* 1.7 (July 1904): 277-79.

Byron, Dora. "From a Cabin in the Cotton." *Opportunity* 14 (April 1939): 125.

"Call to the National Federation of Afro-American Women." *The Woman's Era* (November 1895).

"Charitable Institutions." In *Progress of a Race*, ed. William H. Crogman and H. F. Kletzing. J. L. Nicholas, 1898.

Chivers, Walter. "Neighborhood Union: An Effort of Community." *Opportunity* (June 1925): 178-79.

_____. "Northward Migration and the Health of Negroes." *Journal of Negro Education* 8.1 (January 1939): 34-43.

"A Club Model." *The Woman's Era* (November 1895), 10.

"Colored Women at Waldorf Astoria Meet." *National Association Notes* (January 1928).

"Convention of the Southern Federation." *National Association Notes*, February   1902.

Cooper, Anna Julia. *The Social Settlement, What It Is and What It Does*, Washington, DC: Murray Brothers Press, 1913.

Crogman, William H., and H. F. Kletzing, eds. *Progress of a Race*. Naperville, IL: J. L. Nicholas, 1898.

Crogman, William H. and John Gibson, eds. *Progress of a Race*, Naperville, IL: J. L. Nicholas 1929.

Culp, D. W., ed. *Twentieth Century Negro Literature*. 1902; Miami, FL: Mnemosyne, 1969.

Daniels, John. *In Freedom's Birthplace: a Study of the Boston Negroes*. Boston: Houghton Mifflin, 1914.

Davis, J . E. "Fertilizing Barren Souls, the Industrial Home School for Delinquent Colored Girls of Virginia." *The Southern Workman* (1914): 463-77.

Dexter, Robert C. "The Negro in Social Work." *Survey* 46 (25 June 1921): 440.

Dillingham, Pitt. "Black Belt Settlement Work: I. The Settlement." *Southern Workman* 31.7 (July 1902): 382-88.

Domingo, Wilfred A. "A New Negro and a New Day." *Messenger* 2 (November 1920), 144-45.

"Dr. Mary F. Waring to Head Women." *Baltimore Afro-American*, 3 August 1935.

Du Bois, W. E. B. "The Conservation of the Races." In *W. E. B. Du Bois: Writings*, ed. Nathan Huggins. 1897; New York: Library of America, 1986.

_____. *Some Efforts of American Negroes for Their Own Social Betterment.* Atlanta, GA: Atlanta University Publications, 1898.

Eaton, Isabel. "Robert Gould Shaw House and Its Work." Crisis 6.3 (July 1913): 142.

Elzy, Robert L. "Social Work in Brooklyn." *Opportunity* 5 (August 1927): 238-39.

Fauset, Jessie. "The Thirteenth Biennial of the N.A.C.W." *The Crisis Magazine* 24 (October 1922): 257-60.

Fernandis, Sarah Collins. "Colored Social Settlement." *Southern Workman* (June 1904): 346-50.

_____. "A Social Settlement in South Washington." *Charities and the Commons* 15   (7 October 1905): 64-66.

Ford, Mattie. "The Atlanta Woman's Club." *National Association Notes* (April/May 1917), 12.

Hammond, L. H. *Southern Women Radical Adjustment*. 1917; 2d ed. Lynchburg, VA: J. P. Bell, 1920.

Harris, Judia Jackson. *Race Relations*. Athens, GA, June 1925.

Haynes, Birdye E. "Lincoln House: Its Work For Colored Americans." *The Standard* (October 1918): 122-24, Lillian Wald Papers, Columbia University.

Haynes, George E. "Negro Migration." *Opportunity*, (October 1924): 273.

A History of the Club Movement among Colored Women of the United States of America. 1902; Washington, DC: NACWC, 1978.

"Home for Negro Girls Planned." *New York Evening Post*, 27 November 1912, 21.

"The Howard Orphan Asylum," *The Colored American Magazine* 10 (April 1906): 238-43.

Hunton, Addie. "The National Association of Colored Women." *Crisis Magazine* 1 (May

1911): 16-7.

"Industrial Home for Wayward Girls," *New York Age*, 3 July 1915.

Jones, Anna H. "The American Colored Woman," *The Voice of the Negro* (October 1905): 692-94.

_____. "How We as Women Can Advance the Standing of the Race." *The National Association Notes* (July 1904).

_____. Jones, Eugene Kinckle, "Social Work among Negroes," *The Annals of the American Academy of Political and Social Science*, 140 (November 1928): 287-93.

_____. "The National Urban League," *Opportunity* 3 (January 1925): 12-15.

Kellor, Frances A. "Assisted Emigration: The Women." *Charities* (7 Oct. 1905): 11-14.

_____. "Association for the Protection of Colored Women. *The Colored American Magazine* (December 1905): 695-99.

_____. "Opportunities for Negro Women in Northern Cities." *Voice of the Negro* 2 (July 1905): 470-73.

_____. *Out of Work*. New York: G. P. Putnam's, 1905.

_____. "Southern Colored Girls in the North: The Problem of their Protection." *Charities* (18 March 1905): 584-85.

Keyser, Frances Reynolds. "What One Woman Has Done for the Young Girls of Florida." *Competitor* (March 1920): 55-57.

Koven, Louise de. "The Colored People of Chicago." *Survey* (November 1, 1913): 117-20.

Lattimore, Florence. *A Palace of Delight: The Locust Street Social Settlement for Negroes at Hampton*. University Archives, Hampton University, 1915.

Lewis, Mary. "The White Rose Home and Industrial Association: the Friend of the Strange Girl in New York," *Messenger* 7 (April 1925): 158.

Locke, Alain. *The New Negro*. 1925; New York: Atheneum, 1992.

Logan, Adella Hunt. "Why the National Association of Colored Women Should Become a Part of the National Council of Women." *The National Association Notes* (December 1899).

Logan, Gussie Mims. "The Carrie Steel Orphanage." *The Voice the Negro* 1.11 (November 1904): 538-40.

"Mary F. Waring to Head Women." *Baltimore Afro-American*, 3 August 1935.

Matthews, Victoria Earle. "The Awakening of the Afro-American Woman," address at the Annual Convention of the Society of Christian Endeavor, San Francisco, July 1897, Beineke Rare Books and Manuscript Library, Yale University.

_____. "Dangers Encountered by Southern Girls in Northern Cities," Hampton Negro Conference, Proceedings, July 1898.

_____. "Value of Race Literature." Address before the first Convention of African Boston, 1895, Beineke Rare Books and Manuscript Library, Yale University.

Miss Cornelia Bowen. In *The National Cyclopedia of The Colored Race*, ed. Clement Richardson. Montgomery, AL: National, 1919, 22-3.

Miller, Loren. "Jim Crow in Relief." *Social Work Today* 2 (May 1935): 28.

Moore, Rose. "A Pioneer Settlement Worker." *The Southern Workman* 52.7 (July 1923).

Moton, Robert. "Negro Women in America, a Study in Interracial Cooperation." *Southern Workman* (December 1922): 573-81.

"Mrs. Barrett Entertained at Tea by Jane Addams." *Chicago Defender,* 22 April 1910.

"Mrs. Bethune Asks Race Women to a Conference." *New York Age* 21, 21 December 1929, 3.

Mrs. Booker T. Washington, "The New Negro Woman." *Lend-a-Hand* 15 (October 1895): 254-60.

"National Association of Wage Earners." *Competitor* (1928): 399-402.

"Negro Women Entering Trades and Business." *New York Post*, 1917, 6.

"Negro Women in New York Industry." New York Post, 21 March 1919, 3.

"Our New Teachers." *The Bulletin of Atlanta University*, (October 1904).

Ovington, Mary White. *Portraits In Color*. New York: Viking Press, 1927.

"Partial History of the White Rose Home and Industrial Association, 1911." n.d., Board of Directors, White Rose Home and Industrial Association, typescript.

Penn, Irving Garland. *The Afro-American Press and Its Editors*. 1891; Salem, NH: Ayer, 1988.

Records of the National Association of Colored Women's Clubs, 1895-1992. Bethesda, MD: University Publications of America, 1997; microfilm..

"Report of the Empire State Federation of Women's Clubs." *The National Association Notes* (March/April 1915).

Richardson, Clement, ed. *The National Cyclopedia of the Colored Race*. Montgomery, AL: National, 1919.

Richings, G. F. *Evidence of Progress Among Colored People*. Philadelphia: George S. Ferguson, 1897.

Richmond, Mary. *Friendly Visiting Among the Poor*. New York: Macmillan, 1898. _
_____ . *Social Diagnosis*. New York: Russell Sage Foundation, 1917.

Ridley, Florida Ruffin. "Memorial to Josephine St. Pierre Ruffin," *The National Association Notes*, September/October 1928, 18.

_____ . "The Negro in Boston." *Our Boston* 2 (January 1927): 1-20.

"Ruffin Incident at the Fifth Biennial of the General Federation." *National Association Notes*, November 1900.

"Saving the Girl Who Comes to Chicago." In *The Negro in Chicago, 1779-1927*. Chicago: Chicago Washington Intercollegiate Club, 1922, 154-55.

Scott, Emmett J. "Mrs. Booker T. Washington's Part in Her Husband's Work." *Ladies Home Journal* 24 (May 1907): 42.

Scruggs, L. A. *Women of Distinction*. Raleigh, NC: L. A. Scruggs, 1893.

"Settlement at Hampton, Virginia." *The Commons* 9 (September 1904): 438.

"Settlement Workers are Segregated: Negro Delegates Withdraw from Meeting When Jim Crowed." *Kansas City Call*, 1934, 25.

"Social Service Fellowships." *Opportunity* 1.4 (April 1923) : 4.

"Social Work in Harlem," *Survey Graphic* (1925): 7, 699.

Terrell, Mary. *A Colored Woman in a White World*. (1940; Washington, DC: NACWC, 1968.

_____ . "The National Association of Colored Women." *Howard's Magazine* 4 (November 1899): 26-31.

_____ . "The Progress of Colored Women." *The Voice of the Negro* (1 July 1904): 291-94.

Thrasher, Max. "Women and Their Work." *New York Evening Post*, 23 August 1900. 8.

"Training Dusky Griseldas: Mrs. Booker T. Washington's Missionary Work among Negro House-Wives," *San Francisco Bulletin*, 2 August 1903, also in *The Booker T. Washington Papers*, ed. Louis Harlan. Urbana: University of Illinois, 1974.

"The Utopian Neigborhood Club." *Crisis Magazine* 25 (1923): 203-10.

Washington, Booker T., ed. *A New Negro for a New Century*. Chicago: American
    Publishing House, 1900.
_____. *Tuskegee and Its People*. New York: D. Appleton, 1905.
Washington, Josephine. "Some Things Our Women Are Doing." *The National
    Association* Notes (November).
Washington, Margaret Murray. "The Negro Home." Address before the Interracial
    Conference, Memphis, TN, October 1920, 1- 7.
_____. "The New Negro Woman." *Lend-a-Hand* 15 (October   1895): 54-60.
_____. "The Organization of Women's Clubs." Tuskegee, AL, 22 June 1910, Box 132
    A, Convention Reports, Margaret Murray Washington Papers.
_____. "Social Improvement of the Plantation Woman." *Voice of the Negro* 1 (July
    1904): 288-90.
_____. "The Tuskegee Woman's Club." *The Southern Workman* 49 (August 1920): 365-69.
Weller, Charles, "Neglected Neighbors: In Alleys, Shacks, and Tenements of the
    National Capitol." *Charities and Commons* 21 (1908-1909): 323.
White Rose Industrial Association. "An Appeal to Our Friends," 1920, Schomburg
    Center for Research and Black Culture, New York Public Library.
"White Rose Mission Settlement." *New York Age*, 6 July 1905.
Williams, Fannie Barrier. "Club Movement among Colored Women." In *A New Negro
    for a New Century*, ed. Booker T. Washington. Chicago: American
    Publishing House, 1900.
_____. "Club Movement among Negro Women." In *Progress of a Race*, ed. John
    Gibson and William Crogman. 1902; Miami, FL: Mnemosyne, 1969.
_____. "The Colored Girl." *The Voice of the Negro* 2.6 (June 1905): 400-3.
_____. "Colored Women of Chicago." *The Southern Workman* 43 (October 1914): 565.
"The Woman's Era Club." *The Woman's Era* (March 1894).
Wood, L. Hollingworth. "The Urban League Movement." *Journal of Negro History* 9.2
    (April 1924): 117-26.
Woods, Robert A., and Albert J. Kennedy, eds. *Handbook of Settlements*. New York:
    Charities Publication Committee, 1911.
Woofter, Thomas J. "The Negroes in Athens, Georgia," *Bulletin of the University
    of Georgia* 14.4 (December 1913): 5-41.
Woolley, Celia Parker. "The Frederick Douglass Center, Chicago." *The Commons* 9
    (July 904): 329.
"The Work before Mrs. Judia Jackson Harris." *The Atlanta University Bulletin*
    (March 1928): 4-6. Archives and Special Collections, Robert Woodruff Library,
    Atlanta University Center.
"Work of the Neighborhood Union." *Spelman Messenger* (November 1916),
    Archives and Special Collections, Robert Woodruff Library, Atlanta
    University Center.
Yates, Josephine Silone. "The National Association of Colored Women." *The Voice of
    the Negro* 1.7 (July 1904): 283-87.
_____. "A Personal Letter from our President." The *National Association Notes*
    (January 1901).

Secondary Sources

Andrews, William, ed. *Sisters of the Spirit: Three Black Women Autobiographies
    of the Nineteenth Century*. Bloomington: Indiana University Press, 1986.

Aptheker, Bettina. *Woman's Legacy, Essays on Race, Sex, and Class in American History.* Amherst: The University of Massachusetts Press, 1982.

Baker, Lee D. *From Savage to Negro: Anthropology and the Construction of Race. 1896-1954.* Berkeley: University of California Press, 1998.

Berkley, Kathleen. "Colored Ladies also Contributed: Black Women's Activities from Benevolence to Social Welfare, 1866-1896." In *The Web of Southern Relations: Women, Family, and Education*, ed. Walter J. Fraser, R. Frank Saunders, and John Wakelyn. Athens: University of Georgia Press, 1985.

Berry, Mary. "Twentieth-Century Black Women in Education." *Journal of Negro Education* 51 (Summer 1982): 288-300.

Best, Lasalle. "History of the White Rose Mission and Industrial Association." WPA Research Paper, n.d., Schomburg Center for Research and Black Culture, New York Public Library.

Blair, Karen. *The Clubwomen as Feminist: True Womanhood Redefined, 1898-1914.* New York: Holmes and Meier, 1980.

Blassingame, John. *Black New Orleans, 1860-1880.* Chicago: University of Chicago Press, 1973.

Bodin, Ruth. *Women and Temperance: The Quest for Power, 1873-1900.* Philadelphia: Temple University Press, 1981.

Boer, Albert. The Development of USES: A Chronology of the United South End Settlements, 1891-1966. Boston, MA: United South End Settlement.

Bremner, Robert. *From the Depths, the Discovery of Poverty in the United States.* New York: New York University Press, 1972.

_____. *The Public Good: Philanthropy and Welfare in the Civil War Era.* New York: Alfred A. Knopf, 1980.

Bremner, Robert, John Braeman, and David Brody, eds. *The New Deal: The National Level.* Columbus: Ohio State University Press, 1975.

Brian, Scott. "The Origins of Social Group Work." In *Encyclopedia of Social Work.* 16th ed. Washington, DC: National Association of Social Workers, 1971.

Brown, Elsa Barkley. "Womanist Consciousness: Maggie Lena Walker and the Independent Order of Saint Luke." *Signs* 14.3 (Summer 1989): 610-33.

Brown, Ira. "Cradle of Feminism: The Philadelphia Antislavery Society, 1833-1840 ." *Pennsylvania Magazine of History and Biography* 102 (April 1978): 143-66.

Bunche, Ralph. "The Programs of Organizations Devoted to the Improvement of the Status of the American Negro." *Journal of Negro Education* 8 (July 1939): 539-50.

Caraway, Nancie. *Segregated Sisterhood: Racism and the Politics of American Feminism.* Knoxville: University of Tennessee Press, 1991.

Carby, Hazel. "Policing the Black Woman's Body in an Urban Context." *Critical Inquiry* 18.4 (Summer 1992): 738-55.

_____. *Reconstructing Womanhood: The Emergence of the Afro-American Woman Novelist.* New York: Oxford University Press, 1987.

Carlton-La Ney, Iris. "Notes on a Forgotten Black Social Worker and Sociologist: George E. Haynes." *Journal of Sociology and Social Welfare* (September 1983): 330-31.

Chafe, William. *The American Woman, Her Changing Social, Economic, and Political Role, 1920-1970.* New York: Oxford University Press, 1972.

Chambers, Clarke. *Seedtime of Reform: American Social Service and Social Action, 1918-1933.* Minneapolis: University of Minnesota Press, 1963.

_____. "Women and the Creation of the Profession of Social Work," *Social Service Review,* 60 (March 1986): 1-33.

Chitty, Arthur Ben. *A Brief History of St. Augustine's College*. n.d., 15, Raleigh, NC.

Chow, Esther Ngan-Ling, Doris Wilkinson, and Maxine Baca Zinn, eds., *Race, Class, and Gender, Common Bonds, Different Voices.* Thousand Oaks, CA: Sage, 1996.

Christian, Barbara. *Black Feminist Criticism: Perspectives on Black Women Writers*. New York: Pergamon Press, 1985.

Cohn, Al. "Money Woes Revisit an Ex-Slave's Church." New York *Newsday,* 23 October 1983, 8.

Collins, Patricia Hill. *Black Feminist Thought: Knowledge, Consciousness, and the Politics of Empowerment.* New York: HarperCollins, 1990.

Cook, Blanche Wiesen. *Eleanor Roosevelt, 1933-1938.* vol. 2. New York: Viking Press, 1999.

Cook, Samuel Du Bois. "The Socio-Ethical Role and Responsibility of Black College Graduates." In *Black Colleges in America, Challenge, Development and Survival*, ed. Charles Willie and Ronald Edmonds. New York: Columbia University Teachers College Press, 1978, 54-55.

Connolly, Harold X. *A Ghetto Grows in Brooklyn.* New York: New York University Press, 1977.

Conway, Jill. "Women Reformers and American Culture, 1890-1930." *Journal of American History* 5 (Winter 1971-72): 164-67.

Costin, Lela B. *Two Sisters for Social Justice: A Biography of Grace and Edith Abbott.* Urbana: University of Illinois Press, 1983.

Coulter, E. Merton. *A Short History of Georgia.* Chapel Hill: University of North Carolina, 1960.

Courlander, Harold. *Negro Folk Music, U.S.A.* New York: Columbia University Press, 1963; Dover Books, 1991.

Crocker, Ruth Hutchinson. *Social Work and Social Order: The Settlement Movement in Two Industrial Cities, 1889-1930.* Urbana: University of Illinois Press, 1992.

Cross, Robert D. "Grace Hoadley Dodge." In *Notable American Women*, ed. Edward James, Janet James, and Paul Boyer, vol. 1. Cambridge: Belnap Press of Harvard University, 1971, 489-92.

Curry, Leonard. *The Free Black in Urban America, 1800-1850: The Shadow of the Dream.* Chicago: University of Chicago Press, 1981.

Dahl, Linda. *Stormy Weather: The Music and Lives of a Century of Jazzwomen.* New York: Limelight Editions, 1984.

Daniel, Sadie. *Woman Builders.* Washington, DC: Associated, 1931.

"The David T. Howard Family." *The Negro History Bulletin* 17.3 (December 1953): 51-5.

Davis, Allen. *Spearheads for Reform: The Social Settlements and the Progressive Movement, 1890-1914.* New York: University Press, 1967.

_____. "Settlements: History." In *Encyclopedia of Social Work.* 16th ed. Washington, DC: National Association of Social Workers.

Davis, Angela. *Blues Legacies and Black Feminism*. New York: Pantheon Books, 1998.

_____. *Women, Culture, and Politics*. New York: Random House, 1989.

Davis, Elizabeth. *Lifting As They Climb*. Washington, DC: NACW, 1933.

Davis, Leonard G. "The Politics of Black Self-help the United States: A Historical Overview." In *Black Organizations: Issues on Survival Techniques*, ed. Lennox Yearwood. Lanham, MD: University Press of America, 1980, 37-50.

De Costa-Willis, Miriam, ed. *The Memphis Diary of Ida B. Wells*. Boston: Beacon Press, 1995.

Degler, Carl. *Out of Our Past, the Forces that Shaped Modern America*. New York: Harper and Row, 1962.

Delany, Sarah A., Elizabeth Delany, and Amy Hill Hearth. *Having Our Say: The Delany Sisters' First 100 Years*. New York: Kodansha, 1993.

Deutrich, Mable E., and Virginia C. Purdy, eds. *Clio Was a Woman: Studies in the History of American Women*. Washington, DC: Howard University Press, 1980.

Diner, Steve. "Chicago Social Workers and Blacks in the Progressive Era." *Social Service Review* 44 (12 Dec. 1970): 393-410.

"Dorothy Boulding Ferebee, M.D." *Journal of the National Medical Association* 62 (March 1970): 177.

Drake, St. Clair and Horace A. Clayton. *Black Metropolis: A Study of Negro Life in A Northern City*. 1945; Chicago: University of Chicago Press, 1993.

Du Bois, W. E. B., "Black Folk and Birth Control." *Birth Control Review* 17 (May 1938): 8, 90.

du Cille, Ann. *The Coupling Convention: Sex, Text, and Tradition in Black Women's Fiction*. New York: Oxford University Press, 1993.

Duster, Alfreda. *Crusade for Justice: The Autobiography of Ida B. Wells*. Chicago: University of Chicago Press, 1978.

Dye, Nancy Schom. "Creating a Feminist Alliance: Sisterhood and Class Conflict in the New York Women's Trade Union League, 1903-1914." *Feminist Studies* 2. 2-3 (1975): 24-37.

Ehrenreich, John H. *The Altruistic Imagination: A History of Social Work and Social Policy in the United States*. Ithaca, New York: Cornell University Press, 1985.

Fanon, Frantz, *Black Skin, White Masks*. New York: New Grove Press, 1967.

Farley, Reynolds and Walter R. Allen. *The Color Line and the Quality of Life in America*. New York: Oxford University Press, 1989.

Fields, Mamie Garvin. *Lemon Swamp and Other Places*. New York: Free Press, 1980.

Fishel, Leslie H. "The Negro in the New Deal Era." In *America's Black Past*, ed. Eric Foner. New York: Harper and Row, 1970.

Fisher, John A. *The John F. Slater Fund: A Nineteenth Century Affirmative Action for Negro Education*. New York: University Press of America, 1986.

Fisher, Walter. "Madam C. J. Walker." In *Notable American Women*, ed. Edward James, Janet James, and Paul Boyer, vol. 3. Cambridge: Belknap Press of Harvard, 1971, 533-35.

Fleming, Sheila Y. *The Answered Prayer to a Dream, Bethune Cookman College, 1904-1994.* Virginia Beach, VA: Donning, 1995.

Flexner, Eleanor, and Ellen Fitzpatrick. *Century of Struggle: The Woman's Rights Movement in the United States.* Cambridge: Harvard University Press, 1996.

Fox, Stephen, . *The Guardian of Boston: William Monroe Trotter.* New York: Atheneum, 1971.

Franklin, John Hope, and Alfred A. Moss. *From Slavery to Freedom.* 6th ed. New York: McGraw-Hill, 1988.

Frazier, E. Franklin. *Black Bourgeoisie.* New York: Free Press, 1957.

_____. "The Negro and Birth Control." *Birth Control Review* 17 (May 1938): 8-90.

_____. *The Negro in the United States.* New York: Macmillan, 1966.

Fry, Gladys-Marie. "Harriet Powers: Portrait of a Black Quilter." In *Missing Pieces Georgia Folk Art 1776-1976.* Atlanta: Georgia Council for the Arts, 1976, 16-23.

Gaines, Kevin. *Uplifting the Race: Black Leadership, Politics and Culture in the Twentieth Century.* Chapel Hill: University of North Carolina Press, 1996.

Garvey, Amy Jacques. Editorial. *The Negro World* (24 October 1925), In *Black Women in White America, a Documentary History*, ed. Gerda Lerner. New York: Vintage Books, 1973, 576-79.

Gates, Henry Louis. "The Face and Voice of Blackness." In *Facing History: The Black Image in American Art, 1710-1940*, ed. Guy McElroy. Washington, DC: Bedford Art and the Corcoran Gallery of Art, 1990, xxix-xliv.

Gates, Henry Louis, and Cornel West. *The Future of the Race.* New York: Alfred A. Knopf, 1996.

Gatewood, Willard. *Aristocrats of Color, the Black Elite, 1880-1920.* Bloomington: Indiana University Press, 1990.

Giddings, Paula. *When and Where I Enter, the Impact of Black Women on Race and Sex in America.* New York: William Morrow, 1984.

Gilkes, Cheryl Townsend. "If It Wasn't for the Women: African American Women, Community Work, and Social Change." In *Women of Color in U.S. Society*, ed. Maxine Baca Zinn and Bonnie Thornton Dill. Philadelphia: Temple University Press, 1994.

Gilmore, Glenda. *Gender and Jim Crow: Women and the Politics of White Supremacy in North Carolina, 1895-1920.* Chapel Hill: University of North Carolina Press, 1996.

Glazer, Nathan, and Daniel P. Moynihan. *Beyond the Melting Pot, a Study of Blacks and other Ethnic Groups in New York City.* Cambridge:

Massachusetts Institute of Technology Press, 1963.

Gordon, Ann, Bettye Collier Thomas, John Bracey, Arlene Avakian, ed. *African American Women and the Vote, 1837-1965*. Amherst: University of Massachusetts Press, 1997.

Gordon, Linda. *Woman's Body, Woman's Right, a Social History of Birth Control in America*. New York: Grossman, 1976.

Gordon, Milton. *Assimilation in American Life: The Role of Race, Religion, and National Origin*. New York: Oxford University Press, 1964.

Grossman, James. *Land of Hope:Chicago Black Southerners and the Great Migration*. Chicago: University of Chicago Press, 1989.

Gutman, Herbert. "Persistent Myths about the Afro-American Family." In *The American Family in Social-Historical Perspective*, ed. Michael Gordon. New York: St. Martin's Press, 1978, 467-89.

_____.   *The Black Family in Slavery and Freedom, 1750-1925*. New York: Vintage Books, 1976.

Guy-Sheftall, Beverly, and Jo Moore Stewart. *Spelman: Centennial Celebration 1881-1981*. Atlanta, GA: Spelman College, 1981.

Hall, Jacqueline Dowd. *Revolt Against Chivalry, Jessie Daniel Ames and the Campaign Against Lynching*. New York: Columbia University Press, 1979.

Halliburton, Cecil D. *A History of St. Augustine's College, 1867-1937*. Raleigh, NC: St. Augustine College, 1937.

Hamilton, Donna Cooper. "The National Urban League During the Depression, 1930-1939: The Quest for Jobs for Black Workers." Ph.D. diss., Columbia University, 1982.

Hamilton, Tullia. "National Association of Colored Women, 1896-1920." Ph.D. diss., Emory University, 1978.

Hammonds, Evelyn. "Missing Persons: African American Women, AIDS and the History of Diseases," *Radical America* 24 (1987): 8-13.

Harley, Sharon. "Beyond the Classroom: The Organizational Lives of Black Female Educators in the District of Columbia,   1890-1930." *Journal of Negro Education* 51 (Summer 1982): 254-65.

_____. "For the Good of Family and Race: Gender, Work, and Domestic Roles in the Black Community, 1888-1930." In *Black Women in America: Social Science Perspectives*, eds. Micheline R. Malson, Elisabeth Mudimbe-Boyi, Jean F. O'Barr, and Mary Wyer. Chicago: University of Chicago Press, 1988.

_____. "The Middle Class," In *Black Women in America: An Historical Encyclopedia*, eds., Darlene Clark Hine, Elsa Barkley Brown, and Rosalyn Terborg-Penn . Brooklyn, NY: Carlson, 1993, 786-89.

Harris, Barbara. *Beyond Her Sphere: Women and the Professions in American History*. Westport, CT: Greenwood Press, 1978.

Hartnick, Allen. "Catherine Ferguson." *Negro History Bulletin* 35 (December 1977): 176-77.

Henri, Florette. *Black Migration: Movement North, 1900-1920*. Garden City, New York: Anchor Press/Doubleday, 1975.

Hewitt, Nancy A. "Beyond the Search for Sisterhood: American Women's History in the 1980s." *Social History* 10 (March 1985): 299-321.

Hewitt, Nancy A. and Suzanne Lebsock, eds. *Visible Women: New Essays on American Activism*. Urbana: University of Illinois Press, 1993.

Higginbotham, Evelyn. "African American Women's History and the Metalanguage of Race." In "*We Specialize in the Wholly Impossible*": *A Reader in Black Women's History*, eds. Darlene Clark Hine, Wilma King, Linda Reed. Brooklyn, NY: Carlson, 1995, 3-24.

_____. "Nannie Helen Burroughs (1879-1961)." *In Black Women in America*, ed. Darlene C. Hine et al. Brooklyn: NY: Carlson, 1993. 201-15.

_____. *Righteous Discontent: The Women's Movement in the Baptist Church, 1880-1920*. Cambridge: Harvard University Press, 1993.

Hill, Adelaide. "Josephine St. Pierre Ruffin." In *Notable American Women, 1607-1950*." eds. Edward James, Janet James, and Paul Boyer, vol. 3. Cambridge: Belknap Press of Harvard, 1971.

Hill, Kathleen, Evelyn Green, and Marcela W. Daniels. *Breaking the Barriers in Pursuit of Excellence-Howard University School of Social Work-A Force for Change*. 50th Anniversary Brochure, Washington, DC: Howard University School of Social, 1987.

Hill, Robert, ed. *The Marcus Garvey and Universal Improvement Papers*. vol. 1. Berkeley: University of California Press, 1983.

Hill, Ruth. "Inabel Burns Lindsay (1900-1983)," In *Notable American Black Women* ed. Jessie Carney Smith. Detroit: Gale Research, 1992.

Hine, Darlene Clark. *Black Women In White: Racial Conflict in the Nursing Profession, 1890-1950*. Bloomington: University of Indiana Press, 1989.

_____. "Rape and the Inner Lives of Black Women in the Middle West: Preliminary Thoughts on the Culture of Dissemblance." *Signs* 14.4 (Summer 1989): 912-20.

Hine, Darlene Clark and Kathleen Thompson. *A Shining Thread of Hope: a History of Black Women in America*. (New York: Broadway Books, 1998.

Hine, Darlene Clark, Elsa Barkley Brown, and Rosalyn Terborg-Penn. eds. *Black Women in America: an Historical Encyclopedia*. Brooklyn, NY: Carlson, 1993.

Hine, Darlene Clark, Wilma King, and Linda Reed. "*We Specialize in the Wholly Impossible*": *A Reader in Black Women's History*. Brooklyn, NY: Carlson, 1995.

Hofstadter, Richard. *The Age of Reform: From Bryan to F.D.R.* New York: Vintage Books, 1955.

_____. *Social Darwinism in American Thought*. 1944; rpt. Boston: Beacon Press, 1955.

hooks, belle, *Ain't I A woman: Black Women and Feminism*. Boston: South End Press, 1981.

Horton, James O. *Free People of Color: Inside the African American Community* Washington, DC: Smithsonian Press, 1993.

_____. "Freedom's Yoke: Gender Conventions among Antebellum Free Blacks." *Feminist Studies* 12.1 (Spring 1986): 51-76.

Hull, Gloria. *Color, Sex, and Poetry, Three Women Writers of the Harlem Renaissance*. Bloomington: Indiana University Press, 1987.

_____. *Give Us Each Day: The Diary of Alice Dunbar-Nelson*. W. W. Norton, 1984. Hunter, Tera. "The Correct Thing, Charlotte Hawkins Brown and the Palmer Institute." *Southern Exposure* 11.5 (September/October 1983): 37-43.

Hutchinson, Louise Daniel. *Anna J. Cooper: a Voice From the South*. Washington, DC: Smithsonian Institute Press, 1981.

Hutson, Jean Blackwell. "Victoria Earle Matthews." *Notable American Women, 1607-1950*, eds. Edward James, Janet James, Paul Boyer, vol. 1. Cambridge: Harvard University Press, 1971, 510-11.

Jacoway, Elizabeth. *Yankee Missionaries in the South, the Penn School Experiment*. Baton Rouge: Louisiana State University Press, 1980.

Jagger, Allison, and Rothenberg, Paula, eds. *Feminist Frameworks: Alternative Theoretical Accounts of the Relations Between Women and Men*. New York: McGraw-Hill, 1984.

Johnson, Audrey. "Catherine (Katy) Ferguson." In *Black Women in America, an Historical Encyclopedia*. ed. Darlene Clark Hine, et al. Brooklyn, NY: Carlson Publishers, 1993, 426.

Johnson, Charles. *The Urban League Story, 1910-1960*, Golden 50th Anniversary Yearbook, New York: NUL, 1960, National Urban League Papers.

Johnson, Daniel, and Rex Campbell. *Black Migration in America, a Social Demographic History*. Durham, NC: Duke University Press, 1981.

Jones, Beverly Washington. *Quest for Equality, The Life and Writings of Mary Eliza Church Terrell, 1863-1954*. Brooklyn, NY: Carlson, 1990.

Jones, Jacqueline. *Labor of Love, Labor of Sorrow: Black Women, Work, and the Family from Slavery to the Present*. New York: Basic Books, 1985.

_____ . *Soldiers of Light and Love, Norther Teachers and Georgia Blacks, 1865-1873*. Chapel Hill: University of North Carolina Press, 1980.

Jones, James. *Bad Blood: The Tuskegee Syphilis Experiment*. New York: Free Press, 1981.

Jones, Maxine and Joe Richardson, *Talladega College*. Tuscaloosa: University of Alabama Press, 1990.

Kellogg, Charles Flint. *NAACP: A History of the National Association for the Advancement of Colored People, 1909-1920*. Baltimore: Johns Hopkins University Press, 1967.

Kennedy, David. *Birth Control in America: The Career of Margaret Sanger*. New Haven: Yale University Press, 1970.

Kerber, Linda, and DeHart, Jane, eds. *Women's America: Refocusing the Past* 1982; New York: Oxford University Press, 2000.

Knupfer, Anne Meis. "If You Can't Push, Pull, If You Can't Pull , Please Get Out of the Way": The Phillis Wheatley Club and Home in Chicago, 1896 to 1920. *Journal of Negro History* (Spring 1997): 223-31.

_____ . *Toward a Tenderer Humanity and a Nobler Womanhood: African American Women's Clubs in Turn-of-the-Century Chicago*. New York: New York University Press, 1996.

Lamon, Lester. *Black Tennesseans, 1900-1930*. Knoxville: University of Tennessee, 1977.

Lasch-Quinn, Elizabeth. *Black Neighbors: Race and the Limits of Reform in the Settlement House Movement, 1890-1945*. Chapel Hill: University of North Carolina Press, 1993.

Latimer, Catherine A. "Catherine Ferguson, Black Founder of a Sunday School." *Negro History Bulletin* 5 (November 1941): 38-9.

Lemert, Charles, and Esme Bhan, eds. *The Voice of Anna Julia Cooper*. New York: Rowman and Littlefield, 1998.

Lerner, Gerda, ed. *Black Women in White America, A Documentary History*. New York: Vintage Books, 1973.

_____ . The Creation of Feminist Consciousness. New York: Oxford University Press, 1993.

_____ . "Early Community Work of Black Club Women." *The Journal of Negro History* 59. 2 (April 1974): 158-67.

_____ . *The Female Experience, an American Documentary*. New York: Oxford University Press, 1977.

_____. *The Majority Finds Its Past: Placing Women in History*. New York: Oxford University Press, 1979.

Leuchtenburg, William E., ed. *Franklin D. Roosevelt: A Profile*. (New York: Hill and Wang, 1967.

Levine, Lawrence. *Black Culture and Black Consciousness Afro-American Folk Thought from Slavery to Freedom*. New York: Oxford University Press, 1977.

Lindsay, Inabel Burns. "Some Contributions of Negroes to Welfare Services, 1865-1900." *Journal of Negro Education* 25 (Winter 1956): 15-24.

Lissak, Rivka Shpak. *Pluralism and Progressives: Hull House and the New Immigrants, 1890-1919*. Chicago: University of Chicago Press,1989. Locke,

Loewenberg, Bert, and Ruth Bogin. *Black Women In Nineteenth-Century American Life*. University Park: Pennsylvania State University Press, 1976.

Logan, Rayford. *The Betrayal of the Negro*. New York: Collier Books, 1963.

_____. *The Negro in the United States*. Princeton: D. Van Nostrand, 1957.

Logan, Rayford, and Michael R. Winston, eds. *Dictionary of American Negro Biography*. New York: W. W. Norton Co., 1983.

Lovett, Bobby L. *The African American History of Nashville, Tennessee, 1780-1930*. Fayetteville: University of Arkansas Press, 1999.

Lubove, Roy. *The Professional Altruist: The Emergence of Social Work as a Career, 1880-1920*. Cambridge: Harvard University Press, 1965.

Luker, Ralph. "Missions, Institutional Churches, and Settlement Houses: The Black Experience, 1885-1910." *Journal of Negro History* 69.3, 4 (Summer/Fall 1984): 101-13.

_____. *The Social Gospel in Black and White, American Racial Reform, 1885-1912*. Chapel Hill: University of North Carolina Press, 1991.

"Madam C. J. Walker to Her Daughter A'Lelia Walker-the Last Letter." *Sage* (Fall 1984).

Majors, Monroe. *Noted Negro Women: Their Triumphs and Achievement*. 1893; rpt. Salem, NH: Ayers, 1986.

Mann, Susan A. "Slavery, Sharecropping, and Sexual Inequality." *Signs* (1989): 792-98.

Manning, Marable. *Race, Reform, and Rebellion: The Second Reconstruction in Black America, 1945-1990*. Jackson: University of Mississippi Press, 1991.

Marks, Carole. *Farewell-We're Good and Gone, the Great Black Migration*. Bloomington: University of Indiana Press, 1989.

Matthews, Glenna. *The Rise of Public Woman: Woman's Power and Woman's Place in the United States, 1630-1970*. New York: Oxford University Press, 1992.

McBride, David. *From TB to AIDS: Epidemics among Urban Blacks since 1900*. New York: SUNY Press, 1991.

McCarthy, Kathleen, ed. *Lady Bountiful Revisited: Women, Philanthropy, and Power*. New Brunswick, NJ: Rutgers University Press, 1990.

Meier, August. "Negro Class Structure Structure and Ideology in the Age of Booker T. Washington." *Phylon* 23 (1962): 259-66.

_____. *Negro Thought in America, 1880-1915*. Ann Arbor: University of Michigan Press, 1978.

Meier, August and Eliott Rudwick. *From Plantation to Ghetto: An Interpretive History of American Negroes*. New York: Hill and Wang, 1966.

Moore, Jessie Thomas. *A Search for Equality: The National Urban League*. University Park: Pennsylvania State University Press, 1981.

Moses, Wilson. *The Golden Age of Black Nationalism, 1850-1925.*   New York: Oxford University Press, 1978.

Moss, Alfred A. *The American Negro Academy, Voice of the Talented Tenth.* Baton Rouge: Louisiana University Press, 1981.

Neverdon-Morton, Cynthia. *Afro-American Women of the South and the Advancement of the Race, 1895-1925.* Knoxville: University of Tennessee Press, 1989.

_____. "Self-help Programs as Educative Activities of Black Women in the South, 1895-1925." *Journal of Negro Education 51* (Summer 1982): 207-21.

Nimmons, Julius. "Social Reform and Moral Uplift in the Black Community 1890-1910, Social Settlements, Temperance, and Social Purity." Ph.D. diss., Howard University, 1987.

Obituary, Elizabeth Davis, *Chicago Defender*, 29 July 1944.

O'Farrell, Brigid, and Joyce Kornbluh. "We Did Change Some Attitudes: Maida Springer-Kemp and the International Ladies' Garment Workers Union." Women's *Studies Quarterly* 23.1,2 (Spring/Summer 19995): 41-70.

Osofsky, Gilbert. *Harlem: The Making of a Ghetto, Negro New York, 1890-1930. New* York: Harper and Row, 1971.

Parris, Guichard, and Lester Brooks. *Blacks in the City.* Boston: Little, Brown, 1971.

Peebles-Wilkins, Wilma and E. Aracelis Francis. "Two Outstanding Black Women in Social Welfare History: Mary Church Terrell and Ida B. Wells-Barnett." *Affilia 5.4* (Winter 1990): 87-100.

Perkins, Linda. "Black Women and Racial Uplift Prior to Emancipation." In *The Black Woman Cross Culturally.* ed. Filomina Steady. Cambridge, MA: Schenkman, 1981, 317-34.

_____ . *Fanny Jackson Coppin and the Institute for Colored Youth, 1865-1902.* New York: Garland Press, 1987.

Philpott, Thomas Lee. *The Slum and the Ghetto, Neighborhood Deterioration and Middle-class Reform, Chicago, 1880- 1910.* New York: Oxford University Press, 1978.

Pivar, David. *Purity Crusade: Sexual Morality and Social Morality, 1868-1900.* Westport, CT: Greenwood Press, 1973.

Porter, Dorothy. "The Organized Educational Activities of Negro Literary Societies, 1828-1846." *Journal of Negro Education* 5 (October 1936): 556-66.

Potocky-Tripodi, Miriam, and Tony Tipodi. *New Directions for Social Work Practice Research.* Washington, DC: NASW Press, 1999.

Quarles, Benjamin. *Black Abolitionists.* New York: Collier Macmillan, 1987.

Rabinowitz, Howard. *Race Relations in the Urban South, 1865-*1890. Urbana: University of Illinois Press, 1980.

Read, Florence. *The Story of Spelman College.* Princeton, NJ: Princeton University Press, 1961.

Richardson, Marilyn. *Maria W. Stewart, America's First Black Women Political Writer.* Bloomington: Indiana University Press, 1987.

Robinett, Belinda. *How Long? How Long? African American Women in the Struggle for Civil Rights.* New York: Oxford University Press, 1997.

Rodrique, Jessie. "The Black Community and the Birth Control Movement." In *Passion and Power: Sexuality in History,* ed. Kathy Peiss and Christina Simmons. Philadelphia: Temple University Press, 1989.

Rosen, Ruth. *The Lost Sisterhood: Prostitution in America, 1900-*1918. Baltimore: Johns Hopkins University Press, 1982.

Ross, B. Joyce. "Mary McLeod Bethune and the National Youth Administration: A Case of Power Relationships in the Black Cabinet of Franklin D. Roosevelt." In *Black Leaders of the Twentieth Century*. eds. John Hope Franklin and August Meier. Urbana: University of Illinois Press, 1983.

Ross, Edyth, ed. *Black Heritage in Social Welfare, 1860-1930*. Metuchen, NJ: Scarecrow Press, 1978.

Rouse, Jacqueline. *Lugenia Burns Hope: A Black Southern Reformer*. Athens: University of Georgia Press, 1989.

Rousmaniere, John P. "Cultural Hybrid in the Slums: The College Woman and the Settlement House, 1889-1894." *American Quarterly* 22 (1970): 45-66.

Rudwick, Elliott. *W.E.B. Du Bois, Propagandist of the Negro*. New York: Atheneum, 1969.

Russell, Kathy, Midge Wilson, and Ronald Hall. *The Color Complex: The Politics of Skin Color among African Americans*. New York: Harcourt Brace Jovanovich, 1992.

Ryan, Mary. *Womanhood in America, From Colonial Times to* the Present. New York: New Viewpoints, 1979.

Salem, Dorothy. "To Better Our World, Black Women in Organized Reform, 1890-1920." Ph.D. diss., Kent State University, 1986.

Sanders, Charles L. ed. *Crossing Over. Proceedings, 50th Anniversary*. Atlanta: Atlanta University School of Social Work, 1970.

Schwalm, Leslie A. "Sweet Dreams of Freedom: Freedwomen's Reconstruction of Life and Labor in Lowcountry South Carolina." *Journal of Women's History* (1997): 9-38.

Scott, Anne Firor. "Most Invisible of All: Black Women's Voluntary Associations." *The Journal of Southern History* 56. 1 (February 1990): 3-22.

_____. *Natural Allies: Women's Associations in American History*. Urbana: University of Chicago Press, 1991.

_____. *The Southern Lady: From Pedestal to Politics, 1830-1930*. Chicago: University of Chicago Press, 1970.

Seraile, William. "Susan McKinney Stewart: New York State's First African American Woman Physician." *Afro-Americans in New York Life and History* 9.2 (July 1985): 27-44.

Shaw, Stephanie. *What a Woman Ought to Be and to Do: Black Professional Women Workers during the Jim Crow Era*. Chicago: University of Chicago Press, 1996.

Sklar, Katheryn Kish. *Florence Kelly and the Nation's Work: The Rise of Women's Political Culture, 1830-1900*. New Haven, CT: Yale University Press, 1995.

Smith, Elaine. "Mary McLeod Bethune." In *Notable American Women, the Modern Period*, eds. Barbara Sickerman and Carol Hurd Green. Cambridge: Belknap Press of Harvard University Press, 1980, 76-80.

_____. "Mary McLeod Bethune and the National Youth Administration." In *Clio was a Woman, Studies in the History of American Women*, eds. Mable Deutrich, and Virginia C. Purdy. Washington, DC: Howard University Press, 1980, 149-77.

Smith, Elaine and Audrey Thomas McCluskey, eds. *Mary McLeod Bethune, Building a Better World*. Bloomington: Indiana University Press, 1999.

Smith, Susan. *Sick and Tired of Being Sick and Tired: Black Women's Health Activism in America, 1890-1950*. Philadelphia: Temple University Press, 1995.

Sollors, Werner, ed. *The Invention of Ethnicity*. New York: Oxford University Press, 1989.

Southern, Eileen. *The Music of Black Americans: A History*. New York: W. W. Norton, 1971.

Spear, Allan. *Black Chicago: The Making of a Negro Ghetto, 1890-1920*. Chicago: University of Chicago Press, 1967.

Steady, Filomina, ed. *The Black Woman Cross-Culturally*. Cambridge: MA: Schenkman, 1981.

Stein, Judith, *The World of Marcus Garvey, Race and Class in Modern Society*. Baton Rouge, LA: 1986.

Sterling, Dorothy, ed. *We Are Your Sisters: Black Women in the Nineteenth Century*. New York: W. W. Norton, 1984.

Strickland, Arvarh E. *A. History of the Chicago Urban League*, Urbana: University of Illinois Press, 1966.

Taylor, Arnold. *Travail and Triumph: Black Life and Culture in the South since the Civil War*. Westport, CT: Greenwood Press, 1976.

Taylor-Owen, Sandra. "The History of the Profession of Social Work: a Second Look." Ph.D. diss., Brandeis University, 1986.

Terborg-Penn, Rosalyn. "African American and the Vote: An Overview." In *African American Women and the Vote, 1837-1965*, eds. Ann Gordon, et al. Amherst: University of Massachusetts Press, 1997.

_____. "Discrimination against Afro-American Women in the Woman's Movement, 1830-1920." In *The Afro-American Woman Struggles and Images*, eds. Rosalyn Terborg-Penn and Sharon Harley. Port Washington, NY: Kennikat Press, 1978.

Terborg-Penn, Rosalyn, and Sharon Harley, eds. *The Afro-American Woman: Struggles and Images*. Port Washington, NY: Choanocyte Press, 1978.

Thomas, Bettye Collier. "Annie Turnbo Malone." In *Notable Black* Women, ed. Jessie Carney Smith. Detroit: Gale Research, 1992, 734-727.

Thompson, Daniel C. *A Black Elite: A Profile of Graduates of UNCF Colleges*. Westport, CT: Greenwood Press, 1986.

Thornbrough, Emma Lou. *T. Thomas Fortune: Militant Journalist*. Chicago: University of Chicago Press, 1972.

Thurman, Michael. *A Story Untold: Black Men and Women in Athens, Georgia*. Athens: Clark County School district, 1978.

Timberlake, James. *Prohibition and the Progressive Movement, 1900-1920*. New York: Atheneum Press, 1970.

Trattner, Walter. *From Poor Law to Welfare State: A History of Social Welfare in America*. New York: Free Press, 1974.

Trolander, Judith. *Professionalism and Social Change: from the Settlement House Movement to Neighborhood Centers, 1886 to the Present*. New York: Columbia University Press.

_____. *Settlement Houses and the Great Depression*. Detroit: Wayne State University, 1975.

Trotter, Joe William, ed. *The Great Migration in Historical Perspecive: New Dimensions of Race, Class, and Gender*. Bloomington: Indiana University Press, 1991.

Valentine, Charles. *Culture and Poverty: Critique and Counter*-Proposals. Chicago: University of Illinois Press, 1968.

Walker, Alice. *In Search of Our Mothers' Garden*. New York: Harcourt Brace Jovanovich, 1983.

Washington, Mary Helen. *Invented Lives: Narratives of Black Women, 1860-1960*. New York: Doubleday Press, 1987.

Weibe, Robert. *The Search for Order*. New York: Oxford University   Press, 1968.

Weiss, Nancy. *National Urban League, 1910-1940*. New York: Oxford University Press, 1974.

Wesley, Charles. *The History of the National Association of Colored Women's Clubs*. Washington, DC: NACWC, 1984.

West, Cornel. *Race Matters*. Boston: Beacon Press, 1993.

White, Deborah. *Too Heavy a Load, Black Women in Defense of Themselves, 1894-1994*. New York: W. W. Norton, 1999.

_____. "The Cost of Club Work, the Price of Black Feminism." In *Visible Women: Essays on American Activism*, eds. Nancy Hewitt and Suzanne Lebsock. Urbana: University of Illinois Press, 1993.

Wolters, Raymond. "The New Deal and the Negro." In *The New Deal: The National Level*, eds. Robert Bremner, John Braeman, and David Brody. Columbus: Ohio State University Press, 1975, 170-217.

Young. G. M. *Victorian England, Portrait of an Age*. London: Oxford University Press, 1960.

Wilson, David Harris. *A History of England*. Hinsdale, IL: Dryden Press, 1972.

Wilson, William Julius. *The Truly Disadvantaged: The Inner City, The Underclass, and Public Policy*. Chicago: University of Chicago Press, 1987.

Yee, Shirley. *Black Women Abolitionists, A Study in Activism, 1828-1860*. Knoxville: University of Tennessee Press, 1992.

Zinn, Howard. *New Deal Thought*. New York: Bobbs Merrill Company, 1966.

_____. *The Twentieth Century, a People's History* (New York: Harper and Row, 1980.

Zinn, Maxine Baca and Dill, Bonnie Thornton, eds. *Women of Color in U.S. Society*. Philadelphia: Temple University Press, 1994.

Zinsser, Judith P. *History and Feminism: A Glass Half Full*. New York: Twayne, 1993.

Index

About the Author

FLORIS BARNETT CASH is an Assistant Professor of Africana Studies and History at the State University of New York, Stony Brook. She teaches in the Department of Africana Studies and has courses affiliated with Women's Studies.